IN PURSUIT OF
weightlessness

A Rogue Trainer's Secrets to Transforming the Body,
Unburdening the Mind, and Living a Passion-Filled Life.

TOM FAZIO

ISBN: 1726313840
ISBN 13: 978-1726313841

Dedicated

To Michael: *For the Dice Club*

To Monika: *For Enso Temple.*

And dedicated

*To my generous teachers and dedicated clients who inspired the
stories and lessons within this book.*

CONTENTS

Book 3 – The Unfettered Mind

Book 4 – Weightlessness

Epilogue

UPDATE TO THE SECOND EDITION

What's Happened Since the Writing of In Pursuit of Weightlessness:

In Pursuit of Weightlessness was a turning point in life and business for me. Writing it allowed me to scratch off a bucket list item, but more importantly, it forced me to struggle with the concepts of Weightlessness I'd put on the back burner for nearly a decade. Like many, I had overlooked a number of my convictions about life in the all-consuming process of survival known as entrepreneurship. Writing the book sparked new life in me and set the stage for things that I couldn't have anticipated. Looking back now, it was a defining moment.

Prior to writing it, I'd been personal training in Shanghai and Hong Kong for many years. I was customizing programs for individuals with a wide range of interests and requests in the mind-body or martial arts domains. All of the stories in Book 2 of *In Pursuit of Weightlessness* reflect that phase – a creative yet very direct application of developmental principles.

While the philosophy governed many of my programs in principle, I had not yet taught to a single soul the comprehensive system that is now Weightlessness. Nor was the system itself developed enough to be elucidated at the time of writing. The system, in its entirety, is now laid out in the sequel to this book, *The Essence of Lightness*.

It was the attempt to teach Weightlessness in full in the years that followed that unveiled its incoherencies, gaps, and rough edges. It was the insistence on teaching Weightlessness exclusively (and declining all other training requests) that showed me where my own gaps in understanding lay. But I could nonetheless clearly see what it could become. The theories and principles in this book are as true today as they were when first written, but their systematic application and integration required a great deal of tinkering. Since I wrote this book, the system of Weightlessness has been thoroughly fleshed out. It has become a coherent, fully integrated, scientific approach to mind-body development and peak performance that changes lives.

System aside, the spirit and lifeblood of Weightlessness run through these pages, and I do believe that to understand the thing you need to know where it comes from. This isn't a system born of speculation or a priori insight and deductive reasoning. It's a system that has been tried and tested, refined by fire. There has been glory. And there has been fallout. But most importantly, there has been skin in the game for myself and many other pioneers.

In the years after first publishing this book, I began teaching Weightlessness through extremely intense 100-day programs to tribes of committed individuals in Shanghai. These years were a roller coaster ride, and generated stories of transformations that some would find hard to believe. Whatever the results I had produced prior to this, they were amplified tremendously through training in the integrated system. The program was called Weightless in 100, and it delivered.

Weightlessness has since been taught to leaders worldwide, ranging from a Young Professionals Organization (YPO) forum in Shanghai to the MBA program at the École des Ponts in Paris, and remotely to peak performers (and those aspiring to be) residing around the world in over 20 countries.

It's only the beginning.

A Rough Chronology

It has become evident that a timeline might help the reader understand the book a bit better. While my hope is that the stories herein can be considered educational and timeless, I can see that their coherence might be improved with context. I'd also like you to approach many of the stories in Book 3 with a sense of levity, as mere snapshots and insights acquired during the early stages of my journey. They should not be taken as static, concrete portraits of a weightless person or the embodiment of the method and philosophy that Weightlessness as a whole has become. Here's a very rough chronology of the pursuit:

Weightlessness Formative Years: 2000-2003

- The stories from Book 3
- My time in the jungle
- My time at the Shaolin Academy

Enso Temple Years: 2011-2015

- All chapters in Book 2
- The Dice Club chapter from Book 3

In Pursuit of Weightlessness first published: 2014

2nd Edition: 2018

Between 2003 and 2011 I was doing a variety of things I see as tangent to this storyline, but which nonetheless added perspective to my assumptions on the necessity of unburdening in life, including: teaching English at a university in southern China for two years, commodities futures and options trading for two to three years, and launching my martial arts and fitness coaching business in Shanghai three years prior to the Enso Temple years. My catastrophic coffee futures experience and mention of my university teaching are included in the book, though not central to the storyline.

Changes to the Structure of the Book

While this book has been revised to improve tone and message, it's more or less the same structurally – with two exceptions. The first is the relocation of the training programs from the appendix to the more centrally located Chapter 2 of Book 4. I discuss the reasons for this within the chapter itself, but essentially I came to realize that training is not a footnote to narrative. If anything, it should be the other way around. I made a mistake in the first edition of relegating it to a nice-to-have suggestion postscript, rather than a call to action and an integral aspect of the message of the book. This has been fixed.

This relocation also completes Book 4 as one of three chapters that draw together the different pillars and practices within Weightlessness. Book 4, entitled Weightlessness, is about integration. The Manifesto in Chapter 1 provides the theoretical framework of integrated mind-body training. The Programs in Chapter 2 provide the practice and tangible structure required for integration in the whole person. And Chapter 3, A Hundred Days Later, paints the portrait of someone growing in the system and integrating Weightlessness in daily life. This new structure of Book 4 looks at all three essential elements of integration – theory, training, and life-application.

The scope of this book is very broad. Many of the topics herein are usually the sole topic of entire fitness, wellness, or self-help books. The risk I faced in writing it the way I did was that the disparate elements might seem independently dangled in front of the reader without coherent connection and integration to the other facets of development. There are now additional insights and threads that attempt to make this integration more obvious. These are generally done within the stories or original chapters themselves.

The second structural exception is the relocation of the dialogue – *The Businessman and the Martial Artist* – to the Epilogue, due primarily to the fact that some of its content reiterates key points and reflections from elsewhere in the book. That said, there are new contributions in that piece that I believe add insight into the meta-level discussion of Weightlessness, and address the disparate strands of the book. The dialogue overtly identifies those missing threads and sheds light on them.

The outcome I very much hope for with this book is that readers see the various practices and topics within – nutrition, strength, flexibility, meditation, qigong, stress-adaptation, non-attachment, peak performance, mind-body integration, model error, probabilistic thinking, cognitive dissonance, pre-intellectual thought and nonjudgment, skin in the game, etc. – not as independent topics or fields of study, not as nice-to-haves and purely preferential in nature, but as inextricably entwined, indispensable threads that comprise the tapestry of your strongest, most weightless self.

Many of the key themes in this book are embodied, though not overtly analyzed, within each of the chapters. The allegories in Book 3, for example, often drop the reader into a setting meant to pull you through an emotional journey rather than appeal to your rational mind. They are snapshots of meditative moments marked by non-attachment in real time, and leave room for interpretation while still drawing key insights. As such, some of the threads that tie the book together may be overlooked.

This may not be easy to identify within each story, and the reader might miss that it is all about the dangers and fallout of relying fully on a rational, analytic mind without understanding what is being sacrificed: the purity, beauty, and insight of unfiltered meditative moments, which do not stem from understanding (interpretive operations of the prefrontal cortex) but in fact precede it. If this is you, I suggest reading the Epilogue thoroughly and revisiting the stories a second time with that discussion in mind. Don't miss the forest for the trees.

The Evolving System of Weightlessness

Much has been learned since the first edition of this book. In the years that followed publication, I've had the honor and opportunity to teach Weightlessness systematically, without compromise, to leaders and mind-body enthusiasts around the world. When this book was first written, there was a weightless guinea pig of one. And while the theories, principles and tools are well grounded in science and as valid today as they were then, a data set of one is not an inspiring proof.

There have been many heroes and pioneers of this path since, who have experimented and sacrificed just as I have to achieve a sense of weightlessness. They've taken the risks, put skin in the game, and have played a critical role in the filtering and refinement of the system of Weightlessness.

In addition to the relocation of the workout samples in Chapter 2 of Book 4, I've also updated the workouts to account for what I did not know when I wrote the first edition, which is that Weightlessness requires a considerable foundation before some of the advanced training techniques described in this book can be implemented fruitfully. Over the years, I have had to reverse engineer the process preceding the implementation of the pillars outlined in this book. There were risks I had not foreseen prior to testing on others.

When I first discovered Weightlessness in the jungle, it manifested from immersive training in the four pillars. For many years I made the understandable mistake of hindsight bias – assuming with the vantage of hindsight that the factors I identified as prime movers of my experience told the whole story. They didn't. They were not wrong; they just weren't the whole truth. I had undervalued my previous ten years of structural conditioning in martial arts, resistance training, and meditation, and the grit and focus cultivated through years of mind-body risk-taking and competition.

This in no way undermines the content of this book. If anything, it speaks to the accuracy of the insights and information herein while leaving room for greater nuance and sophistication in program design. This book accurately identifies the stuff that makes Weightlessness truly unique. The tools of transformation in Book 2 (with the exception of dynamic stretching and ballistic weight training in Chapter 5, The Weightless Giant), and the principles of mindful awareness and non-attachment in Book 3 are central to Weightlessness, and now comprise the foundational training elements in the Weightlessness Spectrum – the prescriptive framework that organizes the tools of progressive mind-body development across three pillars: strength, flexibility, and meditation.

The Weightlessness Spectrum is the comprehensive conditioning phase of Weightlessness that provides a comprehensive foundation for all mind-body pursuits, while what I first identified as Weightlessness training (the focus of this book) is now relegated to advanced training protocols that I refer to as Lightness Protocols. So in some ways this book is starting at the end.

Lightness training is protocol-based and less progressive in nature, focusing exclusively on the pillars outlined in this book after one reaches a point of diminishing returns across all foundational pillars. Qigong, ballistic weight training, and dynamic stretching are the three practices that require substantial prior foundation and provide additional risk, in terms of both safety and of fruitless practice without proper preparation. These three tools are cleanly situated within Lightness training and therefore reflect a categorically different level of mind-body performance. They shouldn't be attempted without substantial conditioning. This shift is accounted for in the updated programs in Book 4, though the specific changes to method are not added to this book – they can be found in *The Essence of Lightness*.

In Pursuit of Weightlessness tells the story of Weightlessness, a philosophy of living and the spirit of four key pillars that can transform an individual in profound ways, unlocking his or her greatest potential. The changes to the organizational structure of the training method are tangential. And while the stories are mine, at the end of the day they're not about me. The tools and principles uncovered create a context for personal development, self-reflection, and meaningful life choices. The tools and principles matter, but the reason for it all, the big WHY, is the central focus here.

The comprehensive theories, principles, new developmental tools, key metrics, program design algorithms, and overall framework are the central focus of my next book, *The Essence of Lightness*. For those looking to become masters of Weightlessness, that will be a necessary study. For those looking for life transformation, the book you're reading now and the programs in Book 4 contain that indispensable information.

The Science of Qi Omitted

The premise of *In Pursuit of Weightlessness* is to express the essence and spirit of Weightlessness as I discovered it, supported when appropriate with scientific evidence. Despite many references, I do not delve into the science of qi here – that is, the science of bio-electromagnetism, a known, measurable energy that can be correlated with most, if not all, attributed manifestations of that energy known as qi. In *The Essence of Lightness*, I lay out the entire developmental framework of Weightlessness, including the science of, and roadmap to, internal energy development.

In a very rudimentary synopsis, nearly every cell in your body has the special capacity to generate and conduct electricity. Your nervous system communicates throughout your body via nerve impulses (electrical events).

Energy flows in and through you non-stop. Sound health is marked by an organized flow and communication of nerves and cells throughout. Every metabolic function in the body requires electricity to send information or to generate ATP – the molecular energy currency of the body behind cellular metabolism. Ailments and pathologies are marked by impeded energy (electron) flow.

To allay the skeptic's credibility concerns, please consider that I want this book to retain the flow and vigor of my younger truth-seeking self. At the time of my experiences in the pages that follow, the science (in Western terms) of qi was weak, and global consensus something to be desired. Much has happened in the world of empirical science since, marrying traditional Chinese medical theory with modern bio-electric feedback devices that measure and verify electrical conductivity of meridian points and voltage manipulations from acupuncture.

We can no longer deny (in Western terms) that energy flow throughout the body has many implications from health to peak performance, and is in fact our source of life from moment to moment. While the correlation of energy flow within the body to more esoteric and mystical phenomena are nowhere near tight scientific correlations, the energy systems of the body are hard science.

The case made in *Lightness* is that the leap from known energy flow within the body under normal conditions to improved performance capabilities is a leap in degree, not in kind. We're simply operating in a domain that Western science has yet to frame and analyze effectively, a reminder that absence of evidence is not evidence of absence. Science sees what it looks for.

There has been little in the way of research isolating the data distribution of bioelectric output and flow to compare normal and extraordinary individuals, due primarily to the fact that qigong masters (the legit ones) are real outliers, representing a very small data pool. But the applications currently being studied range from increasing intelligence to curing cancer to re-growing limbs (in animals who otherwise don't regenerate body parts) through voltage and charge manipulation. We're on the cusp of massive medical breakthroughs.

A Note on the Manifesto

If you want to jump straight to the heart of Weightlessness training, you'll find my conclusions on holistic mind-body development in the Weightlessness Manifesto in Book 4. If you want to know how I got to those conclusions – well, you're in for a journey through the rest of the book. The Manifesto springs from, but does not rely on, the pages prior. It's designed for quick and dirty reference (or cross-reference) of key mind-body principles, and can be revisited time and time again.

Be weightless!

Shanghai

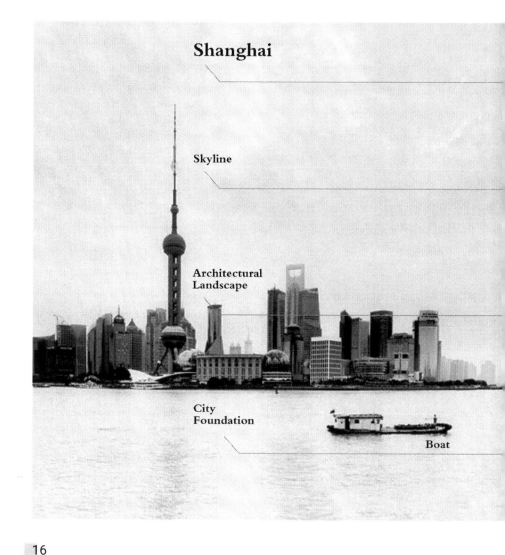

Skyline

Architectural Landscape

City Foundation

Boat

INTRODUCTION

W eightlessness was born over fifteen years ago in the jungle of Koh Phangan, Thailand. The philosophy and training methodology surfaced in solitude, during my grueling efforts to transcend my mental and physical limitations and free myself from the heaviness of life. Weightlessness is my philosophy of life, as well as my salvation. And it can be for you too.

Navigating the Book

While traversing the landscape of this book, you'll encounter a portrait of unified man that is as diverse and visually dramatic as the Shanghai cityscape. My aim throughout is to paint a coherent picture of the mind-body complex, a picture that demonstrates the inherent logic and necessity of Weightlessness training. I'll analyze, in depth, the triune foundation of holistic health and fitness: the psychological domain, the physical domain, and the metaphysical domain (or the intangible). In so doing, I'll methodically construct a case for Weightlessness from the ground up.

D) Book 4 – Weightlessness

Holistic – The future of mind–body fitness and a treatise on human flourishing.

C) Book 3 – The Unfettered Mind

Metaphysical Domain
- Mindful Awareness
- Energy Development
- Randomness

B) Book 2 – Enso Temple

Physical Domain
- Health & Nutrition
- Physical Strength
- Dynamic Flexibility
- Effortless Speed

A) Book 1 – The Phoenix

Psychological Domain
- Self Worth
- Survival Strategies
- Artistic Expression

Each of these domains is covered within its own dedicated section, or Book. The origins of Weightlessness and the psychology of personal growth, as discussed in Book 1, provide a necessary foundation for physical and mental development. Book 2 examines the physical architecture of a weightless person. The metaphysical domain, covered in Book 3, is akin to the negative space of a city skyline, without which the architectural landscape (physical form) would be a dark void. It covers the intangible elements responsible for peace, power, and passion. The foundation, the architectural landscape, and the negative space (internals) of our mind-body complex coalesce in a stunning, holistic portrait of a weightless person. This portrait is painted in Book 4.

The boat (in the diagram) you can ignore for now.

Overview

Book 1, *The Phoenix*, deals with the psychological underpinnings of physical and mental rebirth. It contains the birth of Weightlessness as well as musings on self-worth, survival, and creative expression, the foundations of holistic transformation.

Book 2, *Enso Temple*, elucidates the principles of physical transformation, strength, health, flexibility, peak performance, and lean body mass.

Book 3, *The Unfettered Mind*, provides anecdotes and explorations on our relationship with the present, the subtle energy within, and the potential power of embracing randomness.

Book 4, *Weightlessness*, builds on this triune foundation and provides a concise treatise on human flourishing (the Weightlessness Manifesto), a call to action, and a portrait of a weightless person.

Throughout our journey together you'll encounter explanations of peak performance and descriptions of the human body that are more technical and detailed. In acknowledging the proclivity many have to skip dinner and go straight for dessert, I've clearly marked each one as a *Weightless Tangent*. When I've said my fill, I return to the more exciting narratives so that you can peruse all that Weightlessness has to offer and return later for a more in-depth look at some of the principles of physical transformation and mental development.

Recurring Concepts

The Four Pillars of Weightlessness: The most potent tools of mind and body development known to man. Together they provide a platform for limitless personal growth and freedom. Pillars one through three are of the physical domain, and are discussed in depth in Book 2, *Enso Temple*. The fourth pillar, Meditation, is the subject of Book 3, *The Unfettered Mind*.

- **High-Tension, High-Intensity Resistance Training:** Heavy training in the one-to-six-rep range. Improves strength and health. Lean, fast-twitch muscle fiber is crucial for a healthy metabolism and maintaining joint health. It alleviates feelings of heaviness and lethargy by improving one's strength to weight ratio.

- **Dynamic Flexibility:** Rising kicks. Deconditions the stretch reflex, and creates a confidence in the elasticity and performance capability of the body. It reduces feelings of heaviness and paves the way for full range ballistic efforts.

- **High-Speed Resistance Training:** Ankle weight training. Shortcuts the acquisition of speed by allowing the body's natural intelligence to find the path of least resistance (refined coordination). It relieves feelings of lethargy and heaviness, and is the key to transcending all physical boundaries methodically.

- **Meditation:** Qigong and mindfulness. Liberates and concentrates the mind, increases internal energy, and allows an immediate, unbiased experience of your present reality. It reduces stress, fear, and self-doubt. It is the pathway to peace, power, and happiness, the key to transcending all mind-body limitations.

Antifragility: Nassim Taleb has made the greatest contribution to applied philosophy in recent times with *Antifragile* (both the book and the philosophy). The antifragile are those things that gain or benefit from disorder or stress.

Weightlessness is antifragility applied to the mind-body complex. While I don't mention the term until the latter third of the book, the concept itself perfectly encapsulates my philosophy of fitness, self-defense training, and personal development, and has for nearly two decades.

The human mind and body are antifragile. The appropriate degree of stress elicits adaptation. It makes us stronger. Weightlessness training and the principles of transformation and personal development throughout this book all rely on the notion that methodical stress leads to an antithetical adaptive response (weightlifting, for example, breaks down muscle tissue, which causes the body to overcompensate by constructing bigger, stronger muscles). The weightless person is reborn in the fires of focused training and methodical stress.

The Weightless Man: The embodiment of all of humanity's greatest strengths and freedoms. While the four pillars are tools for peak mental and physical performance, Weightlessness training should not be reduced to an elite performance regimen. I genuinely believe it is for all people everywhere, and that it contains the principles and tools we all need to be free from feelings of stiffness and heaviness, as well as commonplace inhibitions stemming from stress, fear, and insecurity. We can all become weightless!

The Weightless Man: A New Era

Legend has it that Bodhidharma brought Buddhism to China from India. After educating his first followers, he realized the limitations of spiritual advancement if unaccompanied by physical training. Legend also has it his monks routinely passed out while meditating. So Bodhidharma, after observing and mimicking the physical movements of animals, as monks are known to do when no one is looking, created the five animal forms for strength and health that later became the foundation of Shaolin martial arts.

With time, the internal and external practices became inextricably entwined. A warrior who lacked awareness, sensitivity, creativity, and – at higher levels – internal energy control and freedom from fear, was incomplete. A monk who lacked the physical strength to endure extended bouts of concentration and the discipline to follow the path of compassion was also incomplete. The Taoist principle of nurturing peace by preparing for war, as expressed in Sun Tzu's *The Art of War*, is a paradoxical and seemingly contradictory notion. But it underlies all monastic martial arts traditions. Mahatma Gandhi, pacifist bar none, elucidated this dichotomy best when he said, "Forgiveness adorns a soldier" but "abstinence is forgiveness only when there is the power to punish; it is meaningless when it pretends to proceed from a helpless creature."

Warrior monks developed the bodies of lions and the minds of lambs. They forged their spirits in the fire of grueling training. They cultivated innocence and passion through meditation. They did not, as many meditation proponents these days advocate, detach from or try to transcend reality. They felt it. They felt all of the pain and punishment a body can feel, and they learned from it. They learned that pain is an immediate, temporary phenomenon, a gust of wind that tickles the skin. The mind can feel – should feel – it fully, and then let go. Each new moment comes with new sensations, new challenges, and new beauty.

Physical training and combat preparation were a means of facing and overcoming the fear of pain and death. A mind free of these things was free in an absolute sense. The barriers that kept people apart could be broken down. Ideologies that caused separation and conflict could be left behind. Peace and happiness could flourish.

The monastic warrior tradition has all but died out. You find masters of combat and gurus of meditation, and almost nothing in between. These are the two dialectical elements of the same species, isolated, trained in exclusivity, preventing the unification of body and mind.

Today the virtues of man are more fractured than ever. The world has become accessible in all ways to all people, and we have become stronger, faster, and more physically capable than ever before. The knowledge of internal practices and mental development has become readily available to all seekers. If someone can't afford a plane ticket to Thailand or India for a meditative retreat, they can find a YouTube guru with just as much insight in thirty seconds (not counting the time needed to sort sage from charlatan). While this convenience has democratized information of all the arts and sciences, it has also become an uncensored, overwhelming supply of information, further distracting our schizophrenic minds.

Where is the balance?

I'm not an advocate of the monastic life. I've known too many monks to wish that on anyone. But I believe that the tools of the warrior monks, the meditative and physical practices for self-actualization, don't need to be relegated to temple life. I imagine free, strong, independent men and women with the power and agility of their monastic predecessors, along with the mental fortitude, creative insight, and cultivated non-attachment required to flourish in our becoming world.

I hope that Weightlessness will usher in a new breed of urban ascetics, sophisticated individuals with the intellectual and practical traits of education, refinement, worldliness, and, when necessary, gritty toughness and elite physicality. The pillars of Weightlessness will find a home in the hearts and minds of the focused businessman, the passionate artist, the indomitable athlete, teaching them to maintain a healthy distance from the dramatic inessentials that distract our minds and influence our emotions. They will become individuals with the knowledge to capitalize on modern technology without becoming captive to it; they will fill themselves with passion and creativity, no longer governed by the fear of loss or failure.

The weightless man.

BOOK 1

The Phoenix

The psychological underpinnings of mental and physical rebirth.

In *The Phoenix* we explore the birth of Weightlessness, notions of self-worth, survival strategies in the game of personal development, and creative expression.

Chapter 1

THE BIRTH OF WEIGHTLESSNESS

I tore through the jungle, leaping shrubs and dodging coconut trees with the same exhilaration of unbridled speed one feels at 2am racing past streetlights, with a glow illuminating the horizon, a sparkling dazzle of city, suburb, and more city. It was the feeling of committed action and freedom. Three months into my island reclusion on Koh Phangan, I'd long relinquished my inhibition and fear of jungle threats, the massive python nestled behind the next bush, the softball-sized tarantulas, the harmless but ugly geckos on steroids, and let it all go. Now it was just another morning run. The lead weight burdening each of my ankles had become imperceptible and the heaviness of life was all but gone. And with every breath, a taste of pure life.

A few months prior I had been drifting in the precarious void of aimlessness that exists after graduation and before career. After four years of studying philosophy and religion, and with a genuine lack of practical skills, I saw only two paths. I could either tame my wanderlust and join the rat race, or take the road less traveled. I wanted to follow in the paths of men and women who lived their beliefs with unwavering commitment, and not those who pontificated universal truisms while smoking a pipe in a cozy armchair.

I was hearing two contradictory voices. The first, a quote from Henry David Thoreau, resonated deep within me:

> I went to the woods because I wished to live deliberately, to front only the essential facts of life, and see if I could not learn what it had to teach, and not, when I came to die, discover that I had not lived.

It was a haunting call to life that I could not shake off and ignore, spoken by a man of integrity, a man with skin in the game, who risked a bit of life to test his values.

The other voice was that of my father, who summed up Thoreau's *Walden* in three New York words: "Guy's a bum."

"He's not a bum," I objected. "He's living off the land, living life, developing himself. Isn't it cool?"

"Did he have a job?" my father inquired.

"Well he grew beans and shit," I explained. "I think he sold some. But most of his time was spent reading, writing, and walking through the woods for several hours a day."

"Anyone who walks in the woods all day and doesn't have a job is a bum," he confirmed, putting an end to the conversation.

But I couldn't shirk that voice, that call to life, to test myself, my principles, and seize the day. *I have today, only today.* I knew that. The past was dead, the future a mere abstraction. So I left the world I knew behind, reduced all expenses to under $100 a month, and sojourned to the jungle of Koh Phangan, Thailand. I was armed with only a pair of ankle weights, a few changes of clothes, the collections of Krishnamurti and Chopra, some Qigong texts for secular and martial practices (authored mostly by Yang Jwing Ming), a few pocket readers on meditation, Taoism, and Zen, and a handful of martial arts classics, including *The Book of Five Rings* by Miyamoto Musashi, *The Art of War* by Sun Tzu, and *The Art of Peace* by Morihei Eushiba, founder of aikido.

The one book I did not bring, regrettably, was the laughably simplistic, cartoon-laden summary of ancient Chinese martial arts energy practices that I'd stolen from a local Fort Collins library and then misplaced. This book changed my life. I can't recall the name, and despite countless attempts over the last decade, I have failed to find another copy of it. I believe it's long out of print, and for good reason. It smacked of bullshit: monks so light they can leap ten feet in the air, sprint ten miles with ease, run on water, and endure strikes to vital targets and razor-sharp sword slashes on naked skin. It was a fun fifteen-minute read and excellent toilet paper.

There was, however, one line in the chapter on speed running (which I thought was at first a silly translation of sprinting – I know now that it refers to a type of training that allows the extension of anaerobic performance into the realm of endurance training) that was so subtle that had I not already been using ankle weights periodically for ten years, I would have breezed over it like all the rest. It connected all the gaps for me. It made sense of the disparate training elements that are taught in isolation today but once defined the whole, undivided god-man: "Before sprinting, begin with five minutes of stationary jogging, *concentrating on deep abdominal breathing.*"

Why did this matter so much to me? Because athletic performance requires copious amounts of oxygen to fuel muscle contraction and recovery. Oxygen delivery demands an elevated heart rate, which typically requires heavy, upper chest breathing. Deep abdominal breathing, on the other hand, most typically found in traditional meditative and internal martial arts practices like tai chi, is energy-enhancing, yet relaxing. It relieves tension and stress, concentrates energy, and stills the mind.

In yoga and various external martial arts that also incorporate qigong, a technique called reverse abdominal breathing is sometimes employed, in which the lower abdomen draws in upon inhalation, and expands slightly upon exhalation. This type of breathing, in theory, massages the internal organs for improved digestion and adrenaline production. It is a difficult practice at first, but seems far less mystical once you examine how your own breath functions before giving a speech or trying to talk to the girl or boy you've been eyeing at the local coffee house. You'll notice that your breath creeps into the upper chest and the lower abdomen draws in, causing a slightly unsettled stomach (butterflies in the stomach). This is our natural power breath, your biological fight-or-flight response. Digestion is shutting down, adrenaline is being released, and blood and oxygen are filling skeletal muscles.

Watch full contact fighters and American football players do their thing. They are huffing and puffing, their chests heaving, shoulders slouched to protect the vitals throughout the torso. Admittedly, a full-contact fight is more dangerous than starting a chat with someone attractive, but your body doesn't know the difference until you're skilled at both. Stress, whether it emerges from real physical danger or personal insecurities and fear, elicits the same biological response. Upper chest breathing is exciting, and it prepares the body for high-stress situations. So why in the world were elite warrior monks, masters of breath control and physical specimens bar none, dropping their breath to the lower abdomen during maximum effort exertions, a technique long relegated to static or slow-moving meditation?

Coordination.

The loudest sound arises from the deepest silence. A contracted muscle cannot contract. A tense muscle is incapable of generating power. It's encumbered by its own tension. Tension and relaxation are necessary correlates. Without one, the other cannot exist. The Tao of extreme physical power lies in one's capacity to actualize deep relaxation. From the stillness explodes a scream of power, committed and holistic as a newborn's cry or a lion's roar before battle.

It has long been known that few individuals actualize their immediate physical potential. Most people call on less than 30 percent of their muscular capability when performing physical feats like lifting weights or playing sports. Elite athletes are able to activate a much greater potential, upward of 80 percent. This higher level of activation is in theory enough to tear your body apart from the force of conscious muscular contraction alone. Why do you think Olympic sprinters pull hamstrings and tear tendons?

What if we could activate all this untapped potential, and more importantly, control it? If this potential is present and no additional muscle fiber is required to tap into it, then how can we activate it safely? The answer is three-fold. First, as explained above, we can maximize relaxation, the emptiness from which maximum contraction comes. If water is the substance of power, then the cup that holds it is relaxation. The larger the cup, the more water can be held. The greater the state of relaxation, the greater one's power potential.

The second key lies in dynamic stretching, which is essential for controlling your body's extreme capabilities and protecting muscle and connective tissues from being torn apart by your own physical power. The third is mental focus and awareness, which work on the control centers of physical power.

Deconditioning the stretch reflex through dynamic stretching preserves the integrity of your tissue by eliminating the panic button. It removes your body's impulse to pull back, tighten, and freeze when reaching its known limits. Generally speaking, the stretch reflex is a natural protection mechanism that keeps us from performing beyond safe limits. It also prevents us from reaching our fullest potential.

Relaxation, the release of tension, the empty cup, the ebb of an ocean that gives rise to a tsunami, the deepest valley that bows before the highest summit, the calm before the storm. Warrior monks discovered the path to weightlessness – not by becoming the strongest men on Earth (though pound-for-pound they are formidable), but by emptying their cups. It was through the vehicles of relaxation and deep abdominal breathing within the context of anaerobic, maximum-effort exercise that legendary skills were born. It is in this same context that you and I can become god-men, as our warrior-monk predecessors were before us.

Or was this all astrology based on a puerile comic book?

This was the question I asked myself in the fall of 2003, at the age of 23, prior to beginning my experiment with Weightlessness. I was determined to find answers, to live boldly. If I could not find and study under these men of legend and learn their secret methods for elite mind-body living, perhaps I could be bold enough to risk everything and become one of them.

I remained in my secluded jungle hut on Koh Phangan for three months, resolved to test my theories in full. I awoke with the sun every morning, strapped eight pounds to each ankle, and jogged through the jungle to the beach with a relaxed, long stride, focusing on sinking my breath and releasing tension throughout my body. I stood before the clear azure of quiet waters and breathed deeply for fifteen to twenty minutes, hugging an imaginary golden bell, concentrating qi in my *dantian*. As I did this, I sensed the extended energetic strings that connected my parted fingers, which were slowly oscillating six inches apart from one another.

On my way back, I sprinted as if being chased, leaping fallen coconuts, twisting and drifting past low-hanging branches, holding nothing back. Relaxed, focused, the fresh and humid jungle air fueling my speed, I felt the weight on my ankles hit my core like the most focused abdominal machine, burning and tearing muscle fibers from thighs to chest. The threshold to my domicile was marked by a thirty-foot tall coconut tree that grew at a forty-five degree angle until it discovered a small clearing of open blue sky amid its stronger brothers and sisters, at which point it straightened into a vertical ascent. It found a way. It reminded me every morning that there is great strength in yielding, great power in non-resistance.

After a minute or two of pacing and breathing while my heartbeat returned to normal, I threw on my backpack, weighted with some thirty pounds of books, and fell into my leaping hole (initially three feet deep, the first stage of the cartoon prescription for extreme leaping skills). I sank my breath, released all identifiable points of tension in my shoulders and back, and leapt in and out, with patient repetitions until the onset of fatigue. Never failure. Each effort was 100 percent, and each rest was sufficient to release all tension. I then performed a few sets of dynamic stretching, swinging my legs aggressively to full height, ankle weights still attached, before scrambling a few eggs on a makeshift gas stove and adding a bit of leftover rice for breakfast.

My days perhaps sound a bit monotonous. I followed breakfast with a couple of hours of martial arts training, leaping, kicking, bodyweight calisthenics, and plyometrics. I conditioned my hands and shins by striking young trees and planks of dead wood.

Training left me covered with itchiness. Suffering hours of mosquito bites is a genuine exercise in mindfulness and a challenge in non-attachment. But this was a small price to pay for paradise, and I could remove the sting in the clear blue salt water every afternoon.

Afternoons were slow and reflective, filled with small bouts of meditation, ruminations on martial and spiritual classics, and sporadic technique training until the early evening. At that point, the ankle weights were fastened on again, the backpack thrown on, and I fell into my leaping hole one more time before dinner. A lack of electricity dictated early slumber and therefore early, well-rested waking with the subtle glow of a new day.

Before weighting my ankles for my morning run, I'd scrape a bit of earth from the bottom of my leaping hole, making it imperceptibly deeper than the day before, yet deeper nonetheless. My performance the day before determined whether more books would be added to my pack come leaping time.

After three months in the jungle, I was a different man. My energy was abundant and flowing. I felt a constant sensation of cool fire in my abdomen, accompanied by an energetic tingling throughout my forearms. My mind was exceedingly clear, calm, and alert. I felt at once prepared to die, yet ready to live with every ounce of my being. Sunrise brought the joy of a new limitless day, and sunset the release of all tension. All things of importance were well done that day. Life was good, and rest was full, well-deserved, and meaningful.

In the beginning, coming home to find a large, menacing snake waiting in bed for me was a real temptation to throw in the towel and return to normalcy. After three months, I could take it in stride and leave the snake in peace until it moved on to a more comfortable bed. It was just passing by.

So often in life we take on tools and practices that help us deal with uncertainty – that snake in the bed, that tiger lurking in the forest, that unforeseen stressor that challenges our assumptions of the way things should be. But there in the jungle I learned that unburdening, not accumulating, was the path to freedom. I learned that relinquishing my sense of control, my emotional attachment to desired outcomes, was the path to peace.

And I learned that this process of unburdening is best adorned by adding weight.

My body had become balanced, strong, flexible, and relaxed. My heart rate was exceedingly low, my confidence exceedingly high. Training was always challenging – it was training, after all – but life outside of training became effortless. Like an institutionalized prisoner, I began to crave the confines of my weights. Without them, I felt too light. Walking became complicated and it required a conscious effort not to sprint everywhere. At that point, I could sprint full-speed for minutes on end without losing my breath.

My energy was so high, my limbs so light, that I needed something to hold me back, to make me feel normal. I no longer needed to warm up or stretch before full exertions. I could swing my leg straight overhead first thing in the morning and do a standing jump of four-and-a-half feet with ease. At all times I was relaxed, yet ready and able to move at 100 percent without inhibition or injury. I felt superhuman. I felt weightless.

Meditation; high-speed resistance training; dynamic flexibility; and low-volume, high-intensity resistance training – the four pillars of Weightlessness training – should be considered on the basis of their rapid effects on mental and physical performance independently. But their symbiosis was magical.

My ability to adapt to progressive stress seemed limitless, assuming it was of an appropriate degree. My antifragile nature (expounded upon in Book 2, *Enso Temple*) – of my muscles post-effort, of my bones when tested against unforgiving trees, of my connective tissues when rapidly stretched to their limits – became an intimate badge of honor that I could rely on. I learned to trust my body.

In releasing my attachments to fixed ideas and egocentric desires (the essence of Book 3, *The Unfettered Mind*) I realized in their wake a world of beauty and peace that was always there, suppressed beneath the surface of my experience. My conflicts of self were carried away with the tide every morning; my damaged tissue restored itself every night. My body was light, my mind free.

But this is not the end of the story.

At the end of fall, the heavy rains came and flooded me out, ending my time in the jungle. I moved to Chiang Mai to practice a bit of Thai boxing and acclimate myself to the real world again. What demonstrated the revolutionary impact of this training protocol was not only my heightened mental and physical state on Koh Phangan, but the fact that three months after leaving, and consequently discontinuing my program,

I had not regressed. My body and mind had changed in substantial ways, reprogrammed if you will.

Despite re-entering the world of normal responsibilities, normal concerns, and distractions that define modern life, I noticed a striking disconnect between events in real time and my emotional attachment to them. Previously I'd get frustrated, impatient, or merely judge harshly (and impulsively) things that did not conform to my expectations. I was disheartened or upset every time something didn't go as I wished, to varying degrees. I was the center of my own world, and my world was burdensome. Those judgments were a pillow pressing me down, a constant heaviness preventing me from taking a full breath.

Now, despite the stark contrast in lifestyle to that of my reclusion, my mind had sustained the clarity, focus, and non-attachment cultivated in the jungle. I wasn't weighed down or blinded with common frustrations. I was free to engage and adapt, to act and innovate. It didn't matter where I was or what I was doing, I discovered, the tools I'd developed were a significant upgrade to my mind-body hardware – and that goes everywhere with me – permeating every experience I had and every decision I made. I hadn't just been training to build capacity and resilience in my body or separate my mind from the things of this world, it turned out. I had been training for life.

This was the first type of training I'd encountered where the results did not rapidly evaporate after ceasing the program. One may maintain high levels of strength, but any athlete can tell you how quickly the 'feeling' dies. Stiffness creeps into the limbs, the mind loses focus, and warm-ups become increasingly important to prevent injury and regain speed and range of movement. So too can anyone returning from a vipassana retreat tell you how quickly the serenity and clarity accessed in silence fade away when returning to normalcy. That had always been the case for me as well... until now.

In harmonizing the breath (via deep abdominal breathing) with explosive movement (burdened with added resistance), intuition and sensitivity become alive. You begin to feel the interconnectedness of fractured body parts. You begin to feel points of tension that, when released, release blinding speed and explosive power. This heightened sensitivity, this intuitive coordination and power, and the waves of relaxation and tension that comprise complex, gross motor movements – this does not die when training ceases. It reprograms your nervous system, which, when accompanied by a calm, concentrated mind, unleashes a power within that angels and demons fear.

Weightlessness was born.

Chapter 2

THE PHOENIX RISES

Mind

It wasn't long after Mei Ling had been raped by her uncle while on an overnight trip to a neighboring city to help him select a new computer that she explained to her boyfriend the futility of speaking out, of acting up. As an American, his blood was burning, churning, bubbling over with anger. He wanted justice. He wanted revenge. She explained the typical course of events like these in her village, and how the best-case scenario would be a small financial recompense from her uncle to her father for his loss of face. Her father's reputation would be in question, not her virtue. And she would have to live with the public embarrassment.

Mei Ling (not her real name) grew up in a small farming village. Her parents were farmers. There was little other commerce in town and a lot of down time. Mei Ling was elected by the village to go to college, and as a community they sponsored her. She was bright, curious, hopeful, and free-thinking. Mei Ling was one of the lucky ones. On the outskirts of her village was a small cave that housed the skeletons of baby girls. Girls weren't strong enough to work the fields, yet they required just as much food as boys. Wasteful. They were more often than not placed in Skeleton Cave and left to die.

Mei Ling recalled when, as a young girl, the village gathered and walked to a field together. They all stood there in silence looking at the naked body of another bright, curious, and hopeful young girl who had just come home from college on summer holiday. One of the village boys had taken the opportunity to establish his worth and put her in her place.

He beat, raped, and murdered her. There was no trial and no punishment. Her father lost face and the boy's family financially compensated him for the loss of his daughter. Mei Ling, standing in a field among a people that couldn't see past their cultural biases and prejudices, wondered with a heavy heart, "Is it not possible that girl had a greater value, a value ignored?"

Body

Rob and I had everything ready. A couple of forties of Budweiser, a little bit of weed, and the channel set to *Jerry Springer*, who was about to interview the thousand-pound man. We'd been anticipating this episode for several weeks and had ditched classes that day to ensure we didn't miss it. This guy was the living definition of morbid obesity, emphasis on *morbid*. But also, emphasis on *obesity*.

The thousand-pound man was grotesque. He was too fat to move. He shit in a bedpan because he couldn't stand or maneuver to an actual toilet. His wife or girlfriend was also morbidly obese, but functional, and fed him constantly, clearly stealing a few bites for herself. She was only five or six hundred pounds if I recall correctly, still sprightly enough to cook him ten egg sandwiches and four packs of bacon for breakfast, twenty sloppy joes for lunch, with a few bags of potato chips (family-size), a couple of liters of soda pop, and for dinner…Jesus, who cares. I'm tired just typing it. And she was sprightly enough to empty his bedpan.

Rob and I were in heaven, listening with a somewhat inebriated understanding to the slurred speech of a man too fat to even articulate his plight. We took turns hitting the pipe and blowing smoke into Rob's beagle's cute face, making him high, confused, and wacky. It was a lot more fun than math class, and I dare say more enlightening.

Jerry seemed genuinely concerned, and he asked the man a very sobering question: "So, why do you eat so much?" As you can imagine, nothing of note came out. The truth was, he was institutionalized. He was living a life dictated by a self-perpetuating inertia. Oh, and his wife kept feeding him. Her reply when asked why? "He likes it. And I can't disappoint him."

That episode of *Jerry Springer* ended as they all should have ended, by cutting the freak out of his trailer and airlifting him to a hospital capable of eradicating such irrational evil. Or maybe they just gave him liposuction, I don't recall precisely. But even then, as I was drunk, high, and loving life, watching a man who'd clearly given up on life, who'd satisfied every immediate craving, who'd lived his life his way, like Sinatra, cause "he liked it," and now was left in his own pile of festering shit, I wondered with a heavy heart: "Is it not possible that man had value, a value he ignored?"

Freedom

Once upon a time there was a legendary race of men and women, alchemists committed to unlocking the door to immortality. Before you get too excited, I'm not speaking of science trolls. I'm speaking of an elite group of warrior-monks who stopped at nothing to reach holistic enlightenment. These masters of weightlessness lived quiet lives and were devoted to actualizing their greatest human potentials. Their methods, which have been ignored for millennia, helped them achieve mental and physical freedom by imprisoning the body and by insisting, day after day, that they seek escape.

Through meditation, they focused their minds and escaped the web of selfish compulsion that stifles and impedes free thought. They were creative, passionate, in love with life. In extinguishing their selves, they nurtured compassion and were uniquely capable of both inflicting tremendous pain and showing profound mercy. Their bodies were raw, sinewy, and elastic, their stamina legendary. As they struggled to overcome increasingly heavy limbs through intense, focused exertion, they realized the freedoms that come with effortless movement and lightness of being.

The masters of weightlessness stated with great conviction: "We have incalculable value, value which cannot be ignored, potential which cannot be squandered."

The Phoenix Rises

Ten years after the birth of Weightlessness, I find myself balancing on a tightrope connecting a world of two extremes. On the one side is the potential for holistic freedom and contentment, and on the other side is a world of extreme bondage. And I don't mean the kinky black-leather type. I mean the depressing, narcissistic, and self-destructive type. People are at war with themselves, amalgams of contradictory thoughts and values, wanting both the sexy as well as the quick and easy, wanting to be loved but unwilling to move beyond the immediate selfish desires and conditioned biases of the ego. We all contain the lethargy and denial of the thousand-pound man. We all contain the deeply imbedded biases that deny life and perpetuate pain and suffering, preventing us from living in the present with power and passion.

I face this dichotomy each and every time someone steps through the doors of Enso Temple looking to make significant life changes. Month after month, I find myself in a familiar dialogue, the stereo set on repeat, listening to the same tune:

CLIENT. Everyone tells me you're the guy to see if I want to get results when all else fails.

YOURS TRULY. How flattering.

CLIENT. Your rates are a bit expensive. Do you happen to offer a trial session?

YOURS TRULY. No. I have a minimum ten-session commitment. No single session can give you a fair assessment of where I can take you over the course of a program, nor is it enough to get results. So I don't provide them.

CLIENT. Well, how do I know if I'll like it?

(Long pause)

YOURS TRULY. Like *what?*

CLIENT. Like the classes.

YOURS TRULY. It's almost certain you will not enjoy the sessions.

CLIENT. Oh... the thing is I'd like to do something I enjoy while getting fit. If I don't enjoy this, I may not want to continue long-term.

YOURS TRULY. I can appreciate that. But I'm not interested in working with you long-term. If we need a long term, I'm not doing my job, or you're not motivated enough to work with. It isn't a consideration for me whether or not you enjoy the training. I only care about reaching your goals as quickly and safely as possible. In all likelihood, this will be an uncomfortable process at best, and at worst one of the most painful experiences of your life. But you will get the results you're looking for, and you'll get them faster and with less time commitment than anywhere else in Shanghai.

For many, this dialogue leads to an about-face and a hightailing out of Enso Temple. The few serious clients that come in, the ones who know that pleasure has led to their pain, who have accepted the reality that the medicine required won't taste as sweet as the poison, stay. And they transform.

I believed my experience in the jungle of Koh Phangan held the key to actualizing untapped human potential, to creating a flourishing superhuman, and to bringing internal peace to the troubled masses. I just never imagined that the four pillars of Weightlessness would find their first home in the demanding lifestyles of China's expat elite, men and women at the highest levels of finance, marketing, fashion, and live performance. It began among men and women who had sacrificed their health and peace of mind to support ambitious careers.

In fact, it was years before I freely talked about Weightlessness, the components of which I felt to be too esoteric and demanding for your average trainee. But I learned that the minds of high-powered executives were uniquely primed to understand and receive the benefits of Weightlessness training. They were extremely driven and had winning habits. They were disciplined in separating effective from wasteful endeavors, were adept at streamlining processes, and skilled in making short-term sacrifices for long-term gains.

Businessmen value smart work while athletes value hard work. Entrepreneurs leverage their time, money, and knowledge, while athletes trade all of the above for days of soreness (which somehow translates into productive training). Businessmen tend to realize that fitness training, while certainly helping you get laid, has the added benefit of improving mental focus and health, and is crucial for balancing a high-stress lifestyle.

While I've had my fair share of physical transformation projects, a large portion of my clientele did not seek me out for physical transformation only. I heard the same complaints year after year. People spoke of a lack of confidence and focus and they believed martial arts training could balance them. Some complained of feeling stiff and heavy, lacking the energy to enjoy a life outside of work. Some needed holistic rehab for complete burnout, with a physical component geared toward strength and health and a mental component for stress relief, energy enhancement, and mental clarity. More often than not, these individuals required training that improved body awareness and coordination, not merely localized strength. Years of living in a caged corporate environment had severed the mind-body tie that marked their youthful passion and vigor.

For every individual that recognizes the tremendous value of health, fitness, and mind-body unity, there are hundreds who cannot see beyond the compulsion to seek immediate comfort and security. One client, in the midst of a grueling session, asked me where my motivation to train comes from. I was admittedly dumbfounded. My motivation to train? I couldn't think of a single alternative, save for meditation, that provided better value for time spent (within reason, and with an efficient approach) than physical training.

I'm a huge fan of efficiency, and even when preparing my physique for a photo or video shoot, I spend less than three hours per week on fitness training, and generally less than two. But as my clients will confirm, these are not a fun couple of hours. I lived just one floor above Enso Temple, so I had no excuses. But I've never been a gym rat who pounds and punishes my body for hours a day. With the results I can provide in three private sessions a week for my clients, I can't think of anything that could be more motivating.

But more importantly, what's the alternative?

I asked softly, "What's the motivation to live in a state you are unhappy with, to be continuously dissatisfied with your appearance, and in which you lack the strength and confidence to fulfill your dreams?"

I had visions of the thousand-pound man being airlifted to salvation. What's the motivation to eat yourself into a state of unhappiness? The client admitted that there was no good motivation to live in a state of discontent with one's condition, and that she'd never looked at it that way.

But she's not alone. There is something tragically wrong with the way people view their health and fitness.

People gravitate toward the quick and easy. They want their five-minute abs and miracle cleanses. Health is a secondary concern to pant size and muscle tone. Even those values are secondary to fast, convenient food. For many, all food is lumped into a flat category of 'bad.' If someone is overweight, his or her solution is deprivation. Overconsumption is considered a known evil. Not eating is seen as an undeniable good (and is often rewarded by overeating). What actually nourishes the body and supports health and fitness seems to be inconsequential, even for those focused on getting in shape. People are at war with themselves. Everyone feels like shit. They want abs, confidence, and sex appeal, and they want that chocolate bar at the same time.

Let the record state that I drink beer, smoke cigars (and other funny things), eat carbs, and binge with the best of them. However, I don't do these things every day, and I don't compromise my mental or physical health for them (too often). Everyone tends to elevate tolerance as the greatest virtue, and I'm not here to argue with that.

I have no problem, not even a little bit, with someone being obese. I have a deep frustration, however, when I see someone who is morbidly obese complain about being overweight, and they don't initiate change. I have yet to meet an obese person who does not betray an insecurity or unhappiness about their state. Tolerance gives us external security, and sustains internal turmoil. It also allows us to slowly kill ourselves. It does not empower change. Furthermore, tolerance ignores a universal law of personal development: stress and discomfort lead to adaptation (and growth).

To cross the threshold from the world of pleasure that leads to discontent into the world of strategic discomfort that leads to health and freedom, one must realize the connection between short-term comfort, security, and satisfaction, and the morbidity that is the thousand-pound man. One must realize the connection between conditioned biases and selfish desires, and the regrettable violence and disregard for human life that occurs as a result. In light of the only glaring alternative, which is to live a life of monotonous mediocrity and risk discontent, one must choose life, and embrace the short-term pain and discomfort required for personal growth. One must affirm, "I have incalculable value, a value that cannot be ignored, a potential that cannot be squandered."

Weightlessness training is a surgical assault on all that impedes physical lightness and psychological freedom. The four pillars of Weightlessness collectively remove all limitations to human flourishing and pave the way for infinite growth and peak mental and physical performance.

The Four Pillars of Weightlessness

- **High-Tension, High-Intensity Resistance Training:** Heavy training in the one-to-six-rep range. Improves strength and health. Lean, fast-twitch muscle fiber is crucial for healthy metabolism and maintaining joint health. It alleviates feelings of heaviness and lethargy by improving one's strength to weight ratio.

- **Dynamic Flexibility:** Rising kicks. Deconditions the stretch reflex, and creates a confidence in the elasticity and performance capability of the body. Reduces feelings of heaviness and paves the way for full range ballistic efforts.

- **High-Speed Resistance Training:** Ankle weight training. Shortcuts the acquisition of speed by allowing the body's natural intelligence to find the path of least resistance (refined coordination). It relieves feelings of lethargy and heaviness, and is the key to transcending all physical boundaries methodically.

- **Meditation:** Qigong and mindfulness. Liberates and concentrates the mind, increases internal energy and allows an immediate, unbiased experience of your present reality. Reduces stress, fear, and self-doubt. It is the pathway to peace, power, and happiness. The key to transcending all mind-body limitations.

Each of these isolated practices can be found in various sports, fitness methods, and the holistic arts, but nowhere outside of the warrior-monk tradition have they been combined into a structured platform for self-actualization. So potent is their union that they can expose one's deepest insecurities and weaknesses, some of which may be too difficult to cope with. Or they can lead to otherworldly insight and power, self-actualization, and an indomitable will.

It's like dipping a newborn baby into a vat of the world's seven deadliest poisons. The child will emerge a scalding mess of leaking flesh and bone like the Nazis who opened the ark in *Raiders of the Lost Ark*, or will surface invincible with the almighty touch of death. Each pillar can be developed with incredible quality-of-life enhancing effects. But to become a master of Weightlessness, mentally focused and physically uninhibited, a beacon of peace and power, all four must be present and balanced.

Weightlessness provides the tools for you and me to stop viewing ourselves as bundles of walking problems and instead begin each day with the innocent optimism of our youthful selves, excited as hell for the day ahead and all of the opportunities that may come. We can awake tomorrow morning with a clean slate, with freedom and passion, unshackled by the pressures of work and the pains that occur within all relationships. We can reignite the fire within and release the pure creative energy that marked our youth. But first we must go on an odyssey of mind and body reflection. We must dig out the skeletons from the closet, those subtle impulses of self-sabotage that prevent us from actualizing our potential and realizing our dreams.

Like the mighty phoenix, part of you will have to die in the fires of focused training, only to be reborn from the battered remains, your strongest self. We must use up all energy storages that weigh us down and build raw, formidable physiques. And we must focus our minds, transcend the conditioned self, and witness the beauty that exists before our eyes.

The strength to accomplish this will not exist prior to beginning your journey; it will arise along the way, amid the pains, frustrations, and self-doubt that will define your rebirth. If we're truly to become weightless, free of stress, anger, and fear, confident with our physicality and sexuality, and free to act with power and precision in any walk of life, we must first find a way to manage our vices. We must find a way to stay the course.

Chapter 3

EVERYONE HAS A PLAN, UNTIL…

I n the fall of 2008 I watched my life savings deteriorate on a daily basis, like many other highly leveraged traders and ignorant speculators riding the coattails of one of history's greatest market bubbles. I was smart enough to play the market with borrowed money and leverage that money to tilt. Fate could have sent my fortune one of two ways, and it sent it straight to hell. But we're always smarter in retrospect, and we're even smarter in retrospect about stupid decisions that others have made. Hindsight biases reign supreme in the wake of economic crises. We all know now what we did not know then. Or so we think.

Information compiled post-trauma is organized to prove what we could have known ahead of time. Other times, it's compiled to prove that events were in fact unpredictably random, and no one is a dumbass because everyone was a dumbass. The verdict is still out as to whether your humble author was a dumbass, but suffice it to say that speculating on coffee futures in 2008 – or rather, buying over a million pounds of coffee with highly leveraged, borrowed capital – was not the makings of a happy year to come. Bankruptcy is an unpleasant curveball in the game of life.

This experience was particularly painful because I did know a few things about coffee. In fact, I'd been making a living trading futures and options independently for several years already. I knew coffee was due for a run to historical highs. I knew that commercial traders had been hedging in historically large positions, indicating the potential for a supply deficit in the coming months and years. I knew that coffee was relatively cheap, at $1.30 per pound, and had yet to experience the inflationary pressures and speculative fervor that other soft commodities like sugar, cotton, and cocoa had experienced. I knew that the goddamn stars were aligned for coffee to run to all-time highs and pay my ass out.

I knew nothing.

Let me rephrase that. I was not prepared to weather the storm of the global financial crisis that ensued. I picked the right market. I was one month too early. Coffee, relative to the stock and commodities markets as a whole, held its ground quite well, but my strategy of pyramiding call options with only six months to one year of time to expiration was a tragic display of hubris. The crash led to a decline and leveling of coffee futures at values not far from my strike price. But coffee, under the pressures of imminent economic collapse, stood no chance of rallying within my time frame. I watched my equity drop on a daily basis, and with it my dreams of early retirement on a Sicilian beach with a beautiful woman on my arm and a warm cup of Arabica lubricating my intestines and sending me to the loo three times before lunch.

The biggest problem was that my market analyses were not entirely wrong. Coffee futures did in fact climb to all-time highs within a year of the collapse, due to all the factors I identified well in advance. But I could not stay the course. My contracts expired a month before the market began to rally, and only three months later I would have made 100 to 200 percent on my investment. It would have been only a small taste of the pie had I been able to then ride the market to the successive heights. I had a great strategy, all the confidence in the world, but I had no measures in place to manage risk. I was completely exposed, vulnerable, and overconfident.

I believe it was the ear-lusting ring scholar Mike Tyson who once said, "Everyone has a plan until they get punched in the face." These words are as true in entrepreneurship and investment, health and fitness, and true love, as they are in boxing. Successful people are not defined in their moments of greatest acclaim; they are defined in the shit, in the gritty trenches of combat, where life, love, and livelihood are on the line. They have something to lose. They take their punches. They get knocked down. And they get back up again.

Had I simply acknowledged my own fallibility, limited perspective, and information blindness, I could have implemented strategies that would have kept me alive long enough to be proven right. Had I not said all or nothing, I would not have wound up with nothing. The best traders, according to my copious research and avid study of market wizards at that time, were not geniuses. They were intelligent gamblers implementing strategies of probabilistic betting and low-risk propositions. The best traders lose all the time. But when they lose, they lose small, and they survive. When they win, they win big.

The worst traders are career professionals who are used to being right most of the time. Doctors, dentists, and lawyers are notoriously shitty traders. These geniuses dump their hard-earned riches in the markets and decide they're going to double or triple it all, because hey, they're winners. They're used to being right. Surgeons who aren't right most of the time quickly get a reputation for killing their patients. Not good for business. A defense attorney who is wrong most of the time winds up with a high conviction rate. Jailed clients don't provide as many referrals as free ones. But trading is not a game of being right most of the time. It's a game of being right some of the time, being wrong some of the time, and making money in spite of one's ignorance and limited perspective.

My first martial arts instructor told me that the first rule of fighting is *never get hit*. He taught a system based on sound fundamentals, and helped me acquire a foundation in martial arts for which I am grateful. But my first instructor was wrong. For not getting hit, while sound in theory, is not a strategy that can always be implemented. Sometimes you are outmanned, outnumbered, sometimes you're drunk or injured, and dare I say, sometimes you are fallible. Ignoring this is a recipe for failure in every single venture in life – love, business, art, self-defense.

I fully accept, as I write these very words, that the first draft of this book is going to be shit. And here I am, still writing a book that I know is going to be shit. But I'm confident there is gold buried deep, and it can be washed out, polished, and held in your hands. Had I resolved to write only gold from the onset, to finish a work of pure inspiration, not a single word would have been typed, not a single passion relayed. The pressure of such a task is suffocating. But if you can accept the prospect of getting hit in the face, well, sometimes you open the door for profound, nonlinear payback. Sometimes you get the man or woman of your dreams, knock the guy out in the first round, or write that bestseller, simply because you've survived the game.

My real lesson in survival and risk management came a decade earlier after a sparring session with Master Scott Yates, hapkido demigod. He complimented me for my skill and chastised me for my reservation. He told me at that time that I was a better kicker than he was, but that I wasn't going to beat him. In fact, he kicked the shit out of me. I fit the mold at that time, and showed him too much respect as my senior. This was in part an act of self-preservation. His skills were legendary even when he was young. But he dominated me at that time, nearly fifteen years ago now, and shattered all my illusions that a strategy based on not getting hit was valid.

Master Yates looked me in the eyes and said, "The difference between you and me is that I know you will hit me, but I'm going to beat you anyway. This game isn't about not getting hit. It's about hitting harder and more often than your opponent." Master Yates accepted, before he squared off with any opponent, that he was going to get hit. His strategies for success did not rely on being unscathed. He accepted that he might be hit, and possibly hurt, before he even began. No surprises to his game plan were possible. He accepted worst-case scenarios. He would still be the last man standing. The consequence, however, after decades of relinquishing all claims to winning without getting hit, was that he rarely got hit. People now see only the legend, but they miss the man who resolved to fight regardless of the consequences, regardless of the injuries that might result. They miss seeing the man who survived on a winning strategy of assumed losses.

As a trainer, I am faced with clients struggling to maintain their identity as strong, successful professionals and well-respected leaders. They struggle to endure the pain of training because they think it should be easier, the results should come faster, and their pant size should be reduced earlier. They think, "I'm good at what I do. People respect me. Why is this shit so hard and demoralizing?"

The truth is, it's hard because you assume a strength you don't possess. It's hard because it is hard. It actually is hard work to be strong, fit, and healthy. For most of us, ten-day master cleanses and five-minute abs, while not total nonsense, are closer to nonsense then they are to truth. We want the quick and easy. We want immediate gratification, the handy Snickers bar or pizza delivery. But this is not the world of health and fitness. Our bodies are not made strong in comfortable environments. They are built to survive, and in order to flourish they must be stressed, tested, and made to feel uncomfortable.

Everyone is perfect for the first two weeks of a fitness program. Some people are perfect for three weeks. A few for four. But everyone gets weak, hits the wall, and looks for an easy way out. Despite answering all questions early on, namely that spot reduction (targeting body fat on one part of the body) is not a practical or even viable approach to fat loss, I am confronted by clients, who, after a few weeks, while pinching a slab of belly fat inevitably ask, "Is there anything we can do for this?" They always look at me cockeyed when I reply in all sincerity and honesty, "Squats and lunges."

Genetics place and remove body fat intelligently, so as to place as little burden on our frames as possible. Where can we carry the most weight without it affecting general mobility? Around our midsections and upper thighs. It requires obesity before fat hands and feet materialize. Reversing this process follows the same logic. Fat leaves the midsection and thighs last, regardless of the type of training or specific exercises employed.

To get to the heart of the matter, to lean up and get abs, one must stay the course and do the hard work first. The abs will be the last to show. The bingo arms are the last to tighten, and cellulite on the thighs the last to vanish. This is your fight. You will lose weight, you will get stronger, and you will still have cellulite and bingo arms. It is your burden, your punch in the face, and your declining futures prices when you expect years of poor nutrition, lethargy, or poor lifestyle habits to vanish after a few weeks of hard training. You are not special. You will have to work hard, sweat, cry, and perhaps even grow to hate certain habits, foods, and friends. It must be addressed and prepared for ahead of time, and managed with callous focus.

Every client who enters Enso Temple says they know this. They all believe they can handle the stress of training and the nutritional changes I suggest. And they are right, so long as they are strong and motivated. Where all plans are set to go awry is in the assumption that this new self, the one that calls the trainer, throws all sugar in the garbage, and shows up the first week of training with the heart of a lion, will be there day after day.

"But I am me, I know what I want, and I'm going to make it happen," you say. Yes, nods the trainer. You are you. Today. But when I'm standing over a *different* you, a weaker you, the you that underestimated the pains of this journey, collapsed on the mats, dripping with sweat, gums aching, doubting, the you that overestimated your own strength, what is your plan for survival? The degree to which you can reduce the risk of *that* self guiding your decisions is the degree to which you will succeed on your path to bigger, better things. It is to that degree that you will become the phoenix, and not a pile of ash.

Anyone can turn down cakes and cookies when sated. Anyone can lift weights when bubbling over with energy. But what is your strategy for survival when your boss asks you to put in overtime, when your boyfriend sleeps with your best friend, when your car gets totaled, when you have a common cold, an ankle sprain, or severe fatigue? At some point the mother of all excuses will arise (or hell, maybe even a weak, convenient excuse), and you will believe it. You will say it's different, it's an exception, it's not the norm. It is the height of self-deception when people cannot tell they've been punched in the face, when they believe they are still winning, that they haven't even been hit.

As a self-defense instructor, I try as best I can to prepare clients for the reality of violence. I teach techniques that mirror gross body movements, such as pushes, pulls, and twists. These movements are enhanced when the fight-or-flight response floods the body with adrenaline and the sympathetic nervous system prepares the body for extreme conditions. Vision and hearing are impaired, pain tolerance increases, digestion ceases.

All blood is sent to the skeletal muscles to fuel superhuman strength at the expense of efficient, well-fed brain function and physical coordination. I teach techniques that become stronger under stress, not weaker. I teach points of anatomical weakness with which to break down an aggressor efficiently. Despite this tool kit for survival, there are still *two of you.*

One self attends self-defense classes, gets the heart rate up, studies techniques, thinks about life, love, and the pursuit of happiness, and ponders the imminent dangers of life-and-death encounters. The other you is primal, base, and raw. Who you are under normal conditions bears no resemblance to who you are when someone has a knife to your throat. A genetic code forty thousand to several hundred thousand years old dictates responses that only soldiers at war, prison inmates, and animals in the wild can fully appreciate. This self must be acknowledged, respected, and developed. In order to do so, the other self, the you as you know yourself, must reach its limits of effectiveness. It must fail, be proven weak, and adapt.

When a self-defense student has been with me a while and has reached a relative level of proficiency, then real training begins. I put them through an hour of brutal training with very little rest. We do intervals of high-intensity, all-out effort until absolutely nothing is left. Their bodies shake and tremble, their eyes lack focus, their movements become sloppy. *And then I make them fight.*

Only when a person is tired, weak, and broken do they find a way to survive and hone techniques that are genuinely practical. No theory can dictate this very personal selection of martial tools. They must be selected from the depths of one's understanding, out of necessity. This weak, broken trainee gets hit. They get hurt. I won't lie to you. But they do survive. And they leave that day, despite all fatigue and pain, with eyes ablaze, with a confidence that cannot be taken away.

The key to winning, again, is how you survive despite getting hit. You will get hit. If you trade, you will take losses. How do you keep them small enough to prevent blowing up? If you fight, you will get hit. How do you survive without being punished so severely that you'll never be whole again? If you undertake a journey of fitness and physical transformation, you will get hit, meet challenges, be faced with unexpected distractions, and confront life-training conflicts. How do you manage the self that dominates in times of weakness, insecurity, and self-doubt? What is your long-term strategy for managing a lack of willpower, motivation, and drive, lacks which are sure to surface?

Some of the most powerful survival tools in the game of health and fitness:

- **Start with the end in mind**. Clearly define your goals within a specific timeline. When a new client tells me their goal is to lose weight, I ask them to tell me in concrete terms what that means and in what period of time. *20 pounds of fat loss in three months* is a well-defined goal. *Lose some weight and get a little stronger* is not. If they cannot define their targets, I ask them to return when they can. A path without a destination is too easy to abandon.

- **Find a community** of like-minded individuals, people who not only care about your progress and support your goals, but who are also willing to keep you accountable. This might mean asking your spouse or partner to commit to lifestyle changes and healthy dinners with you. It might mean joining a group of committed fitness enthusiasts and reducing time spent with friends who have negative habits. It might mean hiring a personal trainer who gives you greater confidence in a structured and effective training plan, provides you with motivation, and keeps you accountable to your goals.

- **Identify primary distractions** as well as less likely but potential distractions (head cold, joint pain, working late, relationship problems, job loss, death in the family, etc.). One or more of these will materialize. Acknowledging these possibilities will remove the shock of being punched in the face and allow you to implement decision-making strategies that override their emotional weight.

- **Make contingency plans** that take into account all potential distractions. You will go to unplanned dinners, take spontaneous business trips, feel too tired to train, be overwhelmed with an insane sweet tooth at times, have frustrating aches and pains, and wind up at places with nothing on your diet menu. I tell all clients that if you don't know what you'll eat for every meal for the next three days, you're going to lose this battle long-term. This year I had two clients with identical objectives. Each was aiming to lose 60 pounds. The man failed, blaming each dietary deviation on external factors. "A friend was visiting and we went to a bar. My wife threw a party last weekend, but otherwise I was good. I had a weak moment but I'm back on now."

The woman, who reached her targets, had greater work pressures and a more demanding lifestyle than the man. She faced all the same challenges. Yet when she knew there was a party she had to attend she ate her planned meal beforehand, so as not to be tempted by cakes and cookies on an empty stomach. She drank water instead of alcohol. When pressured by colleagues to drink, she told them she was on meds that would clash. When she had aches and pains and head colds, which are also sure to arise, she forewarned me every time via text message so I could adjust her workload accordingly. She did not simply cancel. She showed up to every scheduled session unless I told her to rest for health or safety reasons, which did occur on occasion. There were days when she cried, cursed, and voiced her hatred of training. But she showed up even when it was tough. She always showed up.

- **Have skin in the game.** Create a sense of urgency and importance by putting something of value at risk, creating a motivating reward, or both. These must be strong incentives that will override your short-term desire for comfort when you hit the motivational wall, which you will. I won't set a personal physique or performance target without also scheduling a photo or video shoot, which carries the reward of acquiring strong marketing material and the risk of financial loss (the cost of content creation) or social disapproval (not looking like a trainer on camera).

  You might hire a trainer, which carries the risk of lost dollars if you cancel sessions or don't complete your training within an expiration period. You might post public photos of yourself in your current, undesirable state, which carries the risk of that being the last thing people see of you as well the motivating reward of releasing an updated photo with your impressive new physique a couple of months later. You might purchase an active holiday trip where your physical strength and stamina are required in order to enjoy the trip and have the experience of a lifetime. Put skin in the game, and you'll realize a focus and motivation you didn't know you had.

What steps will *you* take to ensure success, despite everything?

Once the comfort-seeking self is put to rest and the mind is resolved to simply show up to the game, day after day, month after month, then a foundation is set for holistic transformation. By managing one's insecurities, fears, and the externals that may affect us, the free, artistic spirit housed in all of us can finally have a chance to express its individuality with confidence, power, and creativity.

Chapter 4

ENSO ORIGINS AND THE ONE-ARMED MAN

The one-armed man swung and punched, blocked and parried, coordinating complex Shaolin forms with catlike grace. No, it wasn't him; he only had one arm. That was everybody else at the live-in Shaolin Gong Fu Academy nestled in the verdant countryside of Siping, Jilin Province. But having one arm didn't stop that man from trying. And it didn't stop his master from teaching him two-armed forms (which led to very interesting phantom techniques suggested by the beautiful lines of a nub that pointed nowhere). Now any compassionate reader would expect this to evolve into a story about overcoming, about doing your best, and accomplishing the impossible.

It's not. And there is no such lesson. The one-armed man and his Shaolin master were idiots.

But that didn't stop them from practicing kung fu. For the uninitiated, the term *kung fu* (more accurately pronounced *gong fu*) was not always applied to martial arts. It's a term that implies deep skill. There's a type of tea in China, *kung fu* tea, that is served with a bit of ceremony, somewhat akin to Zen tea pouring, although generally without the latter's concentrated state of awareness. One may say a good tea pourer has *kung fu*. And kung fu, while generally identified by strict adherence to form, is above form. It is deeply imbedded skill and wisdom. It requires knowledge of the rules, but it also contains wisdom enough to determine when rules should be broken.

The one-armed man had no business practicing two-armed forms. The mere sight of it made me want to slap a monk. Any monk. I wanted to freeze the whole room, grab a megaphone, and scream, "Can you not see that poor son of a bitch has only one arm?" Unequals should not be treated equally. If he is ever to learn real kung fu, he needs to understand his genuine limitations, embrace them, and become whole in spite of them. To deny them is to reinforce his weakness. Fighting with one arm in a two-armed fight is akin to bringing a knife to a gunfight, unless he is capable of employing strategies that only a one-armed man could fully understand and appreciate.

But alas, these monks were not the warrior-saints and masters of legendary skills one envisions when picturing a mystic, rural China. In form, they were profoundly effective, graceful, and explosive. After class, however, they blended well with the cooks who would chain smoke and throw rocks at the chained dogs, or the in-house physician whose cure for every ailment was the heat lamp. Sprained ankle? Heat lamp. Stomach cramps? Heat lamp. Severe sunburn? Heat lamp. Or, treatment number two, non-disinfected needles stuck in random points throughout the body. Science.

I couldn't be too quick to slap a monk. They were human beings after all, and fallible. In fairness, this type of bias is not uncommon for most people in all walks of life. The master taught what he knew. But he only knew what it meant to be a two-armed man, and a kung fu master. Shaolin kung fu was perfect after all, and had to be practiced in its entirety, even if the person practicing it was not whole. The master could see only the form, not the man.

How many forms are we all practicing while ignoring our individual differences?

See the Person, not the Form

I met MF in the spring of 2010, shortly before I left Shanghai for a one-year stint in Hong Kong. She was still in the process of recovering from severe long-term burnout at that time. She told me her story over an hour-long phone call, trying to contain her emotion and frustration. She wanted to become whole again and make significant changes in life. She had always loved kung fu, and her recent experiences had led her to not take time for granted. She wanted to learn. She was also deeply afraid of starting, both because it was new and uncharted territory, but also because she'd lost confidence in her body, a body that was once well-trained when she was a competitive dancer.

Less than a year prior to our first meeting, MF had been hospitalized after completely collapsing on holiday. She'd blacked out and lost the strength to move and even speak. In our first session together, she was shaky with nerves and continuously looked at her hands in front of her as if looking through the eyes of another person, observing a body that wasn't hers. But caged within that frail body was one of the strongest minds I'd ever met. Over the course of a couple months of fundamental martial arts training, meditation, and assisted stretching (which she hates to this day), MF regained confidence in her body and began to feel her fractured parts reuniting. Her holistic transformation manifested in a wellspring of passion and focus that could no longer be sated by the lifestyle to which she'd grown accustomed.

Six months later, over a casual coffee reunion at Starbucks on D'Aguilar Street in central Hong Kong, MF (who was passing through on business) and I started discussing dreams, life goals, and creative interests. After fifteen years as a marketing director of a Fortune 500 fast-moving consumer goods company, and working on the small team that managed the turnaround of their Asia Pacific business, she'd begun to consider realizing her dream of creating her own high fashion brand. She'd been drawing and designing, and showed me her early sketches. Within another six months, they would become the landmark pieces of her bold fashion vision, showcased in her first catwalk show.

MF is a survivor, a petite sparkplug who has a habit of getting what she wants, crushing obstacles, and not taking no for an answer. She dresses boldly with strong asymmetric cuts, always black and white, more often than not of her own design. She balances this strength with sharp wit and a passion for enjoying life. MF's vision for her fashion bore a stronger resemblance to my own vision of martial arts and fitness than anything I could have predicted. It was a resemblance without which I might never have seen fashion as anything more than feminine Friday night fanciness.

She wanted a brand for strong, confident women in tune with their sexuality. She wanted it to be modern, sensual, and marked by asymmetric, black-and-white cuts. Above all she wanted people to be amazed by the women who wore her designs, and not the designer who made them. She wanted a brand that required confidence to wear but also elevated the confidence of women to be themselves – bold, beautiful, sensual, and free. She wanted a place where she could not only launch her brand, but also provide custom tailoring for women, where her ready-to-wear fashion could be altered or new, unique pieces could be designed for greater self-expression. It was in this vision that we recognized an undeniable synergy between our passions.

For years I'd been providing private personal training in Shanghai and Hong Kong. My custom martial arts and fitness programs got fast results and helped clients get to a place of strength, confidence, and happiness. For years, my own martial arts style had been unrecognizable to those who practiced the formal arts. After years of teaching privately, I had been forced to cast aside most of the formality inculcated since my youth. The forms made me in part what I was – strong, structured, flexible, and capable. But they failed to deliver a practical knowledge of martial skills in short periods of time.

My clients have no time to waste. They come to me because they need effective, intelligent programs customized to their unique interests, needs, affinities, and personality types. They need to acquire these skills in a quarter of the time of your average trainee.

My own system of martial arts is heavily influenced by hapkido, tae kwon do, Shaolin kung fu, Thai boxing, Western boxing, and hand-to-hand street self-defense tactics. It is also influenced to a lesser degree by jujitsu, Jeet Kune Do, tai chi, and capoeira. Despite this background, my methods of teaching, transitions, interceptions, and the general structure of my techniques became unique enough that I wasn't sure what to call my art.

I was a personal trainer. I taught martial arts.

I used the tools and principles I'd accrued over two and a half decades of dedicated practice to develop people as unique individuals, individuals with different strengths and weaknesses, different personalities and body types. If at any time I had ten private martial arts clients, they were on ten curricula so distinct that one would be hard pressed to identify a single instructor behind them all.

An indelible seed was planted that day, over spirited dreaming and half-seriousness. MF and I saw clearly the artistic connection between our crafts. We also saw, from a practical perspective, how our services would appeal to a very similar market. We joked about, pondered, and posited an all-in-one mind, body, and image enhancement destination, where people could receive custom fitness and martial arts training programs, sculpt their bodies, strengthen their minds, and get custom-tailored fashion. They would leave showing off fierce new physiques, expressing their inner confidence and individuality. It would be a destination that saw the individual, not only the form. We just needed a name that symbolized the artistic spirit of our mission.

The *enso* is a broken circle, painted with a single brush stroke, that symbolizes beauty as an expression of the moment. Perfect in its imperfection, its simplicity and asymmetry symbolize freedom from form. It suggests that enlightenment is an immediate, personal relationship with the present. The enso is the art principle. It is the symbol of free, creative expression manifested by immediate insight. The height of a Zen master's enlightenment can be seen in the quality of his hand-painted enso. I knew that the enso, in principle, was a central theme to our combined vision, and I was adamant it be included. MF insisted on the inclusion of the word *temple* in the name, symbolizing spirituality and purity of self-expression, and the simplicity that was a central trait of both our crafts.

Eight months later our fashion and fitness lounge was open for business in an old ranch-style colonial house in Shanghai's French Concession. Plenty of light poured into the new MF Fashion Showroom through a wall of glass doors that led to the main garden entrance, secluded and set back from the main street. Adjacent to the showroom was my private training studio – quaint, comfortable, and innocent.

MF designed all the furniture to be consistent with her fashion: simple, modern, elegant, black and white. She also designed furniture for the garden, which glowed in the summer sun, enclosed by bamboo on one side and a stone waterfall on the other. Clients and friends immediately fell in love with the space. Enso was our commitment to the idea that honestly addressing individual differences is the foundation of powerful self-expression and confident living. In our reclusive Enso Temple, we customized fashion, fitness, and martial arts. We elevated and practiced individuality and independence above conformity. We insisted on seeing the people, not the forms.

BOOK 2

Enso Temple

Confidential case studies from the trenches of physical transformation, health, and rehab.

In *Enso Temple* we explore the physical pillars of Weightlessness: the indelible laws of rapid fat loss and muscle gain, the antifragile nature of the human body, primal principles of health and nutrition, and lost secrets of elite physical performance.

Chapter 1

THE POWER OF TRANSFORMATION
(AND THE HUMOR OF FAILED ATTEMPTS)

From the Early Days of Enso Files

T he spirit of Enso and the serenity of its deep blue mats purified everything and everyone who set foot on them. In addition to the flow of bodily juices – blood (rarely), sweat (lots), and tears (hmmm, them too) – my clients, with few exceptions, are spiritually naked before me. Crossing that threshold is a commitment to change, to face pain, to embrace insecurity, and to find the warrior within. The process is not without casualties, but is unparalleled in refining the spirit and molding an indomitable will. Along the way clients admit defeat, curse themselves, vomit sometimes, fall in love, grow to hate me, laugh, cry, expose the darkest corners of their lives, and discover a strength they never knew they had.

Aside from playing the military hard-ass or compassionate friend, my role sometimes evolves to that of a veritable confidant, a neo-bartender who sedates clients with nonjudgmental listening. As I destroy their bodies, their last lines of psychological defense and inhibition go with them. I've been consulted on all topics, from marriage to business decisions. I've seen people black out, and have frequently been privy to decisions of divorce, infidelity, investment, and work-lifestyle changes even before spouses, family, and closest friends are informed. I've been a warm shoulder to cry on when the stress of training causes the release of twenty years of suppressed childhood trauma.

I train people not because I deeply care about the almighty six-pack, but because I have seen, time and time again, the internal transformation that occurs amid the pains of physical growth. I teach because I know the healing power of pain. I teach because of the miracle that occurs after complete defeat and acquiescence. And I teach because I am strong enough not to compromise on the path needed for success, but compassionate enough to let someone reach the depths of hopelessness and self-doubt at the appropriate time, so that together we can pick up the pieces.

Fitness is a constant uphill battle. The body adapts faster than the mind. But there is that magical moment when the mind realizes that old complaints and fears are no longer valid. That moment when it realizes it doesn't belong to the same weak person in need of excuses.

For those who have let themselves stray farther from the path of health and fitness than they intended, there is real soul searching. As soon as the body becomes weak from lunges, push-ups, and crunches, the mind, formerly fortified, becomes exposed and vulnerable. Inhibitions are lost, tears are shed, profanity is slewed, and one of two reactions occurs.

The first reaction is rebellion and anger, usually self-directed. This comes from the realization of one's own weakness, something few people want to acknowledge. This is the tipping point of progress and where most casualties occur.

The second reaction to the suffocating pressure of pain and fatigue is innocence and yielding acquiescence – but of a different nature to prior compliance. When people begin to train they need targets, timelines, defined sets and reps. They follow all orders, though perhaps with a fair amount of griping, and they complete the work. But at this stage they need to know exactly what's expected. They need to process and mentally prepare for pain to come. When all attempts at being strong and winning fail and they begin to realize they're only halfway through a grueling set, having lost all hope of completing it, I ask one pointed question: "Do you have enough inside for just one more rep?"

I am not kind at this stage. Sometimes I release more fire than I intend, and sometimes the pressure is too great and a trainee decides to return to their artificial security. The sight of this weakness repulses me, but not because I cannot accept weakness in others. It's because I see myself, broken, bleeding, doubting, hopeless. I see myself in the jungle of Koh Phangan, in the forest in Jilin, pins and needles in my legs, lacking even the strength to stand up again.

Everything relies on this moment; it can't be overstated. It is the moment of life and death. Which will you chose? Can you stand? Can you give just one more rep and release all fear, forget all hope? Can you, like Sisyphus, condemned to an eternity of rolling a boulder up a hill only to watch it roll back down again, condemned to a life of monotony and pain, can you, at this moment, see some iota of beauty and choose life?

And with that first repetition comes a second, and a third. The *overcomer* is born. A workout deemed impossible is complete, and the doubting self, the self that craves security, is put to rest. After the point of no return is reached, that point of absolute physical and emotional weakness, the trainee surrenders. That is the point from which genuine strength arises. In the same way that existentialism requires nihilism as a precursor, genuine strength requires a mind that has lost all hope, and yet has resolved to carry on, despite all the unknown consequences. A heavy mind is burdened by the fear of failure and the hope of success, since its well-formed identity can be proven a fraud. The warrior, the weightless person, is not concerned with such trivialities. Success or failure is a matter of contingency, of coincidence. The choice to stand and fight, win or lose, this is strength.

But alas, not all sessions reach that existential point of self-creation. Nor do all programs lead to a pinnacle of physical transformation.

The early days of Enso Temple, despite many success stories, were wrought with a fair share of absurdities and frivolous exchanges. Among them was the Betsy incident. Betsy had never exercised before, evidenced by the worst squats I'd ever seen, knees buckling inward with a real possibility of total skeletal collapse. Push-ups, even from the knees, forget it. She was your typical China doll – petite, skinny-fat, raised on dumplings and milk tea. She was sweet enough though, and seemed intent on making real changes. After our first session Betsy was totally broken, but not broken enough.

"So where do you live?" she inquired, batting her long black lashes.

"Well, here, I guess," I replied.

"Oh, that's great. So convenient."

"Indeed, I wouldn't have it any other way. Helps me be on time."

"Can I see your room?" She inched closer.

"Well, it's a bit messy."

"I don't mind," she said. "Can I see it anyway? I just want to see where you sleep."

"Uh, no."

She inched closer still. "Take me to your room. Do you have condom?"

I was beginning to suspect she had ulterior motives.

"Um, nope, no condoms I'm afraid."

"It's okay," she said, grinning ear to ear. "There's a convenience store on your corner, let's go buy some."

"I mean, you're hot, but I'm too tired to go shopping. And it's getting late."

It was 8pm.

"It's not shopping, it's literally thirty meters away. I'm offering myself to you."

"I appreciate that, I do. Just a bit tired. And I really can't sleep with clients, it's a rule I have."

This was mostly true.

The larger truth was I couldn't forget her squats and that shaky awkwardness, her lack of grace and strength. It wasn't gonna happen. She slumped onto the sofa in the MF Fashion Showroom, head drooping into hands, eyes covered.

"I'm so embarrassed," she said. "I don't know how I can face you again."

"Ah, no big deal. We're cool. Shake it off."

Real coachy of me.

"I'll see you in two days."

"I can't, I really can't," she said, nearly in tears. "No one has rejected
me before."

"It's just late, Betsy. And it's policy. Is it really that bad that you can't
train with me again? I thought you were serious about training."

"I can't, I can't come back."

"If I sleep with you, I can train you, but if I don't, you're not coming back?"

"Basically, yeah. I can't come back. Too embarrassing."

I went to my room and returned with a full refund. Things got weird. I
had to kick her out and lock up Enso. Our parting, like her squats, lacked
grace. She rushed out, heart on sleeve, cash in hand, never to return.
Unfortunately, Betsy and I did not traverse the deep waters of pain that
lead to existential ecstasy in the gym or the bedroom. But give me a break,
it was after eight.

There was also Q, a Californian Chinese-American raised by his
mother to be extremely sensitive, polite, and pure crap at sports. Q stole
my towels. This wouldn't be a significant detail in most gyms, but in the
small boutique of Enso Temple, space was limited, towels were numbered,
and since the arrival of Q, they were disappearing at a rapid pace.

Q was particularly sweaty, so much so that after ten warm-up squats,
he was dripping. I don't like sweat. I'd regularly ask Q to dry off to prevent
him slipping and getting injured. Q addressed his sweatiness in the very
strange order of armpit first, face second. I never understood it and was
a bit disgusted. After decades of martial arts training, the compulsion to
treat my training space as myself was deeply ingrained. Etiquette and
hygiene aren't to be overlooked.

"Your towels smell *so* good," Q commented early on in his training.
"What fabric softener do you use?"

"I'm not sure, Q," I replied. "Just regular softener I guess. I'll ask the *ayi*
[cleaning lady]."

"That would be great. I just love this smell, it reminds me of you."

"That's good... I guess."

Where many clients broke under the pressure of training, Q just got weird as winter began to surface.

"So, I only see you in gym clothes," he said. "It's getting colder. Like, what do you wear when you go outside?"

"Uh, I don't know," I said in a nervous stutter. "Long clothes?"

"Cool, I'd like to see that some time."

This conversation was followed by obsequious and insanely courteous text messages regarding the brilliance of each and every session. He sincerely thanked me for everything, reminiscing about how he used to lift less weight, but could now lift more. He wanted me to move to sunny Cali to train him when he returned home. Admittedly, I'm a little slow on picking up the gay vibe. It wasn't until MF, my partner in crime, attributed the missing towels to his being in love that I got it.

Awkward.

Despite his politeness and extreme love affair with my gym towels, I don't like theft. So one day I decided to get to the bottom of things and set a trap for him. I removed all other towels in the hamper before Q's session. If there was no towel in the hamper after his departure, I'd have him!

There was no towel. I sent him a polite text asking if he'd accidently forgotten to drop his towel, as I'd started missing a few. He admitted his "accident." Now keep in mind, Q was a massive sweat monkey, those towels were dripping after every session, fuming with armpit stink and face puddles. Nobody "accidently" places that mess in a bag of otherwise clean clothes and things.

So I pushed a little further. "And did you happen to accidently take any before? Like many?"

"I'll check when I get home," he said. "I may have." Later: "I did have one other towel. Sorry. I will return them both next class."

Regrettably, there is no greater moral to this story. I just want to say: Q, you're a great guy, and if you're reading this and still have my stuff, please send it to Enso Temple at 339 Changle Lu, House 1, Shanghai, China. Thank you.

And then there was Ling, a mainland cosmetics executive. Ling was a tough cookie. She was a tad rotund, with generally round features. Despite a significant language barrier, and as I later discovered cultural barrier, she was determined to train with "the best trainer in Shanghai." Her words, not mine. We had a bumpy start. She was often late, which the martial artist in me does not handle particularly well, and I usually insisted on two to three hundred squats as a recompense.

Ling had a notable peculiarity, a compulsive, guttural, dry-heaving gas problem. She was a goddamned burp factory. I'd never seen anything like it. Ten minutes into every session, she would start convulsing like a ten-year-old on the playground trying to impress his friends with this new skill, aiming for laughs, earning respect. It wasn't working for me. More often than not, she came in after a heavy meal of god only knows what. But definitely garlic. The noxious fumes were peeling paint on the other side of the room and making my eyes water. I couldn't take it anymore.

"Ling!" I shouted. "Don't do that!" She was a thirty-five-year-old exec, educated and otherwise cultured, and I was chastising her like a five-year-old. I had to do it in Chinese too, which I often butcher.

"Huh?" she said.

"That, that thing you do," I said. "Don't do that thing. Too disgusting."

Nervous laughter on her end.

"Why does it happen?" she asked.

"You make it happen."

"It's from training," she corrected me.

"It's not from training. It's not from lunch. It's not from anything. In twenty-five years of training, I have never seen anything like it. In ten years of coaching, I have never had a client that had this reaction to training. It's you. You practice it, so it keeps happening." "How do I stop it?"

"For one month, no disgusting burping, and you'll be okay."

"I can't help it. It's because I have too much qi!"

I look around for a candid camera but don't spot one.

"No, Ling," I said. "You don't have too much qi. I have more qi than you. I don't burp like that. Start the next set."

I was never able to cure Ling of her guttural explosions, but they did wane a bit as her awareness of my disgust improved.

The early days of Enso had their moments of unforgettable honesty as well, ones that came about without any effort on my part. In the first ten minutes of C's first session, she crumpled into the fetal position and released a secret that had weighed on her for two decades. People have always quickly opened up to and confided in me, so it didn't surprise me as much as it should have. But what should have been a forty-five-minute assessment became a two-hour, tear-drenched shoulder session filled with heart-wrenching stories of childhood rape.

C became her uncle's secret plaything before the age of ten. It was a secret deeply locked away after threats of murder should she tell anyone. I was the first person to hear these horrors in twenty years. But crossing the threshold of the deep blue mats is often far more cathartic than the comfort of a psychiatrist's black leather sofa. The mere acts of stepping out and stepping in, of acknowledging poor choices and poor health, of reframing obesity as self-protection against soulless men, these acts open people up to their innermost fears and insecurities. It's like removing shards of shrapnel from an open flesh wound.

C became a regular, seeing me up to four days a week for several months. She became much stronger and healthier. Despite late-night marijuana self-medication for past pain and binges on McDonald's and potato chips, she lost weight, a new body was unveiled, and with it a greater confidence emerged. After only two months, she said that for the first time in twenty years she was able to look at herself in the mirror. She had been the only client at our original Enso Temple who elected to face the open French colonial glass doors that faced our garden while training, to avoid her reflection. It was a glorious moment when, in the midst of a set of jumping jacks, she bounced to face herself in the mirrors. And smiled, never to turn back.

Chapter 2

MONKEY ISLAND AND THE TAO OF NUTRITION

From the Star Wars Files

I love observing animals in nature. Perhaps I think I'll learn something about myself (or all of us) that got lost in the mess of making a living and building the perfect world. On the other hand, with the exception of the mother-infant bond, most animals lack compassion for one another. The alpha takes what he pleases – women, food, or the best perching rock – and the rest is up for grabs. On a recent trip to Thailand I visited a place accurately dubbed Monkey Island, about an hour outside Hua Hin and a twenty-minute canoe trip from the mainland. The island is full of those little bastards. I can't tell you which type they were, but they weren't chimps and weren't the kind with asses for faces. They were strong and curious and free, as monkeys go.

The friend I was traveling with wanted to bring some chips for the long journey. I tend not to eat them, but I figured that since we were going to a deserted island twenty minutes away and would be gone for all of an hour, it wouldn't hurt to stock up on nourishments. My friend had been there before, so she knew that open food there was a bad idea. She buried one open bag and three unopened ones within a duffel bag. Upon our safe arrival, we enjoyed communing with our distant ancestors for a little while, until a father and daughter team rowed up to shore.

Humans.

The little girl hadn't received the open container memo and was chowing down happily as her father rowed them onto dry land. Within a minute she was surrounded by monkeys hunting for chips while her father jabbed and slashed with his oar at the alpha to keep them at bay. *Drop the chips, kiddo, or the monkeys'll getcha.* They spooked, dropped the bag, and got the hell out of Dodge. I sat quietly observing this reverse zoo, waiting for the monkey thumping about to take place. Nature is inspiring.

Naturally, once they got a taste of that girl's chips they started wondering if the other invaders had brought anything. One genius monkey came over to our canoe, unzipped the duffel, and pulled out the plastic bag full of chips, holding them high in the air like a goddamn trophy. In the animal kingdom, brains still don't beat brawn. The alpha went over and took what he felt was his, and the other monkeys sat around afraid, jealous, and hungry until he was well finished. That included a skinny mother with her baby dangling beneath her. The best part was that I found half-eaten bananas not far from where we were sitting and watching.

As thought-provoking as this natural dynamic was, I had only one thought: "Little bastards are one canoe visit away from diabetes. Diabetes Island."

And so it begins. Monkey Island is still relatively desolate, and the monkeys there are still quite lean and fit. But give them time. In twenty to thirty years, they'll be living on chips, getting unemployment for bad knees due to morbid obesity, and shooting insulin into their monkey asses to make use of all the simple carbs that chips can provide.

Okay, this may be a *bit* of a stretch. Maybe.

One of my fitness clients, a Burmese monk from Canada, came to me after a recent four-month stint in Burma. He'd lived on a small bowl of donated food each day. He came in with a rather wasted physique, slightly gaunt. Within two months he had put on twenty-five pounds, most of it muscle, and started looking quite the athlete. During one of our sessions, he told me about the increasing number of diabetic monks throughout Southeast Asia. My immediate thought was, "Jesus, I have no use for monks with diabetes." But he wasn't joking. It's a real problem.

On the one hand, Buddhist monks in the mindfulness camp are committed to nonjudgment, living fully in the moment, and treating all gifts with sincere gratitude. On their morning alms trek through the village, they don't have a large say in which nibbles are placed in their bowls. Therefore they are not at liberty to keep the meat and vegetables and send back the bread. Nor do they always want to. The road to hell is paved with good intentions. Or rather, the road to diabetes is paved with nonjudgmental consumption. The other problem is an overall lack of nutritional education, not an ailment exclusive to Burmese monks. We all have this problem to varying degrees.

But it used to be simple. There were times when Twinkies and instant coffee with added sugar didn't exist, or were too expensive for most people to consume freely. Morning alms meant a bowl full of fresh veggies, lean meat (because fat was a luxury), and rice. My client recalled an episode where his mentor, a renowned monk in his own right, was invited to a meeting with several other monks to discuss monk things (I'm paraphrasing). There were two trays of food. One had fresh fruit, the other candy and junk food. My client was the only one to eat from the fresh fruit tray, which he, after long-term intermittent fasting, devoured. The other monks were puzzled that he'd go for something so banal when all these other goodies were available.

Weightless Tangent

When simple sugars are consumed (and these come in many forms, including pastas, white breads, cakes, cookies, and donuts), your pancreas secretes insulin in order to do something with the surge of sugar within your blood. It works feverishly to reduce blood sugar by ushering it into cells within the liver, skeletal muscles, or, unfortunately, body fat. If you don't need this surge of sugar – that is, if your muscle cell energy reserves are full or you're a sugar junkie – then your sensitivity to insulin quickly becomes compromised. This leads to energy crashes and fat gain. Insulin is a super hormone and a double-edged sword. It can help fast-track rapid body transformation and lean muscle gain when spiked methodically. Yet it can also lead to insulin insensitivity and an inability to use sugar for anything but augmenting body fat.

Eat Real Things

Once considered beacons of spiritual and physical health, monks are now afflicted with many common ailments that stem from poor nutrition. Most of them sport physiques that are far from inspiring. This is an apt microcosm for the developing world at large. Our natural diets have been replaced with grocery stores and fast food where the bulk of foodstuffs are processed and altered to such a degree that you're hard-pressed to figure out how they ever came from the earth. Many of the foods still similar to their original form, like fruit and vegetables, are frozen and transported, losing a large percentage of their nutrition and micronutrient content.

We live when we eat living things. The fresher the thing, the closer it is to drawing its energy from the sun (or if it eats things that get their energy from the sun), the more readily we assimilate it, and the more we flourish.

Don't believe me? Eat fresh, locally grown fruit and veg and freshly butchered (not frozen) meat for just one week. Just that. Nothing else. Only one week. You'll discover a you that you never knew. Your energy will abound. You'll lose a bit of fat. You'll want to exercise, or even better play, due to the added energy from real nutrition. The absurdity is that most people believe the burden of proof lies on the advocates of eating real things. *It doesn't.*

Our DNA has not evolved markedly in the last forty thousand years. Forty thousand years ago we gathered, hunted, and ate. We did not eat in order to hunt (consider this, you advocates of pre-workout meals). We ate real things like fresh fruits, vegetables, nuts, meats, and fish. Food was all fresh because there were no refrigerators or preservatives. Current anthropological accounts of our very early predecessors portray early Homo sapiens as stronger and faster than we are and as well-built as modern Olympic athletes. Their environmental stresses and natural diets built strong, lean, warrior physiques. Women were tall, lean, strong, and hourglass-shaped like today's fitness models, not the runway gals. They also lived long lives if they survived the environment. There were more natural dangers, and people died young. But those who lived and survived the wild lived long and strong.

Dead are the days when you need to eat something or adhere to a diet because 'it works.' What the hell does 'it works' mean, anyway? That it allows you to fit into a smaller dress size or shed a few inches of your beer gut? There is only one thing that works: nourish your body, and avoid things that don't do that. Live, goddamn it! Flourish. A crash diet that aims at dropping pounds denies an element of our humanity that we cannot afford to lose. We are physical beings. We live in this world and survive by converting living things into energy and new living tissue. Celebrate this fact.

A byproduct of eating that which we have evolved to eat is that you'll become strong, lean, and undeniably healthy. Your energy, complexion, and general outlook on life will improve. You'll want to play, to laugh, to fight, to sing, to paint, to have sex, to explore, to live. It works. It fucking works. Eat real things. Avoid sugars and grains.

For how long does one need to maintain this diet, you may ask? Well, forever. It's nature's gift to you, your sword and shield.

The Tao of Nutrition

Luke Skywalker was whiny. It's a miracle he ever acquired knowledge of the Force. Being from the countryside, and uneducated I presume, does lend itself well to an unquestioning acceptance of mysticism. But alas, he was destined to be a Jedi knight, like his father before him. The fascinating thing about the Force is that it is neither good nor evil, but can be used by both for whichever purpose. The biggest problem throughout the *Star Wars* series is not the existence of the evil Sith lords, those abusers and users of the dark side of the Force. The biggest problem is an imbalance in the Force.

An imbalance in the Force (toward evil) threatens the safety of the galaxy and needs to be dealt with through counter-Force. Fortunately, George Lucas never had to deal with an overabundance of good Jedis in need of aggressive rebalancing by the dark side. Convenient. But we understand it, because we still prefer good to evil, and Sith lords and Vaders are generally ugly or super old and not particularly fun to hang out with.

But the Force, like the Tao, is a polar monism, a harmonious union of opposing forces, such as good and evil, light and dark, feminine and masculine, constipation and the squirts, Jedis and Ewoks. Let's look at the latter.

In the classic battle of Jedis vs. Ewoks, Jedis must keep Ewoks from multiplying and infesting the galaxy. So the key is balance, not eradication. Most natural foods are nourishing, but when consumed in excess create excess storage and metabolic complications. Likewise, intermittent fasting is good, but starvation is bad. Acknowledging your body's proclivity toward health and homeostasis is crucial in understanding how you should eat, and as mainstream diets go, determining 'what works.'

Your body's endocrine system is akin to the Force in *Star Wars*. It comprises opposing hormones that, when balanced, lead to perfect health. Some of these, testosterone and estrogen, insulin and glucagon, and a host of anabolic (growth) and catabolic (reductionary) hormones (like growth hormone and cortisol, respectively), work in tandem to control energy levels, muscle growth and maintenance, fat storage or utilization, and sex drive. Most nutritionists, trainers, and even medical doctors encourage people to live consistent lives and eat consistent meals comprised of a specific balance of macronutrients. This approach is the same as assuming that the galaxy is perfect and simply needs to be maintained. But it isn't. Ewoks are breeding like maniacs, and the good side of the Force must retaliate.

Your body is brilliant. It's efficient. It's resilient. And when it's exposed to stresses, discomforts, and inconsistencies – listen carefully – it becomes stronger. More Ewoks equals tougher Jedis. A galaxy with no real threat of darkness is a galaxy of fat, lazy, inaccurate light saber-swinging Jedis. Monks with diabetes.

A lean and strong body is most effectively achieved in an environment of *inconsistency*. In stark contrast to modern bodybuilding theory, which relies on chronic overconsumption with a strict emphasis on protein, our protein absorption and utilization increases dramatically when our bodies are deprived. It's our Jedi response to an Ewok threat. Growth hormone and testosterone, two super hormones that dictate lean muscle gain and fat loss, are commonly injected into the asses of competitive bodybuilders. Do you know what else elevates growth hormone? Fasting!

Weightless Tangent

When calorie intake ebbs, the flow of natural anabolic growth hormones rises. To overcompensate for the threat of starvation and the loss of lean mass, your body produces hormones that heighten nutrient absorption and utilization during one's next meal. The body allocates resources where they are most needed to preserve life, and if this process is accompanied by physical training, it overcompensates by constructing bigger, denser muscle.

On the other hand, chronic overeating and lethargy (as well as overtraining) reduce your body's natural production of anabolic hormones (which is why big guys inject them) and increases your stress hormone levels, setting the stage for muscle loss and fat gain. This can be cushioned considerably by sticking to natural whole foods and avoiding processed foods, grains, and sugars, and keeping to short, intense workouts. Calorie shifting (alternating between high- and low-calorie meals, and high- and low-calorie days) maximizes the benefits of undereating and overeating, and reduces the risk of metabolic decline and excess calorie storage as body fat.

A similar polarity exists in the realm of carbohydrate consumption. Carbs are Ewoks. They can be accepted in small numbers, and there may even be a place for them in excess, like during late-night campfire entertainment. Hell, the more the merrier. But for the most part, get rid of them. Carbohydrates, in particular simple carbohydrates found in cakes, cookies, candy, noodles, rice, and potatoes, cause a rise in insulin, a super hormone and a super-dangerous hormone.

Weightless Tangent

Insulin causes muscles to absorb glucose (a kind of sugar that comes from the carbohydrates and other sugars we consume) from the blood, and is added to energy stores as glycogen. When blood sugar is spiked too frequently and insulin is released in excess, your body becomes less sensitive to insulin and glucose. Rather than energy being stored in muscles, it gets stored as body fat in the form of triglycerides.

Excessive carbohydrate consumption leads to a few possibilities. The first is energy spikes and crashes. Eat a big bowl of pasta or a chocolate cake, and you'll know what I mean. The second is fat gain and with it, stubborn fat that is difficult to remove. The third possibility is diabetes, which can result from excessive insulin release and consequent insulin insensitivity. But we all know this, which is why every crash dieter has a deeply imbedded fear of and love-hate relationship with carbs.

To make myself very clear, your greatest health is achieved by the removal of all carbs that come from grains and sugars, while those that come from fruits and vegetables are okay. Yes, fruits and veggies have carbohydrates, but most of them do not considerably affect insulin levels or blood sugar.

But this is not the whole story, and sometimes a splash of complexity makes the cocktail sing. Insulin, when spiked methodically, can radically shift body composition. How do I know this? Because I have used this as a working theory for years to help male clients gain ten to twenty pounds of lean muscle in less than six weeks, with only one to two hours of training per week. How do I do this? I create temporary states of Ewok overabundance and allow the Force to overcompensate.

Energy deficits, manifested as real hunger, and extreme stress (high-intensity resistance training), followed by carbohydrate intake and a massive caloric surge, are the yin and yang of natural bodybuilding. We prime an anabolic growth state by inducing a catabolic state. Your body, seeking homeostasis, releases mad Jedis (insulin, growth hormone, and testosterone) that, when armed with the light sabers of sound nutrition, beat the living shit out of Ewoks. They construct an indelible tower of strength with their miniature bones.

The muscle cell energy vacuum is rapidly filled with glycogen, amino acids, and micronutrients, resulting from an extreme insulin response. Muscles bulge. Due to a heightened sensitivity and real need for nourishment (the consequence of hunger and heavy resistance training), all incoming energy is used productively to repair and construct new tissue. And the galaxy cheers. Carbohydrate cycling (alternating between a diet of few to no calories from grains or sugars to the occasional spike in complex carbohydrates) in this manner can be a powerful bodybuilding tool, as well as an effective way of maximizing lean body mass.

And this leads me to my next point. Your body is not a furnace. The long-held belief that your body is a machine with set energy requirements dictated by a set energy expenditure is wrong. Your body is not a furnace. Your metabolism is not constant. The *worst* thing you can do is to treat it like it is.

How might you treat it this way? By eating the same things in the same quantities at the same times every day. This is a recipe for a weak constitution. A strong, healthy body, as we've discussed, is exposed to stresses and therefore forced to overcompensate to maintain homeostasis. This is how vaccines work. You want to be immune to chicken pox? Guess what they inject you with? Chicken pox. In a dose sufficient for your immune system to produce antibodies and therefore generate immunity, but not so great that you get full-blown chicken pox.

Strength and vitality are not provided by our lifestyle or nutrition. They are fought for, internally. In terms of caloric intake, something peculiar happens. When you considerably increase your calorie intake, your metabolism actually *increases* – up to a point. You read that correctly. When you reduce your caloric intake, you guessed it, your metabolism *decreases*.

Our bodies are built to survive. When you reduce your caloric intake considerably, your metabolism slows in order to conserve energy. Within this process your body becomes catabolic, eating away at fat reserves, deconstructing muscle and other tissues in the body, and in extreme cases of starvation, it even eats away at brain tissue. If your metabolism did not drop, you would starve to death every time you crash dieted for more than a couple weeks.

Likewise it's commonly assumed that most overweight people have slow metabolisms. In some cases, this is true. For example, if individuals are getting most of their calories from simple sugars, and on the whole are not consuming a sufficient amount of nutritional food (vegetables, meats, and healthy fats), their metabolisms can slow.

This tends to be more common among women, who have a habit of dieting only to destroy their metabolisms. Most overweight men have great metabolisms. When they get off the couch and start eating right and training, the weight pours off. Generally, these men simply eat more than they can utilize, so they store it as fat. Your thyroid function has a feedback loop that down-regulates your metabolism in conditions of insufficient caloric intake and up-regulates your metabolism in cases of surplus. More energy in, more energy required. Less energy in, less energy required.

Balancing anabolism (building) and catabolism (breaking down) is not as simple as counting calories. Your biology is much smarter than your nutrition plan. Each one of these states provides health and fitness benefits, and ought to be *maximized*, not controlled. Intermittent fasting (occasionally skipping meals or fasting up to 24 hours) maximizes fat burning, allows your body to detox, enhances your immune system, improves nutrient assimilation, and subsequently causes a spike in growth hormones. This spike occurs as a response to elevated stress hormones, like cortisol, which dominate when you are stressed or underfed. Occasional overeating provides a surplus of nutrition from which to repair and construct tissue, adapt to environmental stresses, satiate the mind and body, and increases metabolism.

Yes, ladies, if you want to maximize and sustain fat loss or maintain a lean physique, occasional overeating is highly recommended. Yes, gents, if you want to maximize lean muscle gain, you need to capitalize on the benefits of undereating at least some of the time.

Now, for the purposes of constructing a weightless body and mind, let's take a deeper look at hunger and binging. It should be clear that the sensation of physical weightlessness is in part due to an exceptional strength to weight ratio. We're aiming for a lean, muscular body and low body fat.

But it's not only the body that benefits from a lean, muscular physique built on good nutrition, periodic fasting, and occasional overeating. The mind also performs exceedingly well when it isn't clouded with toxins. It's no wonder that a large number of addictions, bad habits, and psychological disorders are cured with healthy diets or the addition of certain vitamins. A weak, malnourished body equals a weak, unhealthy brain. We maximize mental clarity in the same way we maximize physical health and create a lean, strong physique: through undereating and overeating.

The modern detox craze drives me crazy. My clients are constantly going on and off detoxes, or traveling for ten-day detox retreats. What's wrong with this? Nothing, until they come home. Detoxification is wonderful. It's natural and it happens every evening when you go to sleep. It can be enhanced tremendously by intermittent fasting and trying to eat whole, organic foods, excluding grains. But detox plans don't teach this. They simply 'work.' The truth is, they work for a few weeks and then leave many dieters with a slower metabolism unequipped to reacclimatize to their old lifestyle. The result? Fat gain.

Intermittent fasting aids your body's natural healing and detoxifying capabilities. Detoxing does not require the addition of magical herbs and potions, maple syrup, or lemon juice. It needs only deprivation and water.

Contrary to popular belief, the best time for this deprivation is not always at night. Like all other animals, humans heal, recover from stress, and grow while sleeping. Consistently undereating at night, or worse, not eating on a regular basis at night, will jeopardize health and strength. Your body requires resources to reconstruct tissue and rejuvenate cellular health. These resources come from food. Dinner is the most important meal of the day.

The hormones responsible for growth and recovery, like growth hormone, are secreted while sleeping. Stress hormones like cortisol are elevated throughout the day. Cortisol impedes digestion and nutrient assimilation, while growth hormone aids them. In keeping with these natural cycles, it's better to undereat during the day, relying on stored body fat for energy, and to eat sufficiently (once in a while overeating) in the evening to fuel growth and recovery. For a more in-depth discussion of this lifestyle, I highly recommend Ori Hoefmekkler's *The Warrior Diet* and Art DeVaney's *The New Evolution Diet.*

The final dietary factor of note is nutritional insurance. We're all fallible. Despite even our greatest efforts, we are highly unlikely to maximize nutrition by eating exactly what the body needs when it needs it. Sometimes we're lazy. Sometimes we train beyond normal limits and require additional resources. Sometimes we don't get enough sunshine. Sometimes fish is too expensive to eat regularly.

Eating whole foods with a focus on a variety of bright-colored veggies (indicating a high micronutrient content of vitamins and minerals), meats, fish, nuts, seeds, and fruit, while excluding grains and sugars as much as possible, will help you take care of the vast majority of what your body needs. How can you get the rest without constant blood testing?

Multivitamins, sunshine, and fish oil tablets. These are your insurance.

If you eat fish a few days a week, you can probably scratch the omega three supplements. But multivitamins are your shotgun approach to health. Need them every day? No. In fact, like all nutrients, you're better off getting them sporadically and at differing dosages. I can't count the number of times I've warded off colds, staved off fatigue or exhaustion, and kicked myself out of a near-depression just by tripling the recommended daily dosage of a multivitamin for three to five days.

Once upon a time, people ate locally grown fruits and vegetables within a reasonable time from the moment they were harvested. Today, they're frozen and transported long distances, losing tremendous amounts of nutrition in the process. We live by eating living things. The closer something is to expiration, even if it's organic, the less nutritious it is, the less life it gives. Multivitamins are your insurance.

George Lucas, if you're reading this, I'm aware Ewoks aren't supposed to be evil. I just couldn't help myself.

Weightlessness Footnote

Nutrition is the foundation of health and the key to building a strong, weightless body. The primary objectives of the Weightless Nutrition Plan are as follows:

- Eat a diet based on real food, emphasizing fish, meat, raw and cooked vegetables, whole fruit, nuts, and seeds, to optimize health and generate a favorable strength-to-weight ratio. The less nonfunctional bodyweight you have to carry, the more lean muscle mass you have, and the faster (and healthier) you become.

- Remove sugars and grains (at least most of the time). Their removal will help control insulin release, keeping it well below your daily threshold. Insulin insensitivity as a result of excessive carbohydrate and sugar consumption increases fat stores and can lead to blood-sugar imbalances, energy crashes, chronic lethargy, even diabetes.

- Grains and sugars also increase stomach acidity and can reduce the absorption and utilization of protein. Meat, which is also acidic, when consumed with vegetables, which are generally alkalizing, is absorbed to a higher degree. A good strategy is to limit grains and sugars to one meal a day, or less.

- Improve nutrient assimilation by calorie shifting and carbohydrate cycling (if carbs are not removed altogether). Shifting calories creates temporary states of negative energy balance, which increase fat loss. It also stimulates a corresponding release of anabolic hormones to prevent muscle breakdown. Doing so greatly enhances nutrient assimilation and utilization for faster growth and recovery.

- Improve nutrient absorption by incorporating intermittent fasting as needed.

- Create a detoxified body and mind. Detoxification is a natural function of metabolism. We are designed to excrete toxins. That's why we use the toilet, and why we sweat when we're sick. Detoxification occurs every night when we sleep and during every aerobic workout. Water, exercise, rest, and natural, organic foods are the foundations of detoxifying the body. They lead to efficient metabolism, strong nutrient absorption and utilization, and a clean, clear, focused mind.

Chapter 3

THE AUSTRIAN ACTRESS AND THE SHAOLIN IMPERATIVE

From the Rapid Fat Loss Files

erena, an Austrian defense attorney turned stage actress, came to me with three weeks to show time. She looked good to begin with and had been training frequently on her own for a very long time. But now it was crunch time and she had three weeks to fit into a dress that was a couple sizes too small in front of an audience of critical onlookers. She needed a sure thing, and she needed it right away. She wanted to lose seven to eight pounds of fat, which those who know a thing or two about fitness can tell you is exceedingly difficult the closer someone gets to being very lean. Our bodies are reluctant to surrender that last bit of storage around the waist and thighs. During one grueling workout, five sets into a brutal full-body circuit with one set to go, Verena hit the wall.

"We have to do it again?" she asked. "Why?"

"Your dress," I said.

"Is there really a big difference between five and six sets?"

"Yes, about a fifteen percent difference."

"But I'm dying!"

"Unlikely, but possible. It's the last set that makes all the difference, Verena. Your body couldn't care less how you look on stage. It cares about whether you're strong enough to survive this last set. Your body needs a good reason to change as quickly as you want it to, and dress size isn't one."

As I stood there explaining the concept of energy imbalance and turnover to a woman in complete agony, I had a flashback to my own episodic torture under the hands of Shaolin monks. I had known beforehand that the training would exceed anything I'd been through. In anticipation of that, I had trained intensively, stretched, and meditated daily prior to moving to the countryside of Jilin Province, outside Siping. I went there in the best shape of my life, and they still broke me.

All newcomers to the academy are asked to put on a short demonstration of skill. For some, this meant a single shitty punch if they'd never trained a day in their life. For me it meant a second-degree ITF taekwondo black belt form with jump split kicks, 180 hook kicks, and an otherwise elite competitive form. Several students, after watching my demo, asked me why I was there. Clearly I was in a different class.

I was naïve and ignorant. I thought this demo would help sort me into an appropriate class. Instead it put a target on my back that said *cocky motherfucker, break me please.*

While most of us grow up in a modern society with concepts like abuse, discrimination, and empathy, Shaolin monks still carry sticks and rule with an iron fist. The warm-up sessions alone left the gym resonating with the tear-filled cries of broken men. When I say broken, I mean on a flight home the next day to see if the tendons in their groins could be reconstructed by professionals for general mobility again.

"You're not so flexible?" the monks would say. "No problem, we stretch you. Oops, you can't walk? You're not strong enough for Shaolin."

Our days began at 5:30am with half an hour of standing qigong, followed by a breakfast of hard-boiled eggs and oatmeal or Chinese bread rolls. From 9 to 12 was basic conditioning and practice of the fundamentals. It began with a run through the forests and around a brand-new 'ancient' castle, soon to be a popular tourist site. We finished with aggressive, assisted (that is, forced) stretching. After a basic lunch of rice, veggies, and a little bit of meat, most of us passed out for an hour. From 2 to 4pm the training recommenced, alternating between free fighting, weightlifting, and brutal anaerobic and plyometric bodyweight conditioning that left us broken. We sprinted until our legs gave out. We carried each other up thirty-degree hills. We held static squats until we collapsed. If we could still stand, we topped it off with another hour of standing meditation before dinner at 5.

The first few days of training were excruciating, and without one iota of exaggeration, left me in the greatest physical pain of my life. After four or five days of training, I physically couldn't get out of bed. My legs had pins and needles running through them, my back and neck were stiff and locked out. My arms were destroyed. I was so broken that I lost all lines of defense and caught a severe head cold. I could barely make it to the dining room for meals, and skipped several as a consequence. I lay there in bed wondering what the hell I was thinking, leaving friends and family and moving to a place where this was the norm, not the exception. I wondered if I was actually going to recover or if I'd need extended care in a local hospital, no doubt under the strict supervision of heat lamp guy.

After two full days of immobility and one of slightly better active rest, I awoke on the fourth morning a transformed man. It was my own overnight Spider-Man experience. From the time I came to, my head felt clear, my throat was no longer sore, and my body... was that my body? I tore the covers off to examine what had been a broken and battered slab of muscle and bone, and saw veins running atop a ripped sixer. When I pinched a vein to see if it was real, I noticed my arms had become much thicker, as if I'd spent an hour in the gym and worked up a serious pump. I looked further down to find my legs. Jesus Christ, my legs were huge. They were 30 percent thicker, striated, and vascular. I couldn't believe it. I lay back in bed and just laughed. I had survived.

From that morning, I could run all day and train with the academy veterans. The lactic acid that burned my quads and made me want to vomit in the first few days had become a mere fraction of what it was. I had new confidence that my body would flush it out after enduring whatever torture the day brought. I had the confidence to persist. The severity of the stress I suffered had stimulated an adaptation of similar proportions.

I don't think it's an exaggeration to say that if I had not grown when I did, death was not an unreasonable possibility. It was there in the countryside of Jilin that I learned the primal nature of fitness: survival. I saw clear as day that fitness is a survival mechanism, an adaptive response to environmental stresses.

I also learned that many dietary rules espoused by Western nutritionists are utter bullshit. My resting metabolic rate is 2,500-2,800 calories a day. It has been in that range for a very long time. In Jilin I was training five hours a day and standing in meditation for a couple more. Collectively, this put my daily caloric expenditure at well over 5,000 calories a day, and possibly over six or seven thousand. Our diet at the academy was lean. There was very little complete protein. It was so lean that there were a few near-riots in the cafeteria when management got cheap and filled our meat dishes with scraps of skin and bone. I was dying in bed that particular evening, but apparently several monks were defending the cooks from a group of angry trainees.

My daily protein requirements at my current body weight, according to Western nutrition standards, range from maintenance numbers of about 130 grams a day to over 200 grams (if I wanted to 'bulk up'). These are general guidelines for people living normal lives, not for someone breaking their body down for sport five hours a day, creating an amino acid requirement of double those figures just to prevent muscle waste, let alone actual muscle reconstruction. On a daily basis I'd be fighting to get even close to 100 grams of complete protein. The rest was white rice and mixed veggies drenched in oil. Yet this diet reinforced that primal law of fitness: survival. Fuck rules and calculations. Our bodies are exceedingly resourceful, and when resources are scarce they will find a way to assimilate and allocate with great efficiency, given some source of real food. You will survive.

I learned first-hand that it's possible to build muscle on a caloric deficit, and that one does not need copious amounts of protein in order to reconstruct and build new tissue. When energy turnover is consistently high enough and our nutrition is more healthy than not, our bodies perform with natural intelligence. They preserve muscle for extended durations and under extreme stress. They rapidly metabolize body fat, our long-held energy stores. At our next feeding, our bodies assimilate nutrients with healthy, empty, and ravenous digestive tracks. We absorb greater percentages of nutrients and utilize them more effectively, out of necessity.

After my extreme Shaolin fitness transformation, I found a way to quantify the stresses of training in such a way so as not to need the extreme environment of the Shaolin torture camp to ensure consistent progress. I tested a wide variety of nutrition principles on countless clients and myself until I saw clearly the prime movers of health and fitness. Regardless of whether someone was a run-of-the-mill housewife or supercharged time-constrained executive (lifestyles which in no way reflect the physical demands responsible for my transformation), I discovered the principles of fitness are uniform.

We are dealing with a difference of degree, not of kind. All that is required is the custom implementation of primal principles, not a fundamentally different approach to fitness and nutrition, since there are no others worth considering. The human body is bound by biological forces that dictate health and growth. Personal affinities for this or that fitness approach have little or nothing to do with it.

With only three sessions a week for three weeks and light supplemental jogging on the days she didn't see me, Verena lost nearly eight pounds of fat by the eve of her performance. Admittedly, she felt like shit near the end, which is a natural consequence of running on a prolonged energy deficit. For people who need rapid results, there's always a risk of depleting essential resources. Without testing your vitamin and mineral stats on a daily basis, I recommend all rapid body transformation clients to up their multivitamin intake, drink a lot of water, and go to sleep as early as possible (assuming an otherwise weightless diet).

In Verena's more hardcore case, she was taking two or three vitamins on training days to ensure she wasn't wearing too thin. She still ate three to four times a day, predominately vegetables, fish, and meat, though in small proportions. The only time she was allowed any form of carbs, let alone simple carbs (including fruit), was within an hour of finishing her sessions with me. She generally took this window to enjoy a piece of dark chocolate, her one dietary release.

High-intensity training drains glycogen stores. However, if there is one time when your body can utilize simple carbs, even the bad stuff like cakes and cookies (assuming their fat content is not too high), it's in that free window following hard training. Your muscle cells are sensitive and screaming for glycogen, so spiking your insulin helps usher most of the badness (sugar) into muscle instead of body fat storage.

All food is energy. Consumed at the right times, even things like chocolate, cookies, and pizza can be used constructively. Eaten at the wrong times, they give you a one-way ticket to Diabetes Island with potato chip-lovin' monkeys.

Verena completed her three weeks of hell lean, toned, and smoking hot. She wore her dress and delivered her lines with fullest confidence. And she realized the primal rule of rapid body transformation. When an inadequate body meets environmental stresses that exceed its ability to handle them, and your nutrition is insufficient to fuel physical effort and recovery, your body will adapt by becoming stronger, fitter, and rapidly eating into the energy storages we call *body fat* in order to survive. You will survive.

Weightlessness Footnote

Rapid body transformation requires high energy turnover and progressive overload. Intensity is paramount. It requires caloric oscillation, which allows the emptying of storages. But it also requires ample nutrient injections at the right time, to support growth and recovery, to maintain a highly active metabolism. This should be seen as a weightless warrior's toolkit for rapid peak fitness. It should not be considered a healthy long-term strategy for strength and growth, as it draws too deeply into one's recovery capability, potentially jeopardizing health. Energy conservation is the warrior's way, not practicing progressive states of exhaustion. It should be seen as a short-term path to foundational fitness only.

Chapter 4

FROM BUSINESSMAN TO BEAST

From the Strength Files

Once in a while, a project comes along that allows me to ride the line between applied science and art that makes me love my job. Michael, proud beer-drinking Dane, CEO of Industreams, and the only other dedicated member of the Shanghai Dice Club, with its noble commitment to furthering mindfulness, randomness, and antifragility over beer-filled conversations and challenging dice challenges, visited Enso with a very clear objective (more on the Dice Club in Book 3).

"I'll give you one hour a week for six weeks, to transform my body and teach me everything I need to know about fitness for the rest of my life. I'll do anything I need to do on my own to supplement or complement my time with you."

Now this is something I've heard more times than I can count. The majority of prospective clients start a program with a confidence that has no rational foundation. They overestimate their ability to control their schedules and their cravings, and their ability to maintain that same state of motivation when the training actually gets tough. And it does. They're used to controlling their environments, environments that fall under their domains and become increasingly easier as they dissect, understand, and manage. But fitness, my friends, at least transformative fitness, does not get any easier with time. It's a constant uphill battle that requires continuous adaptation for survival.

But Michael was no ordinary client, because he is no ordinary man. I'd never met anyone with greater willpower and focus. Industreams and Enso Temple were siblings of sorts. They were born less than a year apart, both infused with a creative energy and passion that came from difficult dice-dictated protocols and assignments used to enhance growth and expand product offerings. When he's not wheeling and dealing with big swinging dicks in investment banking, he's generally fixated on some philosophical, economic, or more recently fitness query. But he's never been one for reading and leaving.

Michael implements every single point of interest that he cannot rationally discredit, and he does so by scheduling tons of five-minute focused efforts throughout the day. These are mini-timelines with clearly defined goals. If he wasn't brilliantly effective, one might call him neurotic. But he tests and experiences everything first-hand with a healthy skepticism, much of it guided by the die.

When Michael told me he would do everything necessary for transformation, giving me only an hour of his time each week, I smiled. He's a doer, not a sayer. So it was no surprise when, after six weeks, Michael had gained fifteen pounds of weight and considerably reduced his body fat. I never take body fat measurements because they pale in comparison to strength and stamina metrics when designing a progressive program, and the sense of confidence, or lack thereof, that you feel standing naked in front of a mirror trumps any number a little gizmo might display about how lean you are. But this isn't rocket science. If someone gains weight and their tone improves (which is predominately a byproduct of reduced body fat), then lean muscle gain exceeds the number of pounds added on the scale. Michael, in six weeks, gained about twenty pounds of lean muscle and lost five to eight pounds of body fat.

His transformation was so rapid that friends believed he was on steroids. His own physical strength, performance, and confidence skyrocketed. His girlfriend thanked me. His before photo was a portrait of your average desk jockey, with poor posture and no meat to speak of, a bit of cushion around the midsection. When we made a video synopsis of Michael's results six weeks later, he was lifting weights that in some cases reflected gains of 100 percent or more. His frame had filled out to that of a conditioned rugby player with thick, full biceps, well-developed traps and shoulders, and a thick thoracic region. His before and after images were so impressive that his video testimonial alone sent me several similar projects over the following years.

The irony is that Michael's friends were not entirely wrong. While I didn't have Michael sticking needles into his ass, the training regime I had him on, coupled with extreme calorie shifting, did cause his body to release copious amounts of anabolic growth hormones. While Michael was in the game to get fit and transform himself, my goal was simple: make him as strong as possible, as quickly as possible, by doing as much damage as possible. Nature couldn't care less how good you look naked or what dress size you wear. Nature respects power, strength, and stamina. It just so happens that the default physique of a strong, powerful human is a lean, ripped physique with a good deal of muscle. I was sending a very clear message to Michael's neuromuscular system: Grow or die.

This is where most novices (and I dare say many trainers) go terribly wrong in the gym. They believe they can train for bigger muscles. Size is not a virtue that nature respects. More size is more weight. Nature much prefers a strong and very lean physique, making individuals lighter and faster. To add significant bulk, there must be a real biological threat to your health and an overabundance of nutrition. Stress must be great enough that your body has no option but to build up a wall of protection – that is, fast-twitch muscle fiber – in order to accommodate your environmental needs. If you train to become bigger, you'll probably fail. If you train to become stronger, you'll probably succeed, with the unintended consequence of adding a good bit of muscle.

So how did Michael add approximately twenty pounds of lean muscle in six weeks?

- Fundamental compound exercises
- High-tension, high-intensity resistance training (heavy weights)
- Calorie shifting and carbohydrate cycling, while eating real food

Weightless Tangent

Compound exercises are those that use multiple muscle groups to perform a certain lift. A triceps extension is an isolation exercise. The bench press is a compound lift. A bicep curl is an isolation exercise, a pull-up and a bent-over row are compound lifts. There is almost no reason, save for elite bodybuilding, to use isolation exercises. In sports, combat, and play, we all use the many to attack the few, the coordinated whole to accomplish a single end. Dividing and isolating our strengths weakens us. I'll admit that isolation exercises may have a place *within* a program to supplement compound weightlifting, but they should never replace or supersede the larger compound movements. For the needs of the masses, isolation exercises are totally unnecessary.

From the time a child begins to move, it moves in synchronicity. A head doesn't turn without the entire body turning along with it. Reaching for a toy is a fully committed action, with both arms extending and the knees bending to support. It's only as we mature that we begin to fracture this natural muscular union. We become stronger, so we use less energy. But the question we should be asking ourselves is the following: how did we become stronger in the first place? The first movement a baby performs is a modified push-up, lifting the head and shoulders off the ground. This is followed by a crawl (resembling that much-dreaded exercise, the mountain climber), and later by the almighty squat as babies begin to stand. When old enough to play, they pick up toys with textbook deadlift form.

To this day, when clients travel and ask what they should do to maintain their practice while away, my response is always, "Squats and push-ups." They can be done in any hotel room or park. There are no excuses. They are the foundation of fitness. Why? Because they're what humans do. Dogs run like hell, cats stretch and leap. Humans push, pull, squat, and press. If you aren't pushing and squatting, you're not training. This always seems to elicit a sigh of frustration; they want a sexy little circuit to carry with them. But there's nothing sexy about it. We grew from infants to children on squats and push-ups. You'll grow from unfit to fit following the same method.

Without needing to learn anatomy in depth, you can break down the necessary compound movements according to five vectors of force: push, pull, squat, press (overhead), and twist. These vectors, when performed as compound lifts, exercise every muscle in the body. When weight is sufficient, they can develop a perfectly lean and muscular physique. No machines, gadgets, or esoteric techniques are necessary. Have a look at the physiques of power lifters (non-heavyweights), and you'll see beacons of symmetry and health. These athletes focus on the primaries: the squat, bench press, and deadlift.

Since the beginning of time, warriors and military men have been conditioned on the bread and butter of fitness – push-ups, squats, pull-ups, sit-ups, and running. Simple? Yes. Effective? Nothing is more effective. When someone needs fitness for survival, as a soldier does, you'd better believe they'll implement the most efficient and effective exercises. I don't recall anyone complaining about the physiques of military men recently. Furthermore, they concentrate on exercises that directly involve moving their own bodyweight through space, not exercises performed while locked into a machine. Why? Because fitness has everything to do with performance, with powerful movement in the real world, and not with an occasional photo shoot.

To make it even simpler, only one exercise in each vector (assuming the weights used are heavy enough) is sufficient for complete muscular development. You don't need three or four different exercises per vector. You can pick one from each of the following lists:

Push

- Push-ups (and if strong enough, one-arm push-ups)
- Bench press
- Incline press
- Dips

Pull

- Pull-ups
- Bent-over row

- High pull (upward row)
- Shrugs

Squat (add weight to increase intensity and resistance)

- Squats
- Deadlift
- Lunges

Press

- Shoulder press

Twist (use the muscles required for stabilizing twisting movements. Actual twists are not necessary)

- Plank
- Crunches
- Oblique crunches
- Supported decline twists

After Michael's first session, he looked like absolute shit. He was trembling, unstable, and weak. Destroyed. The first session contained only three lifts – the dumbbell chest press, the dead lift, and the shoulder press. Each exercise was performed for four to five sets to failure, with repetitions ranging from three to fifteen (depending on his level of fatigue). Every effort was 100 percent to failure. He rested and repeated. Following our session he went for a large bowl of pasta and chicken, followed two hours later by a large plate of meat and veg. He had two full dinners in the course of four hours, and more than 60 percent of his daily caloric needs in the same period of time.

We sent every signal to his nervous system that his current physique was inadequate to handle the stresses of his environment. In providing an immediate carbohydrate meal, his glycogen stores were quickly replenished and his insulin spiked, increasing his cellular receptivity for recuperative nutrients. Two hours later, he received all the nutrients he needed to reconstruct damaged tissue with mixed vegetables and lean meat. He consumed no juices or powders. He ate real food when his body needed it most.

Michael couldn't walk or move well for the following three days. He cursed and condemned me via text message. But he kept his word and finished two short supplementary workouts before I saw him next, each consisting of less than fifteen minutes of high-intensity bodyweight circuits, focusing on push-ups, jump lunges or squats, and mountain climbers.

You avid gym goers out there may be wondering why there isn't any core work. The reason is simple. Core work is bullshit. The venerators of the esteemed core have grown into a cult of modern mystics. Few can explain what the core actually is. Even fewer can explain what it does. But everyone thinks they have a weak one, due to muffin tops squishing out over their belt line.

Weightless Tangent

Let's demystify the core a bit. The muscles of your midsection (most notably the abdominals, the internal and external obliques, and the muscles of the lower back) have one coordinated function – to stabilize movement. Without the core, no complex motor movements are possible. As such, it's always working. When you're doing a push-up, what do you think keeps your hips and thighs off the ground? Your core. When you're performing a squat with weight on your back or held in your hands, what do you think keeps your upper body from collapsing under the weight? Your core. When you're pressing heavy weight above your head, what keeps your spine from twisting and collapsing under you? Yep, still the core.

It's the most overrated region of the body to train, and the least understood. My clients constantly tell me they have a weak core and ask if we can spend more time on it. When I ask why, they point to belly fat. At this point, we have a gentle heart-to-heart on the differences between fat and muscle and how they are diametrically opposed in form and function. One can have a very strong core and still look very soft on the outside. Pudge is fat – energy stored as a result of the overconsumption of certain foods and poor nutrient selection. It has nothing to do with strength or stability. If someone is capable of holding a plank for a minute or more with no lower back pain, their core strength is sufficient to prevent injury through general mobility and bodyweight exercises. Period.

Compared to most trainers, I give very little direct attention to the core. However, my method of training constantly calls on the muscles of the core to act as they are intended, namely to stabilize complex movement. It isn't until weeks into a program, once my clients begin to develop a trim waistline and a lean, toned midsection, that they stop asking for more core work. The way I teach people, using their bodies to push, pull, and control their own weight through resistance training and a variety of short, intense, cardiovascular exercises, provides indirect but highly effective core work. Only those who rely on isolating gym equipment, which removes the core from compound exercises, require extensive supplementary core work.

You want a strong core? Do a standing shoulder press, not a machine press. Use heavy weight. You want a strong core? Perform a heavy deadlift, not a seated leg press or (even worse) a leg extension. Lift and move as you would if you were actually lifting and moving in the real world, and you'll be amazed at how strong you are as a whole. Two to five minutes of concentrated abdominal work at the end of a comprehensive full-body workout a few times per week is sufficient for a strong, lean core. Hell, if you're training properly, you may never need to crunch or plank, as your abs and obliques are contracting like hell to stabilize high-resistance movements.

Week after week, Michael sported a thicker, more defined physique. What mattered to me more was the direction of his stats, and those too were climbing at a rapid rate. As his recovery time improved, we added other vectors, until he was including a big pull, like the bent-over row, and a weighted squat (holding the weight in front of his chest with straining and trembling biceps). All the while his core was being used to stabilize extremely intense efforts with weight extended above or in front of him.

Weightless Tangent

Now, how do we define intense? The definition is exceedingly simple. If you can't continue the effort for very long, it's intense. By definition, then, nothing exceeds the intensity of a one-rep max. This is lifting as heavy a weight as you possibly can.

Ever wonder why power lifters (excluding heavyweights) sport such well-developed physiques when they only practice three basic lifts? They lift extremely heavy weights. The muscle fibers that grow larger from stress, fast-twitch muscle fibers, are targeted with heavy weight. Slow-twitch muscle fibers are responsible for walking, jogging, reading, writing, and playing mahjong. They don't have the growth potential of fast-twitch fibers. But fast-twitch fibers need a reason to grow. They are only called into action and recruited to perform their duty when slow-twitch fibers are insufficient to complete an effort. Therefore the amount of weight lifted and the intensity of the exercise are directly related to fast-twitch fiber recruitment, damage, and subsequent muscular hypertrophy or adaptation.

If you can't safely lift to your maximum muscular potential with certain muscle groups, time under tension becomes an increasingly important factor. I had Michael perform his lifts with a slow cadence, where the eccentric (stretching) and concentric (shortening) phases of the lift lasted about five seconds each. When newbies enter the gym, they get so excited to pump iron that they throw weight around like a toddler on the playground – but momentum is the enemy of strength. A fast, explosive muscle requires some ballistic training, but the strength required for fast, explosive movement is best trained under sustained tension, which may include a static contraction with no movement whatsoever.

Our primitive ancestors were incredibly strong. Do you think they did repetitions of exercises? What for? What's a rep?

When you need to lift, move, or chop, you hold, stabilize, and move the object as quickly as possible. If I ask you to move a boulder, you'll find a way to jockey it up to your chest, squeezing with your arms, and deliver it to its destination post-haste. All the while, you'll be fighting the insane burn in your biceps and upper back. You won't lift and curl, release and repeat, checking yourself out in the mirror looking for perfect form. You'll fight to complete the assignment, and you'll rest fully.

If you were hunting, you wouldn't jog lightly for extended periods of time and then, when the clock dictates, slash repeatedly in defined sets and reps. You would walk leisurely until you corner your prey (which seems to be the preferred method of hunting in hunter-gatherer societies), conserving as much energy as possible for the kill. You would approach quietly. And in one all-out burst you would sprint, and stab the creature until its life was extinguished. Then you would commune for Friday night dice club over prehistoric beer and burgers.

Intensity and tension are required for both strength and power. With every set, Michael's muscle fibers were screaming for release. His face was straining, his body shaking, his voice occasionally growling. He held nothing back. Week after week, his numbers went up. Most novices make the mistake of linking soreness or fatigue with a productive workout. That's generally because at the beginning of any program, these are coincidental sensations. Most people can't walk after the first session. Some people puke. And they realize rapid growth. But after you're somewhat conditioned, feelings of exhaustion and delayed-onset muscle soreness begin to wane. But trainees still chase the sensation of feeling like they've been hit by a train, because they believe that's what training is all about. Pain means gain.

It doesn't, necessarily.

In the beginning, pain *accompanies* gain. As you become increasingly conditioned, soreness and fatigue become non-indicators of progress (although they *may* and often *do* accompany productive work). The only factors that indicate progress are strength gains – defined by the ability to perform more work – and power gains – defined by the ability to perform more work in the same or a shorter period of time. This generally means a reduction in rest times if all other variables remain the same. I know before I start a session with a client exactly what they need to perform on the day to ensure progress. (If your trainer doesn't, what are you seeing him or her for?)

The caveat is that sometimes clients finish a day's session, reaching all targets, and feel that they have more energy and want to do a bit more work. They are indeed stronger. They've adapted. But the key to intelligent training is not to use your feelings of strength and weakness as factors to determine intensity, but rather to use your numbers. If you've lifted more than last week or performed more sets of a high-intensity cardiovascular exercise, regardless of how you feel, you've done enough to elicit growth or stimulate fat loss. This is a gift. Take it. Go home. Rest. Let your body grow and recover without pushing it more today and eating into limited energy reserves. Doing so won't lead to additional growth. It will merely make you need longer rest and more recovery time.

The master enters the gym, knows his objectives, does his job, and goes home. No more, no less. The novice does as much as possible for as long as possible and goes home feeling exhausted, maybe feeling like shit. He crosses his fingers and hopes. The master grinds out his results, patiently adding to his numbers week after week, the way a professional poker player grinds out his winnings. He rarely goes all-in and risks everything, because long-term health and strength are his priorities. Staying in the game trumps the big win on any single day.

Nearly two years since Michael's rapid body transformation, he's not only maintained his physique, but has established a tremendous base of strength. He no longer needs my assistance with his fitness objectives. He's become an independent, expert fitness enthusiast. At present, I'm only responsible for his martial arts development on Friday afternoons before the Dice Club's weekly burger and beer session.

Weightless Tangent

In the beginning, every push-up and squat is an act of all-out effort, requiring full concentration and maximum strength. After a while, children grow and begin to play, incorporating many push-ups and squats over the course of the day. There's no way around it. For a baby, every movement is a power lift. After they become stronger, those movements become anaerobic strength-endurance exercises, as two, three, four, and more steps become a walk. A while later, these movements enter the realm of aerobic exercise as the child plays for hours on end.

But lets not look only at the result. Let's examine that fascinating stage when one becomes two, becomes three… but not four. Let's examine the realm of strength and power training exhibited by our younger, natural selves.

As children, we rarely lift, squat, or push to failure, because it means we can't do more of it. We play a bit, rest a bit, play a bit, rest a bit, rarely extending our activity into the realm of extreme discomfort or exhaustion. Through this process children become incredibly strong, despite a lack of structure and the drive to train until they get sick.

Russian power lifters employed a similar method for decades. They would perform heavy, maximum-effort lifts for the same muscle groups up to ten times per week. They created an environment that required certain strengths and skills for survival. Children are not under such pressures; they're driven mostly by curiosity. But both are examples of adaptation to environmental stressors.

Michael now sticks to the basics: the deadlift, the bench press, and the shoulder press. He hits each lift a few times a week, and lifts quite heavy during at least two of those sessions, tapering down on the third to provide active recovery. He works week to week to push his three- and five-rep maxes to new heights, and rarely trains with high volume to failure. He's only gotten stronger since his transformation, and his physique has acquired a sinewy taper that gives a thick, lean, and raw impression. He just looks strong. He fuels this sustained growth with a paleo-esque diet of fish or meat, varied raw or cooked veggies, nuts, and the occasional piece of fruit. Grains and sugars are nearly nonexistent for him unless he's visiting his in-laws in the countryside of Chengdu. Beer and whiskey are consumed for business purposes, of course.

Weightlessness Footnote

Strength training should be undertaken with the priorities of improving the contractile force and myofiber density of muscle, and increasing the strength of tendons and connective tissues. To accomplish this, heavy weight training is necessary, with sets of heavy three-to-five-rep maxes at least some of the time. Lifting in sets where repetitions exceed eight puts you in the bodybuilding category, and you'll stand a greater chance of increasing the sarcoplasmic density of muscle cells (the non-contractile muscle cell fluid that stores energy for high volume work). This might be a fine early stage conditioning or rehabilitation rep range, but once conditioned you should diversify with heavier training.

If one is very committed to the path of Weightlessness, most adaptations to strength and physique enhancements can be accomplished with five reps or fewer per set, five sets per vector. How many vectors you can train per day depends on your overall conditioning. As we discussed, the stronger you are, the greater your potential for intense exertions. As such, as you get stronger you'll have to reduce, not increase, the number of vectors trained per day. Each vector should be trained in some form two times per week.

This training protocol ensures the greatest strength increase relative to size. Your strength to weight ratio has a direct bearing on the speed at which you can move, as well as the perception of difficulty within that movement. Being very strong, without being exceedingly heavy, is a defining trait of the weightless person.

Chapter 5

THE WEIGHTLESS GIANT

From the Agility Files

Alistair and I sat beside noisy Changle Road, several blocks from Enso Temple, enjoying a burger and beer, and recapping the last three months of his adventure. Since our last encounter he'd toured the world, hitting the biggest ski slopes and fulfilling a lifelong dream. He'd jumped out of helicopters and plowed down treacherous vertical slopes. He'd hiked into the backcountry with only his standard gear, his coach, and a snow shovel in case they got buried and had to cut their way back home through forests and rock. He got himself into the best shape of his life and went on to enjoy the fruits of his labor, snowboarding powder six hours a day for three months.

His story is inspiring. An ex-Morgan Stanley guy, Alistair realized after several years of high finance, high stress, and a rapidly declining physical state that life is too short to be squandered for an ever-elusive 'higher quality of life.' Alistair had had enough. He was ready to make changes, to take the big leap and commit to actualizing an around-the-world snowboarding trip. He booked his itinerary, purchased his tickets, and was *all-in*, as they say, before he even contacted me. To this day, I have seen no stronger motivating goal than his. It held the promise of the rewarding experience of a lifetime and the risk of wasted time and money if he wasn't fit and healthy enough to burn those slopes.

Eight months prior to our reunion, Alistair walked into Enso at a respectable 340 pounds and in poor overall condition. He sought my help in getting fit enough to handle three months of full-time play and all of the physical demands it entailed. He had several existing injuries to work through, which limited our early training. There was also a constant stream of new pains and discomforts due to using long-dormant joints and muscles, burdened by the added pressure of extra weight. But Alistair was on fire, and every minor pain, discomfort, and failure just put more coal in his stove of motivation.

The early days were marked by run-of-the-mill setbacks. Push-ups, even on the knees, were impossible due to wrist and elbow pain. Lunges hurt the knees. Curls were hindered by a weak grip stemming from serious prior injuries to the wrist and elbow. But Alistair was used to winning and was heavily driven. He would have trained all day, every day if I had let him. I had to hold him back to four sessions a week to start. Just as people always underestimate the difficulty of private training, they overestimate their ability to recover.

A month later we were up to six sessions a week, and shortly thereafter up to eight. Sometimes I would even see Alistair twice a day for three days of the week. He was full-on, living the life of an athlete in training.

Two months after commencing, about sixty pounds lighter, Alistair insisted on incorporating Weightlessness training elements into the program. They were something I'd been reserving for a later date because, quite frankly, I had no idea if it was safe training given his size. I'd never seen a 280-pound guy throw his leg straight up overhead or practice jump squats in rapid succession. I had haunting visions of a blown knee or torn groin.

There was time during these sessions, in the short rest and recovery periods, for soul searching, counseling from both sides, and shooting the shit. My Weightlessness methodology came up on occasion. Despite the fact that I had never considered Alistair's particular demographic, it made sense that a man who'd been big his whole life would be interested in experiencing lightness, physical freedom, and focus.

Could big men become weightless?

By now, all his inhibitory tweaks and pains had been resolved. He was training up to eight times a week, alternating between heavy strength training, high-intensity resistance circuits, and martial arts, and living the fitness lifestyle. He still had another eighty or ninety pounds to drop to hit his long-term goal, but he was very fit. He could push, pull, and squat with stability and power. He could kick and punch, and he'd begun leaping and running. He was pain-free throughout his lower body. He bore all the markings of someone fit enough to undertake Weightlessness training. He was a real challenge to my own understanding and vision of the scope of Weightlessness.

So I crossed my fingers, threw caution to the wind, and strapped five pounds to each of Alistair's ankles. We began with very modest sets of walking and jogging for short distances. At first, ankle-weight training didn't exceed ten or fifteen minutes. Initial trainees always look as if they're carrying heavy weights on their ankles. Big surprise. Every step is a lumbering effort, pulling the legs quickly to the ground with a bit of a jolt through the upper body. Ankle weights initially make people look slow. And then there's the initial phase of skin burn and tearing, which happens regardless of sock thickness or ankle weight design. It's not terrible for jogging, but once leaping and kicking are incorporated, those bastards tear the ankles up.

You scientists out there, make better ankle weights!

In order to unlock his full potential for weightlessness, strength and a modicum of speed were not going to cut it. At his weight, they would only be a recipe for injury if he lacked the ability to safely control his efforts through a full range of movement. Light jogging and a bit of leaping are not terribly dangerous. They're also not terribly transformative. A weightless body is not limited to basic complex motor skills. It's an uninhibited vessel of powerful self-expression. To activate Alistair's fullest physical freedoms, we needed to widen his range of performance and cut the emergency brakes.

We gradually added dynamic stretching in the form of rising kicks, rapid, straight leg swings directly in front of the body, performed as quickly and as high as possible. Incorporating them was also a bit of a stretch for me, curious as hell about whether they were premature given his overall condition. In the weeks prior, Alistair had made tremendous headway in his static flexibility, moving from a pathetic straddle split of around ninety degrees (an *l*-shape), to nearly a full split of about 160 degrees. A full split with legs in a straight line is 180 degrees, and he was nearly there.

We fought through general issues. Like most novices, his tailbone was slightly tucked and his lower back arched, the biggest inhibitors for improving general flexibility. These cause the knees to bend slightly and the toes to point slightly backward when doing the straddle splits (legs spread apart). So when I began to assist Alistair there was no way around over-stressing the tendons on the inside of his knees. This, my dear friends, is extremely painful. As soon as that pain started to manifest, his breath stalled and he did what everyone does when in pain: he tensed up and withdrew.

This reaction to stress and pain is the greatest inhibitor of flexibility and free movement. It's an innate panic button that we're all hardwired with, which intends to preserve the integrity of muscles and tendons by rapidly moving away from an overstretched and compromised position. More often than not, however, it causes injury by too rapidly tensing an overstretched limb. This panic button must be eliminated in athletes who require a large range of movement, and this is most effectively done through relaxation practice. So I taught Alistair to breathe, incorporating abdominal breathing and using our stretching segment as an act of meditation. After a few weeks of stretching and panicking, stretching and panicking, something clicked and Alistair realized he wasn't made of rigid oak, but was malleable like soft bamboo.

Weightless Tangent

And so are we all. The largest misconception for those striving for greater flexibility is that it's a skill that one must forcefully acquire. It isn't. The skill that must be developed is *relaxation*. Flexibility is a necessary consequence of that. To this extent, flexibility should be understood as the contrary of strength. Strength is born of tension, of the rapid contraction of myofibers that occurs as myosin and actin move past one another in grid-like fashion, shortening muscle and moving the skeletal frame. Stretching, on the other hand, is not the pulling of muscle (or, as I've heard from very misguided people, the stretching of ligaments). Rather, it relaxes (and therefore elongates) the same fibers that we contract to perform all movement.

You are probably flexible enough to drop into the full splits... but you will not. You'll get halfway and panic a bit as nerve ends in your tendons and joints fire, sending a screaming signal to your brain to bail out. If you could relax to your greatest extent, you could immediately increase your flexibility by 30 to 50 percent. You just need to relax. Alistair learned after several weeks of assisted stretching, in conjunction with deep abdominal breathing, to relax into the pain. He began to face it without panicking, his natural flexibility manifested, and the pain vanished.

I knew Alistair was ready for dynamic stretching, based on his static splits and the balance of strength he displayed in all exercises. But I had yet to see a man this big throw his legs quickly up in front of him. So we started slow. We began with short sets of only a few reps. We began at slow speeds at lower heights. This got him used to the additional weight that would continue to stretch his hamstrings and pull his leg higher into the air after he reached his physical limit. We began to methodically decondition his stretch reflex, which is far more prominent in dynamic stretching than in static stretching.

Most of us have so much raw strength potential that we could tear our bodies apart. But we have natural self-preservation mechanisms. One is *your brain*, another is *not being a dumbass*, and another is the stretch reflex that unconsciously inhibits movement that could be too damaging. It's the emergency brake that activates every time you put a bit too much weight on the gas pedal. By most studies, we only use 20 to 40 percent of our strength potential even when applying 100 percent effort. In elite athletes, this percentage may creep up to 80 or 90 percent. But the untapped power in our bodies (even without any additional training) is a very inspiring proposition.

Methodically removing the safety brake is the first stage of releasing speed, and therefore of preeminent importance in Weightlessness training. We need bodies that are not only fast and strong, but also have no inhibitions or constraints and allow the fullest expression of our will.

So Alistair, learning how to breathe from his lower abdomen and remain relaxed, graduated from inflexibility to swinging his legs at full speed over his head with eight to ten pounds on each ankle. As these weights were a small percentage of his bodyweight, he was able to graduate to heavier weights quickly. Most novices working up to this amount of weight safely should take six months to a year of very dedicated practice.

When he removed the weight and did the same exercise, his legs were so light that he nearly threw himself over backward, with a speed and momentum he couldn't believe he possessed.

Weightless Tangent

It's rare these days to meet people who value speed more than strength. But speed provides something strength doesn't: the ability to break the illusion of time. When you're faster, you have more time to think and react. You can be more patient than those who are slower, for you need less time to accomplish your task. For a martial artist, this is a process of self-mastery, and appears to onlookers as a mystic mind reading or telepathy. With that speed comes a confidence and a faster perception of real options. When you move quickly, others seem slow, and your mind begins to process real options faster and faster.

Historically, there have been two paths to elite speed. The first is the improvement of one's strength-to-weight ratio. Very simply, if you become stronger and the weight you have to move remains the same, you can move it faster. If the weight in question is your own body, like the arms of a boxer or the legs of a sprinter, then extra muscular strength manifests as greater contractile force against a fixed weight, and greater speed materializes.

With Alistair we worked on both sides of the equation, making him much stronger through heavy resistance training, while also making him much lighter through intense cardiovascular training and a diet low in grains and sugars. Doubling to tripling his strength in many exercises while losing eighty pounds of bodyweight in four months made Alistair feel light, despite the fact he was still at a weight that would be considered burdensome by most.

The second path, that chosen by martial artists, dancers, golfers, artists, and a host of others who rely on fine motor movements, is repetition. Everyone knows that the more you do something, the better you get. With that proficiency comes speed. The legendary swordfighter Miyamoto Musashi, in *The Book of Five Rings*, set the bar at ten thousand repetitions for mastery of a technique. My guess is that number more accurately reflects an *understanding* of a technique, while *mastery* comes from hundreds of thousands of repetitions over many years of practice.

This method accomplishes speed by refining neuromuscular coordination. It shortens the time required for a nerve impulse sent from the brain to result in an intended physical action. It's why most people learning to dance or kick look like idiots – they haven't done it enough. With more practice, we learn to coordinate movement in waves of relaxation and tension that generate tremendous speed and power.

Here, I humbly present you with a third path to speed: high-speed resistance training. It's what you witness when a baseball player puts a few pounds on the edge of his bat while taking warm-up swings. It's what you see when boxers punch while holding dumbbells. It's also criticized by most doctors, who are adamant that practitioners of high-speed resistance training are begging for injury. They do so, however, without addressing method or nuance, and these matter a great deal.

Your average person should not attempt to run a marathon without serious preparation, whereas the conditioned athlete can manage to run several per year without damaging soft tissue or bone, or experiencing other types of fallout. It's important that resistance is only added atop refined skill and integrity of movement. Even then, slowly progressing with added weight (emphasis on slowly) allows time for soft tissue adaptation, the weakest link in the adaptation equation.

Ankle and wrist weights add targeted resistance to extremities, requiring much greater focus, coordination, and strength from every muscle in the body, from the core all the way to the encumbered limbs. It's a way of cheating the path to speed via high repetitions, and the only way of taking someone from conditioned athlete to demigod. There are no limits to the extent of neuromuscular refinement, and therefore speed, except a theoretical time of zero, which is the ever-elusive target of Weightlessness training.

Ankle weight training reverses nature's intelligent habit of economizing movement and improving what is commonly known as mechanical advantage, where weight, including body fat, is placed as close to the center as possible. Obese people don't have super fat hands and skinny waists. It'd be impossible to move. They pack their excess weight around the gut, upper thighs, and upper arms, but are granted nature's generous gift of mobility. Fitness professionals exploit the corollary of this principle by asking clients to do squats while holding weight straight above the head, or by doing lunges with a steering wheel centered weight extended in front of their chests. This makes the work harder, and it forces the core to stabilize much more weight.

Where this concept becomes exciting is when we begin to practice ballistic high-speed movements, placing weight at our extremities, our ankles and wrists. Imagine the core strength you'd possess if your daily routine was performed with bear paws for hands, and concrete shoes. Now imagine the speed and lightness you'd experience if you traded them back for your hands and feet, and someone told you to run. The burden that impeded your movement would be gone and the muscles used to stabilize the burden would have developed to control the arms and legs of someone much heavier.

Your run-of-the-mill couch potato carries all that weight around the midsection. It provides a little extra resistance when climbing stairs, but mostly for the quadriceps. Once that weight is extended out to the ankles, and ankles only, every muscle group, from your core all the way to the added weight itself, is engaged and coordinated to move in the most efficient way possible. A ten-minute session of light play with this weight will leave you feeling light and fresh. Most novices who do a bench press play with this concept by finishing a heavy set, racking the weight, and then mimicking the same motion without weights to feel the sensation of weightless jelly arms.

Before long, Alistair was performing sets of fifteen to twenty weighted jump squats on concrete, giving him all the strength and stability needed to maneuver steep mountain paths atop a snowboard without wear and tear to his knees. The sight of him leaping in rapid succession gave me the chills. To see a big man leap so effortlessly was awesome. As he turned up the heat for weighted wind sprints down the back alley of Enso Temple, I felt like I was standing in the middle of a pro football field three seconds after kick-off. As I saw this fierce, focused, and powerful beast speeding toward me, I realized that the principles of Weightlessness were far more applicable than I had ever imagined.

After four and a half months, and about 100 pounds lighter than the day he arrived, Alistair left me, well along the path to his long-term physical goals, in the best shape of his life. He was strong, confident, and flexible, with enough strength to crush mountains for months on end. He was strong enough to realize his lifelong dream.

Alistair returned to Enso after his journey to finish up his remaining physical objectives. While his weight loss story is incredible in its own right, he's writing the book on that one.

Weightlessness Footnote

Effortless movement requires free, unconditioned thought, an elite strength-to-weight ratio, and unencumbered mobility. Dynamic flexibility is one of the most overlooked virtues of an elite athlete. Most sports exist within a world of specified rules and confined movement. The martial arts stand alone because they belong to no single domain. Combat has no rules, and the warrior must be capable of responding to an infinite number of unpredictable possibilities with intelligent movement and uninhibited power. Whatever the mind conceives, the body carries out.

Ballistic resistance training (ankle weight training), given a sufficient base of health and physical strength, bypasses the need for years of repetition, assuming strong structural alignment. It forces your body to discover natural economies of movement in order to overcompensate for the burden of added weight. And this profound change is not local. Adding weight to the ankles makes you sensitive even to the role of minute shoulder movements in coordinating rapid footwork or sprinting. These efficiencies result in highly refined neuromuscular coordination and elite speed.

Ankle weights also provide an avenue for progressive resistance. This, given extended training periods, paves the way for sustained growth and development. The challenge I pose with Weightlessness is not the sporadic use of this principle to overcome short-term performance hurdles, but to implement high-speed resistance training as a lifestyle approach. We have discussed the incredible benefits of short-term, methodical practice. Imagine the possibilities of implementing this method not for months, but for one, two, or three years of daily, progressive practice!

Weightlessness, like martial arts, is not relegated to a single domain in life. It isn't external to your life as specific sports, hobbies, and occupations might be. As a philosophy of life, it prepares us for volatility and uncertainty. It prepares us for the complexities of life.

Chapter 6

FOREVER YOUNG

The Secret Science of Cheating Your Way Strong
From the Strength, Health, and Rehab Files

D ave and I sat sipping coffee in the reclusive garden of Enso Temple, watching long-legged Chinese and Russian models come and go from the MF Showroom. It was one of the many nice perks of partnering with a fashion designer. Casting calls always added a bit more life to our secluded Temple and certainly helped convince prospective male clients who could see that Enso was bubbling over with exotic beauties in sensual MF gowns and leather straps and things.

"Nice place you have here," Dave observed.

"Once in a while we get days like this," I answered with a smile.

Dave explained his reason for seeking me out: severe rotator cuff damage in both shoulders. I'd never met anyone who had managed to blow out both shoulders, but heavy kettlebell swings can set the stage for complete destruction. He explained that he'd been in rehab for a while and had reached a point of utter frustration. He wanted to try to be normal, train through it, and get stronger. I told him honestly that his was not an easy problem to work around. Depending on the severity of the injuries, I might not be able to help him at all. I'd have to test him, and wouldn't have a clear prognosis until we'd suffered through a few sessions together. But if he wanted to go ahead, I'd be willing to give it a try. I knew that if he could be helped with anything less than surgery, I could help him.

For me, the question is exceedingly simple – are you healthy enough to train? Most people are. People who are not are those who will be weakened by any degree of stress. I'm no doctor, and this particular diagnosis needs to come from a qualified professional. But if surgery is not immediately recommended, then the individual should not be treated like an injured person. They should be treated like a weak person. All negative connotations aside, weakness should not be avoided or worked around. It should be addressed, stressed, and alleviated intelligently.

In Dave's particular case, he was extremely strong despite his severe limitations. His pulling muscles and lower body strength were well developed. He could bust out several sets of clean wide grip pull-ups, and he could curl and squat. He was just unable to push and press. By *unable*, I mean that he could not do a single push-up, and a full-range shoulder press with ten pounds in each hand caused shooting pain. But he *was* able to stabilize himself for half a minute in a push-up position and statically hold light weights overhead.

This was a beginning. If static contraction is possible near full extension for any length of time without pain, then a foundation for training exists. Without it, surgery or extended rest is probably needed.

So we worked with what we had, and proceeded with relatively heavy short-range repetitions that looked like controlled bouncing at the peak of his shoulder press. The weight was much lighter than a healthy Dave could have handled, but heavy enough that getting the weight in and out of peak position caused twinges of pain. Nevertheless, there was a range (his strongest range) of motion that was pain free. We concentrated on stimulating his deltoids in that range until he completed his sets or until pain set in, which was about half the time.

To anyone peering through the Enso Temple training studio windows while Dave was lifting, I'm sure we looked like a couple of hacks. Anyone with experience would have criticized Dave for his poor form and me for being an incompetent trainer. And while they would have had a case for a man with healthy shoulders, here they'd have been missing a deeper application of biomechanical advantage. By lifting with pulsating repetitions near full extension, Dave reduced the amount of stress on his joints while maximizing his muscular engagement. While this was not a pain-free process, every couple of weeks Dave's range improved, his hands drifted closer to his shoulders, and the weight being pressed increased.

Everyone has seen that muscle-bound guy in the gym curling insanely heavy weight with atrocious form. He swings and thrashes, doing whatever is necessary to get the bar up to his chest. The skinny, hardworking guy in the corner scoffs and criticizes his poor form.

Now with all things you have the rule. We must all learn the rules. But the best in any art, science, or endeavor are those who know when to break the rules in order to create something exceptional. There is a very important place within the world of health and fitness for shitty form. I submit that that place is in the expediting of strength (and size) gains due to the increased leverage provided within certain ranges of motion. This is the secret science of strength and health, as well as a way to look like a novice in the gym. It also (listen carefully) removes the last line of defense for everyone too lazy to train due to weakness, injury, or a lack of time. There are no excuses.

The new rules of cheating your way to health and strength are as follows:

1. **Stress must be sufficient to target fast-twitch muscle fiber, as well as strengthen connective tissue**. Most physiotherapists have patients work on fine motor skills like internal and external rotations for rotator cuff injuries with very light weights. I have two qualms with this approach. The first is that there is no use in the real world for such a weird movement, despite the fact that it is considered to work the joint and composite parts through a full range of motion. The rotator cuff is designed to stabilize, so let it stabilize. Don't isolate it. Shoulders are used for lifting and pressing. Period.

   My second qualm is in the use of light weights. Granted, light is a relative term, but let's just say *light* refers to a weight that doesn't test your limits of strength in fewer than six to ten repetitions (in a full range), or in fewer than fifteen to twenty reps (in the case of short-range partial reps, discussed below). This kind of weight is required at some point to strengthen all the composite parts of a joint: the tendons, ligaments, and fast- and slow-twitch fibers of the primary and secondary muscles.

2. **Mechanical advantage must be increased to an extreme to allow for the heaviest weight training possible, and to reduce pain and the risk of greater injury in problem zones**. *Mechanical advantage* refers to increasing the leverage of an exercise, thereby reducing the stress of a particular exercise and allowing one to lift much heavier weights. It's not complicated, but is generally frowned upon by modern gym rats who prefer full-range movements and mock those who 'cheat' their reps.

However, there's ample evidence that old-school strong men implemented this loophole in biomechanics by constructing equipment that took into consideration strong and weak ranges of motion. For example, they suspended weight by chains at the level of a nearly fully contracted bicep curl. Therefore, the range of each rep was only a few inches and one barely had to lift the weight from the taut chains suspending it. To understand strength in range of motion (which is not a static number), we need to look briefly at the notion of *levers*, since they are what our bodies are constructed of. Levers are how muscles move bone, producing all physical movement.

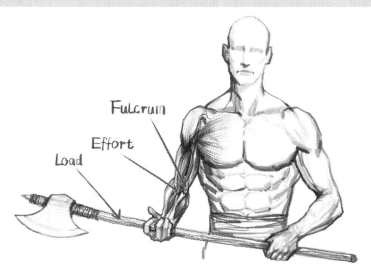

By looking again at that most favored and useless of exercises (revered by the sexy-weak), the bicep curl (or in the illustration above, a bent arm holding a battle ax), we can see how the third-class lever that is your curling arm allows your biceps to lift and hold weight. The strongest range of a bicep curl lies somewhere around a ninety-degree bend in the arm, where the bicep is near full contraction. Mechanical advantage diminishes at the bottom of a bicep curl, which is why considerably more weight can be lifted at the peak of a static hold than at the bottom. Test this for yourself.

Pete Sisco, a long-time advocate of static contraction training (holding weights without movement in a fully contracted position) and short-range partials (short 'cheating' repetitions where the weight is bounced slightly in the strongest range of motion), contributed a rough working model for measuring intensity, one that helps reduce all methods of training to an easily quantifiable measure of stress. Pete is a physics nerd who applies the laws of science to the art of bodybuilding. He coaches elite bodybuilders with decades of tinkering, trial and error, and jail yard rules behind them on how to build muscle more efficiently. And he's made crucial connections between both fields, well worth knowing for the purposes of looking hot and feeling strong into your sixties and beyond.

His methods focus on two factors: mechanical advantage (using the greatest leverage of your biomechanical frame to target fast-twitch muscle in the strongest range of motion), and reducing variables in the formula to the amount of weight lifted multiplied by duration. His own path moved from short-range partials explored in his earlier works to static contraction training in later ones.

This is a useless methodology of training for the general public. However, it's particularly useful in two cases: for those who want to become very strong very fast (starting from a de-trained state), and for those who are rehabilitating injuries. In short, due to the nature of biomechanical levers in the human body, more weight can be lifted in certain ranges. This eliminates the danger of tears or regression due to applying stress in a range of motion ill-equipped to control the weight. Weight builds strength, and more weight builds more strength. But it must be done safely, and that means training in a range where you are strong, not weak.

3. **Take multivitamins (on top of an otherwise ample, whole food diet)**. Most rehabilitation requires the reconstruction of muscle and connective tissue. It also requires strengthening muscles too weak to support the spine and other tenuous joints, such as the ankles, knees, and hips. This process requires raw materials in order to reconstruct and build new tissue. An increase in micronutrients – the vitamins and minerals abundant in all things fed with water and sunlight (fruits and vegetables) – as well as an increase in complete proteins (fish or meat) is vital. Most people starting a program with me are conscious of their macronutrient intake (protein, carbohydrates, and fat), with or without my strict nutritional guidelines. But it may not be enough. I add one supplement: multivitamins, your dietary insurance plan.

   I often encourage clients to double or triple the daily recommended dose of multivitamins (or better yet, a powdered greens supplement) for a couple of weeks, and after that to cycle high and low days, high and low weeks. I don't prescribe specific vitamins. Our bodies have a peculiar response to many things not taken from whole, natural foods. When we medicate ourselves, we sometimes inadvertently cause deficiencies in other essential nutrients. Excessive calcium can decrease iron absorption, causing a host of physical ailments. I am not a biologist or a brilliant nutritionist. I don't want to cause more problems with ignorant applications of partial knowledge. I bypass this issue by embracing my ignorance and loading up on everything for short intervals.

   Here you go, body – a plethora of goodies, more than enough of everything. Take what you need, flush the rest.

   I recommend that you go off your cycle every few weeks to improve nutrient absorption for the next cycle and recover from any potential toxicity or overdose (this would be in a relatively benign, undetectable form).

After four to six weeks, Dave began to realize a considerably improved range of motion and strength. He felt a decrease in general pain. We focused on only one lift, the shoulder press. Humans press. We don't sway our hands in and out with rubber bands, a movement rehab specialists tend to focus on. Show me which natural environmental scenario requires such a weird movement.

Does it matter that science has discovered an ideal way to move the joint through a full range of possibilities? Not to me it doesn't. We're strong. We pull, push, and press. With proper form, pressing will recruit all possible fast-twitch fibers of the deltoids and the trapezius, as well as target and strengthen connective tissues. All other movements and exercises are masturbatory.

This does not mean that Dave's path was painless. In fact, it was excruciating at times, requiring us to call it quits after only one set if he hadn't recovered well from a previous session. This is part of the process. Stress, nourish, and recover. Sometimes recovery requires more than your standard day or two of rest. But Dave did recover, and over time has worked up to a respectable shoulder press weight. He can perform full-range push-ups again and is more often than not pain-free in his daily living, all because we applied short-range partial reps, controlling heavy weight at the top range of his shoulder press for eight to fifteen reps.

If memory serves, he's also up for the Nicest Guy in Shanghai award this year.

Weightless Tangent

Other applications of the principle above might include strengthening or rehabilitating muscles and joints like the shoulders and elbows involved in the big push (the bench, chest press, push-up, or in the case above, the shoulder press). The strongest range of motion for your pushing muscles, in contrast to the pulling muscles of the biceps, lats, and hamstrings, is the near full extension of the limbs. Training the push-up at the top of the range is the early stage of transitioning someone from doing push-ups on their knees to doing full-range push-ups on their feet. You can build all the strength necessary to do full push-ups by pushing to higher numbers of short-range reps at the top of the push-up, given good form. When rehabilitating any weak links, such as the shoulders, elbows, or muscular strains, working the chest press in ten to thirty short, heavy, controlled, and pulsating reps targets fast-twitch fibers without overstressing joints and connective tissue.

In all applications of this principle, emphasis should be placed on large, compound exercises within the five vectors of movement, regardless of injury or weakness type.

In the all-too-common case of knee problems, do squats! Or use sister techniques the deadlift and the lunge. Work up to a heavy squat or deadlift, working the top range of movement only (a very slight bend of the knees while holding weight in each hand, done in short-range partial reps). Lift heavy. High, full-range reps with low weights wear the joints out and make it harder to target the fast-twitch fibers responsible for stabilizing and protecting our joints. This is why long-distance runners are rife with knee, ankle, hip, and hamstring injuries, whereas people who sprint (which targets fast-twitch muscle) tend to have healthy, strong, lean physiques. Heavy equals healthy. Partial equals safe.

A creative, less common strategy for implementing this principle is to use materials or devices that increase resistance as you enter your strongest range of motion. For example, you might attach chains to each end of the bar on a classic bench press. As you lower the bar, the chains coil on the ground, removing their weight from the equation as the bar approaches your chest (at the weakest range of motion). As you push up from the chest, link after link is added to the weight, and you're fighting against considerably more weight as you enter your strongest range of motion.

This is a great technique for becoming powerful in a full range of motion, and is highly recommended for those practicing contact and fight sports. It improves both the power and neuromuscular efficiency of the big push. The same principle can be applied to the squat, shoulder press, and a few others. Rubber bands have a similar power-enhancing effect, which is why taekwondo stylists kick against resistance from heavy rubber bands fastened at the ankles and boxers punch against resistance from rubber bands pulling their arms back. These are both examples of high-speed resistance training as well.

Weightlessness Footnote

The weightless warrior should be forever in control of her body and mind. She should be free of the fear of failure, and of self-pity. One can always train. If an injury is severe, that part of the body is rested while the rest is trained as safely as possible. Armed with a toolkit of cheating repetitions, she should be able to leverage her greatest strengths to overcome short-term weakness. When broken, weak, or insecure, she must find a way to become whole again. Static contraction training and short-range partials can be used for rapid body transformation or the rehabilitation of injured and weak body parts. One can always train. Understanding the body as a system of levers will allow the weightless warrior to remain forever young.

Weightlessness does not distinguish between healthy and injured individuals in the grand sense, unless of course the injury is very recent and acute, or there is palpable structural damage. Rest and recovery are always needed before stress can be applied safely. But for many injuries, especially those that fall into the chronic pain category, we ought to treat them as weaknesses and smartly apply the principles that develop an otherwise pain-free individual. This must be done with a sensitive touch (and some therapists and doctors will disagree), but I have consistently helped rehabilitate a wide range of injuries for years with these principles.

Principles of growth and stress-adaptation don't change just because you're injured. Trust your body. Embrace stress again as quickly (and safely) as you can, so that you can become whole again.

Chapter 7

FROM CATO TO CHAMPION

From the Skin-in-the-Game Files

And then there was Champion…

I needed a potato sack for throwing and hurting and whatnot. After years of travel and private teaching, I felt the need for a serious review of my locking and throwing techniques. While most of my clients came for mind and body training, a minority of them came to study self-defense. The problem on my end was that my predominately professional client base had no interest in learning to receive pain and take falls. They wanted to fast-track progress in the art of killing without your typical pain-exchange learning process. I had neglected rudimentary falling skills in their training and had been left with no one to partner with. The solitary life of a private self-defense instructor.

But there I was in China, the Wild East, and surely there had to be countless happy-go-lucky kung fu men who'd love a little extra cash in exchange for an hour and a half of being thrown around like a rag doll. So I put out an ad for someone with these basic requirements.

"Seeking martial arts training partner," the ad read. "Must be strong, fit, and have a very high pain tolerance. Kung fu experience a plus."

Zhang Ping, English alias Champion, first visited Enso on a beautiful sunny afternoon, a portent for our future cooperation. He was a simple guy, but keen and built like a brick shithouse. He also had a decade of Southern Fist experience. I was grateful for that because it allowed me to teach him to fall from all but the advanced throwing techniques within three weeks. His pain tolerance was extraordinary. It was a match made in China.

When a sadist meets a masochist, magical things happen.

Two to three days a week, for three months, I twisted, bent, pulled, pressed, and threw dear Champion. For those interested, we settled on about twenty dollars for an hour and a half of concentrated physical abuse. He took at least thirty to fifty hard falls per session. Every joint was stretched, nerves were ground, and acupoints were pressed until tap-out or absent-minded pass-out. I fully organized and refined my soft weapons curriculum, half of which consisted of locking, binding, choking, and throwing techniques using a sash, belt, tie, or chain. Thanks to Champion, I know exactly how long it takes to strangle somebody with silk and how deep chain digs into flesh when it is wrapped and tugged.

Let me reassure you that I am a normal guy.

I am.

After helping me film *Art of the Sash*, my comprehensive soft weapons instructional DVD, Champion asked me to be his master (which doesn't sound as strange in Chinese). He'd continue on as my chief rag doll and be paid by learning my system of martial arts, which he viewed as exceedingly practical and effective. Not long after that, he asked to become my assistant and full-time employee, which he is to this day. If you thought the foundation of our relationship was somewhat abnormal, things became much more dubious under Project Champion: preparing Champion to become a champion. It was my focused effort to mold a mini-me – or rather, a master *him* – in record time.

The Cato Imperative

In the *Pink Panther* comedies, inspector Jacques Clouseau has a faithful manservant, highly trained in the martial arts, who attacks him at random in order to keep Clouseau's martial arts and awareness skills at their peak. Cato is fierce and unrelenting, often causing hilarious fight scenes. One fight even begins while Clouseau is making love and destroys the entire apartment. Cato represents a random stressor – a tiger lurking in the forest – that requires a weightless state of mind, calm, focused, and alert.

Before social services starts knocking on the doors at Enso Temple due to Champion abuse... wait a second, I'm in China, no one gives a shit. But I should explain that martial artists and civilians process pain very differently. For most people, there is little difference in processing pain and injury. Both seem to cause psychological suffering (more often than not sustained suffering), weakness, or a loss of confidence. In martial arts, however, there is a clear distinction between the two.

Injury is bad. You do not recover quickly from injury. It weakens you. Pain, on the other hand, is good. Pain is a stressor that contains information. It tells you when a technique is proficient. It also tells you when and how you need to move so as to alleviate it. It allows you to overcompensate mentally and physically, preparing your mind and body for higher degrees of stress. Without pain, there is no knowledge. The more appropriate or relevant the pain is to a desired response, the faster you acquire practical knowledge of martial skill. Beating a student who lacks focus with a stick may be unproductive. Forcing a student to respond to pain as an avoidable, imminent danger is extremely relevant.

One day I applied a wristlock on Champion. It was severe enough for him to initiate a break fall, but he was not mentally prepared. He fell hard. Despite the fact that a takedown is a sign of efficacy, I'm extremely impatient when training lacks aesthetic value. It just looked ugly. He fell flat on his back, which aside from posing the danger of kidney damage and lower back injury, also demonstrates a lack of awareness and control.

A martial artist who is not alert and prepared for such contingencies is not capable of using his skills in uncontrolled situations. And in the real world, there are no controlled situations. I decided from that day forward that I would never again forewarn Champion whether to expect a genuine or a moderately demonstrated throw. He was to maintain constant alertness and be sensitive to the degree of force I applied.

At first he said okay. He always said okay, grinning from ear to ear. A few minutes later, when he had fully realized what I was saying, he investigated.

"What if I guess wrong?" he asked.

"I'll break your wrist," I replied. "Don't guess wrong."

Over the following two weeks, every time I put my hands on him, his demeanor changed completely. His eyes narrowed more than normal, with an air of deep concentration. When he arose from each fall he patted his heart with his hand to express a skyrocketing pulse exacerbated by the fear of injury. Not knowing when he would need to fall, but knowing that when the time came he would need to do so or face severe consequences, was enough of a stressor to safeguard him from extreme danger applied at random times. Not every technique was full-on. Less than 30 percent were, I'd say. But not knowing how intense the throw would be made him ready for all of them. His falling skills escalated from intermediate to advanced in record time. He became unbreakable.

I'm sure that there's a special place in hell for people with my particular methods of personal development. I'm not sure on all the details, of course, but I'm sure I'd be doing something meaningful, a kind of shot caller responsible for inflicting pain for the purposes of growth. The irony of course, which is why it would be hell, is that I would be leading people who could not process pain properly, who did not become stronger through it. Since I would be incapable of assessing that properly ahead of time, it would lead to countless futile attempts at helping people through calculated torture. But I'm not there yet, and in this world I have a knack for seeing real potential and identifying the minimum effort, time input, and stress required to stimulate rapid change. It's why people hire me.

Skin in the Game

In all things important we must find a way to have skin in the game, to put something at stake and be in a position to receive a relevant reward. This is the essence of understanding, integrity, and personal accountability. The CEO with a massive fixed salary plus performance-based bonus more often than not has nothing to lose by being wrong. In some cases, the greatest risk of poor performance is a payout in the millions for breach of contract or early termination. The entrepreneur, on the other hand, has personal capital, time, and knowledge at risk. He has potential gain and a very real risk of personal loss.

I'm not saying that hired CEOs without personal equity in the company or previous entrepreneurial endeavors cannot be men of integrity. I'm only saying that we can't know. In the same way, a martial arts instructor who never applies full force because 'the techniques are too dangerous' or who spares his students body conditioning, full-contact fighting, or high-stress training is a charlatan selling the illusion of martial knowledge.

In the pursuit of wisdom and self-mastery, one must be tested. One must be exposed to stress and in some cases at random intervals or in unpredictable degrees. One *must* have skin in the game, with the risk of real personal loss. In such conditions the body will adapt, and the mind will expand.

This is not a negative judgment of weekend warriors or teachers of martial arts-oriented fitness. It's fantastic for people to move by any means, and I too use martial arts tools and techniques for general conditioning. This is an accountability call to those who claim to study and teach the real thing (in any domain) yet avoid stress tests and technical refinement. The techniques of genuine martial arts are designed to kill, maim, or pacify. This requires a strong and ever-improving knowledge of anatomy, a body conditioned to perform under duress, and a mind prepared to survive in life-or-death situations. Ideally one dually cultivates awareness and compassion in tandem so that self-control is preeminent. But let's not confuse domains of development. Those focused on growth cannot overlook this foundational principle:

It is stress that causes adaptation.

I heard a story once about a group of people stranded in a life raft. They'd been drifting at sea for days, going nowhere, losing hope. The captain took it upon himself to poke a hole in the boat, which caused all members to spring to action and row furiously until they found land or death became their fate. They tore their bodies apart, burned their arms to mush, bloodied their hands, cried out in desperation. But they gathered all that was within them and collectively fought for survival. They were picked up on a small deserted island, alive.

If you can find a way to poke a hole in your boat, to methodically stress your mind and body, an infinite world of possibilities will unfold before you. If your wrist may be broken at any moment, you'll quickly learn to fall or counter as a safeguard. If you have your personal energies, ideas, and finances at stake as an entrepreneur, you won't throw money and resources at problems haphazardly. And if you're going to drown, you'll row your heart out to survive. Find a way to put yourself in sink-or-swim scenarios and you'll be amazed at just how quickly you learn to swim.

Sink or Swim!

My own introduction to the sink-or-swim principle of personal development began when I was in high school, where I began to embrace stress as a prerequisite for growth. When I was fourteen years old, I began breaking boards. When I was fifteen, I fell into the habit of beating my shins with oak batons before bed. When I was in college, I began brick breaking and focused hand conditioning. Naturally, this practice resulted in numerous complaints from other students, as the concussion would resonate throughout the dormitory from my one hundred daily post-study punches on the brick wall.

Years of body conditioning, at times intelligently structured and at other times severe enough to require months of rest and recovery, taught me a great deal about how our bodies respond to stress. It taught me so much, in fact, that my approach to rapid body transformation and self-defense training comes from a stressor-adaptation perspective. When all personal development is seen through this lens, identifying the minimal required dosages of stress to achieve a desired end is much easier.

I don't have a particularly strong bone structure. I have very slender wrists, and when deconditioned, I look very slim. I learned young in life that if I punch things, my hands break. I also learned that when my hands recover, they are stronger than before. Bone, when stressed sufficiently enough to crack, responds by becoming larger and stronger. The methodical calcification of bone has been used for centuries by Thai boxers to toughen their shins by kicking banana trees, by karate masters to harden their knuckles on wood, by iron palm practitioners to harden their palms and fingertips, and by Shaolin monks to harden their heads and build abdomens, throats, and testicles of steel.

Muscle responds to stress in the same way. This is commonly referred to as bodybuilding. Most gym rats understand that time spent in the gym is not constructive – it's destructive. Weightlifting tears muscle, stresses the nervous system, and depletes energy reserves. We are and should be weaker after training than before we began. Thereafter begins the process of adaptation, comprised of sound rest and the assimilation of nutrients to build new tissue. The adaptation phase has an acute phase of four to twenty-four hours and a longer period in which gains that can last days to weeks are solidified. Overemphasizing the destructive element of the stress-adaptation cycle reduces the body's ability to adapt rapidly to physical training, and can result in long-term plateaus or fatigue.

The stress-adaptation cycle is relevant for learning all things of a non-theoretical nature. Anyone who speaks a second language can attest to the fact that the fastest growth curve occurs when language is used out of necessity. You can study vocabulary until you're blue in the face, but if there's no sense of urgency, pressure, or practicality, retention is terrible. If you want to learn how to order in a restaurant, go hungry to a restaurant with no English menu. If you want to learn directions, wander until you are lost, and ask how to get back home. And if you want a Champion to be constantly alert, attack him at random, unpredictable times. It's stressful. And it leads to real ability in record time.

A weightless man is not molded in a comfortable environment. If results occur in response to stress, and if our mission is to become weightless, then great weight is required. One must commit to long-term progress, through exposure to long-term, methodical stressors. One must lift heavy weights to feel subsequent lightness of movement. One must confront the heaviness of internal thoughts and emotions, and the pain that comes from desire, in order to be free of attachments and preconditioned thoughts.

When a weightless man is hit with stone, he becomes stronger than stone. When he faces violence and selfishness within himself, he becomes innocent and pure.

Weightlessness Footnote

The weightless warrior should view pain as a positive stressor to be used for growth, whereas injury is a negative stressor to be avoided. Embrace the antifragile (things that gain from disorder or stress) nature of your mind and body, and implement stresses in a methodical manner that force a desired adaptation. If your body is proven weak, it will become strong. If your knowledge or understanding is proven insufficient, your mind will grow. Embrace it and face challenges with confidence. Create environments that test and challenge. Allow your body and mind to do what they are made to do: adapt and evolve.

Chapter 8

PEACE AND POWER

From the Mind-Body Files

T he warrior-monk tradition was established on the grounds that physical training enhances spiritual development. The evolution of martial skills had extraordinary health benefits and practical applications, but the motivation to develop them came from a desire to keep monks from falling asleep while practicing meditation. What kind of a spirit is housed in a heavy, stiff, and lethargic body? To date, the strongest men and women I've met, those most capable of moral integrity and absolute devotion in the face of adversity, have been fighters or mind-body masters. Their eyes are deep, weathered, and clear, betraying the pain and passion that led them to become the warriors they are.

Peace

Adele played hard to get when I asked her to teach at Enso Temple. Or at least I thought she was playing hard to get. It turned out she *was* hard to get. It took me several months to realize she was no ordinary yogi and that I was lucky to steal a few months of her time to teach at my humble little temple. She had left a corporate career as a creative director three years prior, to dedicate her time and energy to developing her mind and body further. She spread a message of peace and love that she knew to be yoga. She never spoke of her previous life, but as we grew to be close and I began to meet friend after friend after friend of hers, I saw the portrait of a person who was owned by no one, who had resolved to help everyone.

Power

After my first encounter with Master Roena, I knew I'd found a genuine master of martial arts, as well as a shit-kicking hardass. His accolades were legendary. With hundreds of street fights under his belt, he was also a world champion in several national and international full-contact tournaments, a Golden Gloves champion, an ex-bouncer, and an ex-military combat instructor. He was also one of three sheriffs in a level-five security lockdown; his job requirement was to keep the peace in a room of eighty convicted murderers, rapists, and other hardcore felons. He's survived prison riots and armed gang attacks on the streets of Denver, and he's cleared rooms of black belt master instructors when they failed to show him proper respect. Despite it all, he is as humble and courteous as a man of the cloth. But when he teaches or fights, there is fire in his eyes the likes of which ye have never seen. He manifests the will of a man who does not know how to lose. It's at once demonic and angelic.

Peace

You don't get to practice martial arts for a couple of decades without meeting exceptionally flexible people. But the first time I saw Adele's sun salutation I was speechless. Her balance of strength and flexibility, the way she sank into a stretch with no apparent resistance in her body, moved and guided naturally by her breath, was an inspiring sight. It encapsulated the way she lived, guided by the breath, flexible, relaxed, adaptable. For three years she had lived a more hermetic lifestyle, dividing her time between part-time yoga teaching and her home, which she treats as an ashram in the forest, away from the frivolity and chaos of normal daily living. While the world around her was running mad, she would sit quietly watching her breath, observing the flow of energy throughout. At the age of forty-six, she had the body of a twenty-year-old, the charming smile of an innocent child, and honest, serene eyes.

Power

Master Roena, at one of our evening classes, lectured myself and a couple of other instructors under him on the unstated rules of courtesy and respect in the martial arts. He'd attended a masters' black belt class in

Denver in an attempt to mend old relationships and reunite with a previous grandmaster. But he did have a history with this man, and several of the black belt instructors in the group were not happy that Roena showed up, despite his personal invitation. As Master Roena recapped the events, his posture began to change. His shoulders rolled slightly forward in a warrior posture, unconsciously protecting the vital organs and reducing the striking surface of the torso. His eyes were ablaze.

"They tried to hurt me," he said. "Now, when you fight, you show respect. You respect clean shots and don't hurt your partners excessively. But today they came after me. And if someone doesn't respect you, if someone comes after you, you hurt them."

We found out later that Master Roena had taken them all down, a room full of master instructors, one after another. Nobody left whole. Except him.

Peace

One evening during a black belt class, Master Roena called myself and his assistant instructors into the changing room. He was clearly shaken, trying to hold back tears. A week prior he'd adopted a new puppy. Earlier that day, in a grocery store, the puppy had crawled up from his arms, over his shoulder, and fallen to its death. Telling us, he was unable to keep his composure. He would have done anything to undo the events of the day.

I was awestruck. This warrior of stone and ice, of indomitable spirit, was shaken to the core by the death of a helpless creature he'd known only a short time. He blamed himself harshly for a mishap that could have been avoided. I knew him as a man with the power to inflict unimaginable pain, yet here he betrayed heartfelt compassion. Many would hurt at the loss of an innocent creature, but his vulnerability with those of us who bowed to him every time we saw him demonstrated a different side of strength.

Master Roena knew intimately the world of violence, yet he wasn't callous to the suffering of others. Nor was he hiding behind a mask of strength to maintain an air of authority with his students. He was strong enough to stand honest and exposed, asking for support in teaching that class and for our understanding if he wasn't quite himself. Despite his hurt at that time, there was no conflict within him.

Power

Shortly after Adele left the corporate world with the intention to serve and support as a yoga teacher, she suffered a serious knee injury that completely halted her physical practice, as well as her teaching. She couldn't properly walk for several months. But rather than let it crush her spirit, she resolved to face her pain and use her mind when her body was not cooperating. She wished for nothing more and sat quietly in daily meditation. After a decade of dedicated physical practice, experiencing the pains of burning muscle and the angst of discomfort that occurs while sustaining postures, she had become intimate with the presence of pain, and intimately aware of its impermanence. In forging a body of strength, grace, and flexibility, she had honed a concentrated mind and relinquished all attachment to ego-driven desires. She'd become strong enough to yield without resistance, to accept without judgment.

Yoga is a complex practice today, but it was once a philosophy of meditation only. Adele rejected surgery, rehab, and medication. She committed herself to feeling every pain, learning from every hardship. If she were to recover, it would come from the natural healing power of her body and mind, not through aggressive medical intervention. Six months later, when attempting her first yoga class, unsure as to whether she could perform basic postures, she discovered that she had not only healed completely but had grown stronger in her physical practice.

The Unfettered Mind

Adele, long, strong, and fluid in body and mind, is a master of her domain. She rolls with what comes and embraces new opportunities, trips, and challenges with an open mind. If she encounters a roadblock or realizes something doesn't suit her, she flows around or ignores it altogether, like a stream engulfing a boulder. With an all-knowing smile, she constantly reminds me to "just flow with it." Free of insecurity and concern for social conventions, pressures, and judgments, Adele attracts people. They compete for her approval, time, association, insight, and advice, since they can clearly see her strength, power, and freedom.

Most bouncers will tell you that it isn't the chest-beating, hot-headed rabble rouser looking for attention and a moment of fame you need to worry about. It's the quiet guy in the corner. It's that unassuming, soft-spoken gent who is silent until he cannot be silent anymore. When that man stands up, you'd better clear the whole bar out.

No earthly danger could intimidate Master Roena. He's been tested by fire for decades. He's been shot at, stabbed, and has defended his life on many occasions. He has learned to let go. He has learned to live in the moment, for to carry anything into that moment of truth was just useless baggage. One needs complete freedom to think and react quickly. After a lifetime of fighting, he'd become the eye of a hurricane, the point of peace and calm in a world of chaos.

When asked what was going through his mind before every fight, he asserted, "I never cared if I won or lost a fight. At those times, I have only one thought in my mind: that the man across from me will never forget my name!"

Weightlessness Footnote

Through the discipline of physical training, we complete ourselves. The yang of physicality, aggression, and fierceness, followed to its natural end, will dissolve all insecurity and egotism. When fear is confronted fully, when the body is fully tested, the mind finds peace. It must learn to let go in order to adapt and survive.

The inner strength and self-control of men and women of advanced physical dedication is unparalleled in other walks of life. Nothing develops more inner strength and focus than extensive training in holistic lifestyle arts. It is the gateway to strength, peace, and happiness. It is also a necessary prerequisite for mental development. The heights of insight, focus, and awareness can only be housed in a strong body.

This is the spirit of the warrior monk tradition, and the spirit cultivated with Weightlessness training. We don't all need to construct bodies of steel, but we should consider the internal strength and fortitude forged in the pain of physical training, as well as the willpower of an individual who cannot be intimidated by physical danger. It creates individuals capable of unlimited devotion and integrity, individuals who can remain steadfast to their values and beliefs. Individuals whose insight penetrates like rays of light tearing through a thunderstorm.

BOOK 3

The Unfettered Mind

Narratives chronicling the passions of a meditative mind.

In *The Unfettered Mind*, we explore the metaphysical pillar of Weightlessness: we become aware of the beauty that resides beneath the surface of experience, we cultivate the subtle energy within, and we discover an aggressive tool for drawing on the creative power of randomness.

A man traveling across a field encountered a tiger. He fled, the tiger chasing after him. Coming to a precipice, he caught hold of the root of a wild vine and swung himself down over the edge. The tiger sniffed at him from above. Trembling, the man looked down to where, far below, another tiger was waiting to eat him. Only the vine sustained him.

Two mice, one white and one black, little by little started to gnaw away the vine. The man saw a luscious strawberry near him. Grasping the vine with one hand, he plucked the strawberry with the other. How sweet it tasted!

A Zen Parable

Chapter 1

STEPPENWOLF AND THE
SHOELESS FLORENTINE

The shoeless Florentine, wayward wanderer with no home or nation, no love or life to call his own, treaded lightly atop empty cobblestone paths beneath a weeping heaven. He'd have no respite this evening. The strength to move was not a conscious strength born of physical power. He was compelled by a primal innocence devoid of selfhood, led by the same spontaneity that leads a child to start sprinting or a cat to leap at a ball of yarn. A deep sadness filled his heart, but amid the pains of a life without attachment there were moments of eternal joy and delight, subtle beauties of circumstance that the sane, organized world cannot detect. The shoeless Florentine, wayward wanderer, fragile heavy-hearted outcast and warrior poet, would endure.

I met Tara while meandering through the majestic Boboli gardens. We had crossed paths a couple times while navigating the labyrinth of brush and sculpture, sharing soft moments of brief eye contact. I took a seat after an hour or so in the sun. Tara passed by again and after another warm smile she decided to sit next to me. You never know what will happen during spontaneous encounters abroad when you open your mouth. Is she Italian? Does she speak English? It was worth a try. She was a petite blonde, an ex-gymnast as I later found out, with a tight and curvy build.

She was American, like me. She was traveling alone, like me. She was a law student, taking a break before taking the bar exam. A smart, petite, blonde ex-gymnast. She was a bit feisty and fun, a perfect holiday adventure. We decided to meet again that evening in the Piazza della Signoria over pasta and a bottle of wine. There were an appropriate number of uncomfortable silences, fueling a growing sexual tension. After dinner we stumbled through the streets of Florence back to her hotel, holding hands, laughing childishly, pausing occasionally to grope and kiss.

We fumbled around at her hotel entrance, prolonging our fiery tension as long as possible. In retrospect, signs do not come any clearer. She needed me to invite myself in. She just didn't want to be the girl to invite a random pick-up in for a one-night stand. Instead, I suggested we visit Pisa the following day. She agreed, with an odd, swirling combination of lust and disappointment in her eyes. What did I think, that my grand gesture would lead to something bigger and better, a life of hand holding and salads?

The following day was a disaster. She felt obligated to play out a role that should have ended as suddenly as it began. The day was memorably uncomfortable, laden with terse conversation and anti-chemistry. Kids were running and screaming, chasing pigeons all over the place, nails on a chalkboard for a hungover mind. I held my guidebook in front of the leaning tower, and yep, still leaning, more pigeons.

During the train ride back to Florence it began to rain. I remembered I'd checked out of my hotel that morning and left my things at the train station, assuming we would travel on together. Another chump move brought on by the hope of sustained romance from yet another agreement made while drunk. I didn't feel comfortable letting her walk back to her hotel alone in the rain, but as the minutes passed, it meant my chances of finding accommodation were dwindling. Since we returned from Pisa on the last train, I had no chance of moving on or finding an overnight train. I was trapped.

We had a very brief and awkward goodbye on her hotel doorstep, and I turned to face the cool, drizzling night. Within minutes the slight drizzle became a heavy rain. I recalled a couple of potential rooms, but after two failed attempts to get a room, I wandered aimlessly through the streets of Florence, drenched head to toe. My feet were calloused and strong from a decade-plus of taekwondo training on hardwood floors, and my shoes were heavy, soppy, and noisy. I decided to taste the cobblestone as nature intended, barefoot.

Taking my shoes in my hand, I had a flashback of an old woman in Milan who had eerily warned me of that very same thing. I'd been trekking through the city barefoot and, entering a dark, underground walkway, she stopped and warned me, staring into my soul.

She asked right away if I was American, without even a word or gesture between us. She warned me of the dangers of walking through the underground walkways. Drugs, she said, mimicking emptying a syringe of heroin into her forearm. AIDS, she said. It was an ominous portent that I shrugged off until my return from lunch, passing the same underground walkway before ascending to the street above. There, in the glow of sunlight, illuminating the edge of my cave, a demon was escaping into an angelic moment of ecstasy. His shoulders slumped and his body went limp as he fell into the arms of a companion, a needle dangling from his vain. His dealer eyed me with suspicion and aggression.

"Keep moving," his eyes said. I put my shoes back on.

Now I marched on, shoes in hand, sopping wet, with no choice but to weather the night, cold, wet, and alone. The initial discomfort was burdensome. Self-pity arose, frustrations of chump moves and naïve decisions. There was the fear of the unknown. I'd camped in nature before, but I'd never spent a night homeless, let alone in a foreign country with nowhere to turn. But the rain, my suffocating burden, punched and pounded, and gradually transformed into catharsis.

As the rain streamed from my face and dripped from my clothes, deeper burdens that bound my spirit flowed within it. My selfish desires for comfort and security collected in each drop and trailed into the torrential stream that flowed beneath me. What's the worst that could happen, I thought? There are men and animals that know only this world, the world of isolation and discomfort. Who am I to deserve anything more than the poorest of the poor?

Rather than resent my plight, I grew stronger, lighter, and free. I could bear the worst that night had to offer. I felt a burning in my abdomen, and a pure glow emanating from my eyes. It was the kind that I imagine a saint exhibits before he heals, or a murderer before he destroys. It had no rational motive. Qi coursed through my veins, accompanying a sense of raw physical power. The rain washed my mind as it did the streets beneath me, and in that emptiness of self, there was a power and fullness I had never known. I was abnormally alert, with heightened physical senses. I felt connected to all things despite being alone. I marched on Florence as a raw, fearless, and innocent man.

In his novel *Steppenwolf*, Hermann Hesse paints a portrait of modern man, wild, burning with passion and natural instinct, but constrained by a conformist society. His protagonist, an introverted academic, spends years alone in an attic, reading, dreaming, struggling with the balance between a passionate animalism and his rational humanity. He likens himself to a wolf that wanders out from his den and settles on the footsteps of society, the gateway between two worlds. In the absence of a world I knew, I ceased to be the man I was. I was liberated from myself, my memories, my likes and dislikes, my habits and desires. I became my strongest natural self. I became the Steppenwolf.

Dining patrons behind glass walls drank their wine and enjoyed their fine cuisine. The eyes of some could not look directly at me, nor could they look away. I was being judged. I was poor. I was homeless. But the shame was not needed. I am a man. You can look me in the eyes. Sticking your head in the sand does not make the world disappear.

Strangers approached at a distance, a couple taking an evening stroll under the protection of an umbrella. They crossed to the other side of the street and refused to make eye contact. Fear. What had I become? What did they see? A man my age asked for money. His eyes were as strong as mine. He said that I was the only one all night who gave, who even looked him in the eye. I saw my life from the other side, living in the skin of the men I judge.

Rain fell like beads of light, illuminating a greater self, unconstrained, unconfined, raw, pure, compassionate, and capable of great cruelty. I was energy without a self, capable of contradiction. I was the thief in the shadows, the hungry man, the raw, single-minded rapist-murderer-villain. I was the wayward poet finding romance in hardship, the quiet healer willing to give himself completely to relieve an ounce of suffering in another. I was free to be that man, all men. My hunger was real. My loneliness was real. But they were no longer *mine.* They were for a moment and they were gone, fleeting as the pressure of a raindrop.

Had this state endured, I may never have returned to normalcy. Alas, the meditative mind need not seek permanence. Life is present. Enlightenment is a drop of rain that falls with caprice and dissolves into the ocean of infinite memories past. After hours of trekking through the concrete jungle, I returned to the train station and resolved to wait until it opened the following morning. I sat under a small, secluded overhang, and my finite self, with egotistical desires, crept back to the surface. Trying to hold on to my innocence as long as possible, I held my backpack upside down and shook it like a child does with his box full of toy cars, full of curiosity, excitement, and recklessness. I had my fingers crossed that there might be some creature comforts I'd forgotten about.

The contents were absurd. I unwrapped two shot glasses from the Hans Christian Andersen house. Useless. I stared down at a troll doll with a modified troll flag that read *USS Danmark.* It was a token from my friend Kevin – who you will soon become acquainted with - to help me on my journey. Useless. A broken whoopee cushion, split from an over-enthusiastic attempt at disturbing a bus of commuters from Limerick to Dublin. Totally useless. A copy of the *Tao de Ching.* Punched by absurdity again. I shoved each item back in and propped my head up with the bundle of madness. I knew the Steppenwolf was gone when I looked over at the bum a few feet away and wondered where he got his cardboard box from. I drifted happily into darkness with the heartwarming thought of rolling him off and taking it for myself.

Chapter 2

REVIVING THE DUMPSTER BABY

Ugly baby. Squidgy, pug-faced little alien-looking baby. Gross. Gross little ugly baby. Gross face. Gross baby face. Body seems normal though.

We've all been there. You've been invited to a party. Everyone is gathered around the carriage ogling and poking, making funny baby noises and smiling sweetly. You're lured closer by all the excitement. There must be something killer in there. You nudge the father aside and push the mother to the ground and peer in at their little... monster. You can't control the impulse to shriek and gasp. It takes you every ounce of self-control not to implore the parents to get rid of it.

The father, after picking up his wife from the floor, says to you, "You look a little pale. Do you feel okay?"

"Uh... yeah, but the thing is, your..."

"It's okay," the father says.

"Jerk," the mother spits out, scowling.

"It's okay," he continues. "It took me a little time to adjust too. But that little bastard is mine, and I love him." He inches closer and puts his hand on your shoulder. "Try not to think of the cuteness of other babies, just look quietly. Don't judge."

You take another look into the carriage, and rather than grab the poking stick to see what the baby's made of, you maintain a steady gaze. You breathe more deeply and let go. You scroll his features, starting with the obtrusive little pug nose. Kinda like a little pig nose, you note. Kinda cute. It's rosy red, soft little cheeks. Kinda like it's drunk or been slapped around a bit. Pretty cute I guess. Its chin has two parts though. A little bit like an evil villain's chin. Because of the puffy cheeks, it's not as menacing as a proper villain's. Possibly even kinda cute. Its ears seem normal. No complaints. By the end, you can't help admitting that the baby is actually kinda lovely in its own way. There's no need to throw it out after all.

"Somebody fix me a vodka tonic!" you cry out.

Let's be honest with ourselves. Not all babies are cute. We've all seen a baby that looks like it's been beaten with the ugly stick. Our first impulse may be revulsion. The second, more socially correct impulse, is to tell the parents how cute it is. With time, you see past the ugliness to the innocence. You see the beauty and uniqueness of the child. What you don't do (in the developed world) is throw it out because it reminds you of pure evil.

Meditation is the practice of peering into the baby carriage of your experience and looking without judgment at the babies there. Some of them are lovely and some of them are less than lovely. It's the practice of seeing all of them with a full, open, nonjudgmental mind.

In the practice of mindfulness meditation, which I'll define as *a state of preintellectual awareness* or *a state of nonjudgmental perception*, we become increasingly sensitive and alive. What begins with innocent observation of your breath should naturally expand to envelop an array of sense experiences. Your motivation is to experience the present, all immediate happenings, much as you would an intimate, sympathetic relationship with a loved one, without judgment or rationalization. One should feel pain without judging it as bad, without needing to remove it. One should be sensitive to sights and sounds and sensations, even those normally considered annoying, without judging them. Are there horns honking in the distance? Don't wish for silence. Be with them. Observe them (without being absorbed by them). Does your back ache? Feel it.

Your ego will seek to define, to judge, possibly to eradicate or enhance. But the reality before you has no intrinsic value or connotation. It simply *is*. Meditation is not the discovery of peace through the removal of undesirable distractions, sensations, and discomforts. It is not the transcendence of pain by denying reality. It is an intimate relationship with your immediate, present experience in all its depth and wonder. It may at times mean you face physical pain and discomfort, unpleasant sights and sounds. Can you witness them, be with them as you would an innocent child or an ugly baby? For in those continuous moments of true, undivided life, before the mind judges and operates, there is fullness and beauty that cannot be encapsulated in words.

With practice, your sensory perceptions will become more pronounced and consciousness will expand to encompass multiple inputs at one time. You can feel the sensation of air slowly moving into your lungs, the pressure of the seat beneath you, the sunshine on your back, the leaves blowing in the wind. Rather than have each one of these sensations compete for your fullest attention to the exclusion of the others, in mindfulness meditation, they all might exist in simultaneity. That is, of course, if your mind is not spontaneously pulled to one focal point or another, to internal thoughts or external sensations. Sitting quietly and innocently observing the present is tremendously challenging work.

Should your mind wander from present sensations, sit patiently with whatever thought materializes. Observe it the same way you do your breath, the same way you would an ugly baby. Sit with it. Poke it a little. Discover it innocently with an open heart. Do not forcibly draw your focus back to something you deem of higher worth (your breath, for example). This is akin to looking away from an ugly baby because the sight offends you. This may lead to observations and discoveries of self that are brutally honest, saddening, or shameful. Within these honesties, however, there lies genuine awareness and insight. With time and dedicated practice, an innocent mind full of peace, passion, and beauty will surface.

The greatest challenge is to experience the mind's caprice, the spontaneous jumping from topic to topic, from observation to observation, without judging or condemning your thoughts (or the thoughts about the thoughts). Your thoughts, judgments, connotations, and intellectual operations on immediate experiences, for all intents and purposes, are ugly babies. Your thoughts about those thoughts are also ugly babies. When you chastise yourself for a lack of focus and awareness while meditating and try to forcefully cut off your tangential musings, this is an ugly baby too. When you rebuke yourself for criticizing yourself (because there is nothing inherently wrong with a lack of focus), this too is an ugly baby.

Over a lifetime of experience and education, we construct complex paradigms of the world and give everything a value. There is nothing inherently ugly or beautiful about a baby, just as there is nothing inherently delicious about chocolate cake or frightening about a clown. Our identities, constructed over a lifetime of experience, habit, and valuation, however, suggest otherwise. Seeing all things as good or bad, beautiful or ugly, practical or useless, is seeing the world as a reflection of yourself.

This does not mean we condemn all thoughts that appear judgmental (or that your own reflection may not be damn good-looking). Judgmental thoughts are still immediate experiences, in the same way that looking at an ugly baby is an immediate experience. With time, judgments dwindle, the mind becomes still, and the baby doesn't seem so bad.

In the beginning, however, it is important that we don't throw the baby out and we don't judge our immediate experience and our spontaneous thoughts. A thought may even be judgmental. Your attention may have left your breath, may have left all awareness of your body, and may have drifted to work or to a relationship. These thoughts, as spontaneous happenings, are your current reality. If you condemn them and force your mind to come back to your breath, or come back to sitting quietly, you've thrown the baby in the dumpster. You've learned nothing about yourself.

If, however, you are fully aware of the tangent your mind has taken, and observe your mind as it is in the present moment, something profound happens. Those thoughts begin to lose their standard meaning and emotional impact. They become one more aspect of your immediate experience and full of life. Years of conditioning, your web of egotism unveils itself. The real you is revealed. You're free to see the present through the eyes of an innocent being, free from bias and egotistical preferences. The mind naturally becomes alive, still, and passionate again in the wake of letting go.

The baby has been revived. Oddly enough, without self-deceit or condemnation of the object of your attention, without the desire to see it as other than what it is – it *is*, in fact, beautiful.

Chapter 3

YOUR QI BALLS ARE IMPOTENT

(Why Fighters Should Not Be Lovers)

After a week of hard full-time training at our live-in kung fu academy, many of the guys would spend the weekend at the Pink Palace, a brothel in Siping. It was the nearest city, forty-five minutes away by bus. For some of the guys with a little cash, it was a necessary release of pent-up manliness. They went through the whole deal, choosing a China doll (or possibly more than one) from a line-up, feeling like conquerors and kings. Some of the younger guys, with less disposable cash, would settle for a hand job in a public room with the local guys. They sat in comfortable chairs facing a television. I don't recall what they said was on, but it was probably something like *Chinese Idol.*

I was one of the few who maintained my celibacy for my entire three-month stint at the academy, including abstinence from solo nocturnal adventures. This practice was highly encouraged for those practicing qigong, an ancient form of Chinese breathing, self-healing, and internal energy development. Master Su strictly forbade weekend retreats at the Pink Palace, and eerily knew when one of his students dropped a nut. If a student had been very dedicated to his qigong study for many months, it was clear as day the moment he'd fallen off the wagon. His complexion changed, generally growing a bit pale, and he was physically weaker. If someone with lesser investment failed, he still knew. Master Su's typical response was to calmly tell the student how much of his training had just been thrown away, and that he would need to start over.

All instructors, as well as new students at the academy, had to do a demonstration of skill. Master Su, lifelong Shaolin protector monk, demonstrated a feat rare even among qigong masters. He sliced a brick in half without supporting either end. He set the brick on the edge of a table. This would typically be supported by the other hand, the pressure of which would provide a modicum of leverage with which to chop it in half. He didn't need it. He focused for a few seconds and sliced through it like a knife through butter. The half of the brick on the table didn't move. To this day, in all of my thirty years of training, he is one of only a handful of master instructors to both inspire me and scare the living shit out of me.

His eyes were fierce and focused. His posture was perfectly erect at all times. His movements, regardless of which form or weapon, were lightning. His will was indomitable. I was extremely fortunate to establish a quick bond with him, as it led to private chain whip and qigong training in the forest away from the academy. That training almost cost me an eye. His talents commanded respect, and when a master of his caliber gives you rules (like not to touch yourself), disregarding them is just foolish. Dude had *skills*, and if being stingy with his essence contributed to them, it was worth a try.

Over the course of a couple of months, we practiced qigong two to three times a day, for an hour at a time. We usually began at 6am, before breakfast, and would do another session at 4pm, before dinner. Qigong is by far the most challenging component of holistic training, and trumps even the most grueling physical training sessions. Every session began with a light jog or a set of squats to improve blood flow, followed by a few minutes of standing relaxation, with the hands resting on the thighs. We were to take a mental survey of tension throughout the body and consciously relax and release it. The hands were then drawn up to the lower abdomen, hand over hand, connecting body and mind to the seat of energy (*dan tian*) located a few inches below the navel.

Weightless Tangent

Energy work (qigong), as opposed to mindfulness practice, has considerable distinctions. In energy work, attention and awareness do not expand to become all-inclusive (though this may be a natural outcropping of improved concentration). Instead, they are drawn to a tight focal point – to the exclusion, at least initially, of external stimuli. The tongue is pressed against the roof of the mouth just behind the pallet, connecting our primary energy channels, the *governing* and *conception vessels*. When connected, these energy channels run down the center of the front of the body, between the legs, up the spine, over the crown point of the head, and back down again. This loop, known in classical qigong literature as the *small universe*, is said to restore and maintain complete health and immunity when it's alive with qi.

We're discussing qigong within the context of martial arts training, but I should make clear that qigong was adopted and perfected within the martial arts traditions due to the tremendous benefits it provides in regards to health and healing, mental acuity, concentration, physical strength, and holistic performance. But qigong is not exclusively a martial arts practice. Visit any park in China around sunrise and you'll find elderly men and women scattered throughout it with closed eyes and outstretched arms, breathing deeply into their lower abdomens. Qigong is considered by some to be the fountain of youth, and has been used to cure chronic illnesses for millennia. It also rapidly improves digestion, energy, and memory, while simultaneously releasing tension and stress.

Qigong Starter Kit

- Sit or stand with an erect spine. Your head should be drawn up by the crown point as if suspended by a string. This should allow the shoulders to relax and sink naturally. If you are standing, keep all joints slightly bent and your tailbone slightly tucked (which removes a rigid military posture and improves energy flow). If you are seated, the knees should not be higher than the hips and your back should be unsupported.

- Take a mental survey of your body and identify all points of tension. Take a minute to mentally release that tension and relax all regions.

- Press your tongue lightly against the roof of the mouth, just behind the palate.

- Hands may be resting in the lap, on the knees, or hand over hand covering the *dan tian*. All other technical positions are superfluous in the early stages.

- Your focus should be on the *dan tian*, your seat of energy, approximately an inch and a half below the navel, and an inch and a half within the body. Imagine that point to be very dense and vibrant, increasing in density and energy with every inhalation.

- Your physical frame should become increasingly hollow, supported only by your skeleton (visualize being devoid of connective tissues, organs, skin, etc.). With every inhalation energy is drawn from the universe into the *dan tian* through every pore in the body, as if being sucked into a black hole.

- The upper chest should have very little play, placing all emphasis on expanding the lower abdomen during inhalations and contracting the diaphragm to expunge air during exhalations. When you exhale, the lower abdomen does not need to fully withdraw. With time, qi storage will create pressure and make it harder to do so.

- There are no rules for how long one breath should last, but it is helpful in the beginning to work up to a slow continuous inhalation of eight counts, as well as a continuous exhalation of eight counts. This will be very challenging at first (in particular the extended and continuous exhalation), but will help balance your breath cycle and improve lung capacity. Once this skill is well developed, you might follow your intuition or implement techniques like breath holding, tensing body parts, clenching the molars, or reverse abdominal breathing to enhance energy accumulation and channeling capabilities (discussed in the Weightlessness Manifesto in Book 4, and in greater detail in the sequel to this book, *The Essence of Lightness,* where I delve into the science of qi – bioelectromagnetism – for those who would like a strong, evidence-based rationale for embracing qigong).

- Don't practice on a full stomach, or when too hungry to concentrate.

Several months of daily practice should result in genuine sensations and awareness of qi (bio-electricity) within the *dan tian*, as well as in general circulation. Do not chase sensations or mystical abilities. Seek only to improve sensitivity and concentration – to know yourself and master your current faculties. Once sufficient energy is accumulated in the *dan tian*, it should act as a wellspring of energy that overflows into the small universe (comprised of the conception and governing meridians), resulting in improved health, energy, focus, and strength.

During our practice, all joints in the body were bent slightly to ensure constant qi flow. The tailbone was drawn down and the crown point (the uppermost acupoint on the skull) of the head was drawn up, away from the shoulders, as if suspended by a string. This created a posture akin to that of a sloppy old man, and would have got a failing grade from a military posture instructor. After surveying the body and meeting all structural requirements, we drew our arms up to chest level in a wide, broken circle, as if holding a giant fitness ball. The fingers were spread and pointing at one another, some six-odd inches apart, connected only by strings of energy.

At this point, the torture began. As simple as it sounds, five to ten minutes into a Golden Bell qigong session the shoulders burn like hell and the lower back begins to ache. It makes concentration on the *dan tian* exceedingly difficult. After many hours of intensive physical training that inevitably weakened the body and fatigued the mind, the toughest challenge was to stand still, quietly, breathing deeply into the lower abdomen and maintaining a state of concentration.

Many trainees threw in the towel after losing the battle of the Pink Palace. Others were diehard and maintained strict discipline. But for serious practitioners, it wasn't too difficult to maintain motivation. We would practice standing meditation at 5:30am in the bitter cold. I recall vividly the heat emanating from Master Su several feet away. After the first week at the academy, I began to suffer from a problem in my lower back that hindered my standing meditation.

I tried to work through it for several weeks, but the pain was only getting worse. After informing Master Su, he asked me to lie down. Hands hovering inches above my back, he ran them slowly from top to bottom, surveying my energy and noting all blockages. They felt like steaming irons. The session lasted only five to ten minutes. He told me to get some rest and that I'd be fine in the morning. And I was. I had no further pain and no relapse.

It was hard not to take him seriously.

Due to experiences like that one, and many others over twenty years of meditative practice, I have no problem accepting Chinese energy theory (despite lingering inconsistencies between the developing body of knowledge around bioelectromagnetism and Chinese meridian theory). It is the foundation of all Eastern healing arts, including acupressure, herbology, massage, and energy healing. Despite experiences of the borderline mystical variety, there are empirical grounds for accepting the relationship between abstinence and strength, though this is true in men only. The opposite is said to be true for women, which is a cruel cosmic joke if you ask me.

The West is not without its aphorisms. In all Western fight sports, competitors are usually warned to not have sex by their trainers for at least a week before a fight. In part, it is seen as an unnecessary distraction, creating a potential loss of focus. The more easily verifiable reason not to have sex before a fight is that it weakens the legs. Male ejaculation costs a tremendous amount of energy. Why do you think men pass out after sex?

While Buddhist qigong practitioners tend to be celibate (at least the diehards), Taoist qigong practitioners set more reasonable guidelines for release of the sticky stuff. Men in their teens can ejaculate daily without much need for concern. Practitioners believe that once men are more than twenty years old, the frequency of ejaculation should decline every five to ten years. There are differences of opinion among teachers and classical texts as to just how much the rate should change according to age. For men in their twenties, some teachers recommend ejaculating only once a week. Men in their thirties can do so between once every three days to once in two weeks; men in their forties are restricted to anywhere between every five days to only once a month. Semen is said to contain *jing*, man's vital essence. When one ejaculates too frequently, health, strength, and energy decline.

If this sounds like voodoo, think about this: it's reasonable to assume that production of a man's life-creating fluids requires energy that could otherwise be spent maintaining general health and recovering from illness, injury, or training. All men experience a reduced sex drive when they are ill. All people also experience a reduced appetite when they have a fever. Digestion requires tremendous energy, energy that can otherwise be spent healing and detoxifying the body.

I speculate that semen production is similar in terms of energy costs, and that the decline in sex drive when a man is ill is another manifestation of the body's natural intelligence to seek homeostasis, health, and immediate survival over procreation. The degree to which one should abstain is outside the scope of this book, but I believe being aware of the relationship of ejaculation to energy is extremely important, regardless of whether you accept the Chinese principle of *jing* and a loss of vital essence, or see it simply as a biological process that requires a lot of energy.

I have dabbled in celibacy and can attest that, while it is not a practical lifelong practice for me at least, it *is* extremely conducive to energy and strength development. As a general guideline, try to reduce masturbation, which is more often than not an inferior sexual energetic state compared to intercourse with an actual human being. I believe this is sufficient to make a significant difference in your overall energy and health within the context of internal energy development.

In short, try to keep it real.

Chapter 4

A FELON TASTES THE SUBLIME

D amon was built like a brick shithouse, and had eyes cold as ice. He was the second African-American who scared the shit out of me, the first being the one-legged kid I was paired against at my first karate tournament, at age ten. I was from the suburbs of Denver and only saw white kids growing up. I knew one other black kid, Brandon, who was adopted by white parents, so he didn't count: he was good at soccer.

So when I went up against my one-legged opponent, it was as if I'd been asked to fight an alien. To top it off, he had a wooden leg. A black kid with a wooden leg fighting karate, it was all so foreign to me.

"Do I hit him like other kids?" I wondered. I had never punched a black kid before. I had never fought a kid with only one good leg before either. Was it fair? Could he kick? Which leg would he kick with, wooden or normal? Did he have special powers I should know about?

To make a short story shorter, the fight was rigged.

Nevertheless, Damon, pronounced *Dah-mon*, who I met in the summer of 2000, was bigger, scarier, and had two working legs. To my knowledge he had never studied karate.

To top it all off, he was a murderer and convicted drug dealer. He was by far the most intimidating man at Harvest Farm, the drug and alcohol rehabilitation center at which I interned at the time. Damon bypassed the convicted murder charge by waiting until he was in prison before crushing a man's skull with a dumbbell, an act of passion that earned him three years of solitary confinement. I wouldn't accuse Damon of being a particularly jovial man. In fact, he always seemed one wrong look away from crushing another skull.

Despite his callous shell, I was able to get him to open up on occasion. On some kind of a bonding expedition in Colorado Springs, the two other interns and I had a chance to demonstrate just how naïve and different we were from the hardened parolees under our charge. Fate had Damon and I walking at a similar pace to the top of Pike's Peak, a fourteen thousand footer that sorts the all-stars from the subs. It gave me a great chance to talk to him.

"I hear jailhouse rules are that you gotta kick someone's ass or become someone's bitch. I take you as the kick-someone's-ass kind of guy."

He looked at me like I wasn't. He grunted a dubious grunt, undecided as to whether he should chuckle or throw me off the cliff. I gulped and felt a tickle in my stomach. So I followed it up with the more masculine, classic line.

"So you like to work out?"

I knew Damon worked out, and I was lucky we were climbing a mountain, or he may have crushed my skull for trying to pick him up. I knew there was more to him and I wanted to crack the wall. *Of course* he worked out, it's what guys do in prison. He was clearly good at it too, sporting perfect muscular symmetry. He also had a deep understanding of the stress-adaptation process we call bodybuilding.

"You gotta lift heavy," he said. "Not too much, though. Three sets per exercise, same body part three days per week. You gotta lift hard and you gotta eat big."

It was an educational icebreaker that mysteriously segued into the story of his arrest and conviction seven years prior.

Damon was never supposed to be at the exchange. His two older brothers were dealing a lot. Damon stood in for one of them for the first and last time. It was a routine drug exchange that ended in a clean conviction. He was framed and busted, and he refused to give anybody up.

Prison made him hard. Solitary confinement made him harder. He spent three years in isolation with one copy of the Bible and one copy of the Koran. He knew both better than most Bible-thumping fundamentalists or Islamic zealots. He had read them cover to cover many times, and neither had an ounce of relevance for him. Alone with the Holy Scriptures, he had no conversation, no music sounded. He was in the hole.

"Stories," Damon would say every time I asked him about his takeaway from a morning sermon. "Just stories. I read both cover to cover many times."

"How do you *feel* about them?" I asked.

"I feel nothing," he said dryly. "Like reading the newspaper."

"Is there part of you that you would consider spiritual, that hungers for something more than our physical world?"

"There is something more," he said. "But it's not in those books. The day I was released from prison I went to visit a friend in the hospital. While there, I wandered up to the maternity ward and heard a newborn baby crying. It was the most beautiful sound I'd ever heard in my life. I sat down and just listened for as long as they allowed. The strength and purity of her cry brought me to tears. It was the most spiritual experience I ever had."

Damon, hardened from years of being in a level-five-security prison, withdrawn after years in isolation, was dumbstruck by the sound of something that most of us find disconcerting, if not annoying. His senses, deprived of countless colors, smells, sounds, and sensations, were at once overwhelmed. His experience of a weeping baby left him frozen in time, tasting sublimity.

The sensitive mind, liberated from the confines of preconditioned thought, is free to experience the majesty of the mundane as if for the first time. I saw that it was possible to experience life anew, like your first kiss, your first lava cake, the first time a sunset took your breath away.

There was beauty right before me, but was I looking?

It was a puzzling juxtaposition for me, this hardened character who found sublimity in the wail of an innocent newborn. Naturally I felt no recourse but to ask the only question I could think of.

"Do you happen to know anyone with a wooden leg?"

Chapter 5

HOW TO MEDITATE

You.

Yes, you!

At the end of this brief chapter you're going to set this book down for exactly one minute. You're going to breathe your fullest breath in years. You're going to experience the vivid beauty of the world directly in front of you, the world you've been overlooking.

You'll sit quietly.

You'll listen carefully.

You'll feel… everything.

Tension will fall from your shoulders.

You'll see what's in front of you. You'll notice all details. You'll forget all names and descriptions.

For one minute, you'll sit quietly and judge nothing. This is the last minute of your life. The only minute that matters. Don't fill it with nonsense. Be with it, *intimately*.

Observe your breath.

Listen.

Feel.

Empty yourself. Open your heart. Let in the beauty of the moment, your moment, your last moment.

Let it in.

Be.

Chapter 6

A TRIP TO ENLIGHTENMENT

"Dude," a voice said. "Dude. Hey, dude. Dude…" I looked up from the verdure come to life beneath me. "I don't mean to alarm you, but I'm pretty sure there's a tin man over there."

"I'm not a doctor, Kevin," I replied, refusing to turn my head and acknowledge whatever nonsense he was imagining. "But I'm pretty sure there is no tin man over there."

Kevin returned to his cocoon of silence, burrowing in the grass like a gopher, falling back into his mushroom-induced, personal heaven. And I went back to mine.

It was my first experience on mushrooms, and my most vivid experience of the interconnected whole. And where better for it to happen than the queen's summer palace in Aarhus, Denmark. It was a vast expanse of rolling green sporadic gardens with rainbow explosions. It had old monuments and hot topless women set against an infinite baby-blue sea that blended with an even purer baby-blue sky. It's a veritable wonderland that I would not have believed existed had I not experienced it first-hand. Had I not experienced it high as a kite on nature's most glorious hallucinogen, I would not have known that the world I knew was only a shadow of the world that is.

"It's good to eat something," Kevin said. He was hovering over a pepperoni pizza like a chemist, delicately sprinkling dried bits of mushroom. He was always careful when preparing drugs. I can't recall if his t-shirt had blood on it; that would not have been out of the ordinary. Sometimes the blood was from acute nosebleeds, sometimes not. He usually wore the same shirt, his personal favorite, inherited when he noticed a stack of neatly folded clothes on the bed next to his grandfather during a hospital visit.

"What's up with those?" Kevin inquired.

"That guy died yesterday," replied his grandfather dryly.

"So he doesn't need them anymore?"

"Jesus, Kevin. No, I suppose he doesn't. Just ask the nurse first. And wash them."

Kevin has a utilitarian edge that can cause a bit of discomfort for the uninitiated. One of the more notable examples was the time he wore trash bags for shoes during one of Colorado's heaviest snowstorms. His shoes were worn through, but not so worn that they didn't actually stay on, look like shoes, or prevent penetration from rusty nails and whatnot. But they were no protection against the cold, wet snow. My father, with his sardonic New York accent, complimented him.

"Nice shoes, Kevin. I preferred the duct tape ones though."

One time, Kevin accidentally fasted during the month of Ramadan. Kevin liked to refer to intermittent fasting as *snaking himself*. He'd methodically binge and store up in anticipation of an inevitable food shortage brought on by an empty wallet or a state of mind too cloudy to go food shopping. I believe *that* fast was accompanied by a personal record of seventy days without a shower. He wore it as a badge of honor well before hotels started encouraging people to reuse towels and save the planet. Kevin was amazed at how well the same pair of sweatpants held up, but even more amazed by the homeless guy who let himself in to Kevin's house at 2am every night to smoke his weed and watch *Three's Company* reruns with him.

Kevin is a muse, a free spirit who in no way conforms to or observes social norms. With a near-photographic memory, honed I believe by watching *Star Wars* a thousand times, he absorbs information like a sponge. He can easily humble Republicans, conservatives, and square academics with the database of relevant, factual information stored in the intoxicated-hamster-always-on-the-verge-of-falling-off-his-wheel stationed just behind the forehead, and between both ears. Despite Kevin's extreme eccentricities, he has a heart of gold, cares deeply about equality and justice, and has a habit of providing artistic inspiration for anyone strong enough to face his hurricane of creative destruction. Two of those he has mostly notably inspired are Luke and Jesse Miller, the two other members of our youthful wayward crew who are now touring the world as the band Lotus.

"It's good to eat something," Kevin said. "Because some people puke when they eat these." Why is that. I wondered? People puke from eating toxins, from drinking poisons. These are mushrooms. Why in god's name would I puke from them?

"So the peperoni somehow counteracts this side effect?" I inquired.

"No, it just tastes good," he said. "Usually we'd smoke a joint, which keeps you from puking. But we're out of weed, and I'm hungry. Here," he said, handing me a slice of pie with a couple of dried fungi atop it. "Eat this."

I took my trip down the rabbit hole. It wasn't instantaneous, of course. I simply enjoyed some pizza like any other American. Kevin was surprised I didn't vomit. Again, I was confused. Why would people eat things that they know make them sick every time? They're either morons or I'm on my way to a world so much more rewarding than the pains of purging.

And I was.

We enjoyed a nice barefoot walk through the city to the beach, along the ocean side walkway that led to the queen's summer palace. Like any first-time drug user, you wait and wonder. You wonder if it will work for you. You wonder what's going to happen. You wonder if it's already working and nobody told you.

"It takes thirty minutes or so to kick in," Kevin reassured me. "You'll know when that is. Let's toss some disk." Hippies like to play Frisbee because it's non-competitive, casual, and you generally can't get hurt. It's also trippy as hell to watch a disk glide through the air and stall, hovering above you like a spaceship, before it falls softly into your hyper-sensitive, outstretched hands. It's a great excuse to get outdoors, enjoy nature, and get a little hippie exercise. Set against the backdrop of rolling green hills, pockets of Technicolor flowerbeds, and an ocean so clear you can't turn away, tossing the disk was icing on the cake.

I did know when it was.

On one particular toss, Kevin released the disk like a rocket, buzzing it through the air with no real lift but with sharp, accurate power. I impulsively leapt for it and there, in mid-leap, the drug hit me. Time slowed down; the Frisbee stalled. I was weightless, floating horizontally above the Earth, my senses heightened and screaming. In the moments before life-and-death tragedy, time slows, senses are augmented, and memory recalls even the smallest of details, no matter how inconsequential. Our minds have the ability to be fully aware and observant, intuiting and processing information at the speed of light. It's an ability that is almost entirely unrealized, save for rare, life-threatening situations and (apparently) when on mushrooms diving for Frisbees.

As I leapt, I saw the disk rotate slowly. I felt the wind tickle hair on my arms. I could see blades of grass dancing several feet beneath me. All of a sudden, I crushed that disk in a blaze of inebriated horizontality, landing in a fluid dive roll that would make a ninja applaud.

I knew when *it* was.

Kevin howled and applauded, as hippies tend to do when one of them does something cool. My world exploded. I looked through a kaleidoscope of lucidity. Colors were unfathomably vibrant and alive. Waves of energy pulsating in varying degrees, bending the air like steam above a stovetop. It was a gift from the gods. My heart opened and I felt a gratitude that trumped opening the best gift on the best Christmas morning. I felt genuine love without an object.

I looked around, turning gradually, taking it all in, feeling like an inextricable part of a whole that I never knew I belonged to. Kevin rotated into view and the ground beneath him began to pulse, sending a wave of green at me like a tsunami that picked me up off my feet and landed me on my back. I couldn't move. I didn't want to move.

Kevin sat next to me. "How you doing dude?" he asked.

"I felt... did you feel that?" I said. "The earth moved. I fell and the colors and my mouth feels funny and I need... where are we?"

"Queen's house, dude," he said, chuckling. "You're high."

I fell to my side, sinking into the prickly bed of grass as if into a soft pillow. It felt so comfortable, so right, like falling into a mother's arms after hours of jovial play. She held me so tight. The rays of sun warmed my skin. The blades of grass, each so distinct, vibrant, and alive, lived together in symbiosis to create a canvas we all take for granted. There was no longer a *me*, and no longer grass. Language failed, my mind expanded to simply experience the world. I was each and every blade of grass, the warmth of the sun, the love of Mother Earth. My view, half-blinded by grass, was a living, pulsating wave of earth flowing toward me.

In a moment my perspective righted itself.

I was standing. I was not standing. I was standing. I was hugging the earth. No, I was standing upright, pressed flat against a vertical wall of green. No part of me could detect my proper angle. My fingers sunk through prickly blades, prickly blades, soft caressing kisses warm mother earth and sunlight blink blink sunlight in eye blink blink happy blinking funny and my toes are feeling things still blades must be blades of grass alive and laughing and playing with me and god am I lying or standing breathing dead or alive am I me am I me am I meeeeeeeeeeeeeeeeeeee and there is only color caressing warmth there is only now here now no me no *Tom* no past or future just warmth and beauty beads of happy sunrays.

The veil of *self* had been lifted. I was free to be. The gap between subject and object, observer and observed, was gone, disintegrated. My ego melted away, burned by acid, dripped into the pool of Jung's collective unconscious. The symbiotic relationship between all living things, *all* things, was claiming me, insisting I return home. I was Ken Kesey-style connected, sipping from the carafe of electric Kool-Aid. Nirvana was *samsara*. All those assholes on the fringe, the ones strong enough to ask what's left when you cease to be you, were taking me by the hands, lifting me, showing me a world of beauty that existed the whole time but which I refused to see because, like all of us, I always called a blade of grass a blade of grass and had never been taught differently.

"Dude," a voice said. "Dude. Hey dude. Dude…" I looked up from the verdure come to life beneath me. "I don't mean to alarm you, but I'm pretty sure there's a tin man over there."

I ignored Kevin for a few minutes. He was surely up to no good. But he insisted. I knew that when Kevin insisted, regardless of how puerile or absurd the reason, life would be irritating if I didn't acquiesce. I rolled from my heavenly bed of loving fingers and slowly sat up. Kevin was staring with mouth agape, arm extended, and index finger pointing. My vision trailed from his sloppy blond hair to his glowing grey-blue eyes, down the trail of intention, along his shoulder line, and down his forearm toward his extended index finger.

"That's just your finger," I corrected.

"Not my finger, you idiot," he said. "Look at what my finger is pointing to. It's a fucking tin man."

I followed the line further, picking up every crease and wrinkle of his digit, past his glossy nail, slowly, along the plains of topless women, past the tin man, down to the monument before the vast blue. *Wait a second, what the fuck was that?* My eyes sprang back to Kevin's discovery. There was in fact a tin man moving around in the distance. He was carrying a sword, surrounded by villains, heroes, or maybe just ordinary people sitting around watching him.

"Should we intervene?" I asked with a deep concern.

"What does that mean? You fucking see that thing?"

"I see it."

"I'm not completely nuts?"

"Just because I see what you see does not mean you are not completely nuts. Should we do something? Something is terribly wrong over there. You were right about the tin man."

A conquering smile came to Kevin's face. He nodded slowly. He was clearly delighting in the accuracy of his observation, but all sense of action or consequence had gone. He was in a vacuum. A war could have been going on around him and he would have felt right as rain that he did in fact see a tin man. He went back to burrowing, an animalistic burrowing in the grass. What the hell was he looking for?

I too was in a vacuum. What did I mean *intervene*? What the hell was happening? He was smiling. That made me smile. We were both smiling and happy. I looked back again and saw another tin man. Two tin men. Jesus fucking Christ. This was abnormal. I stilled my gaze and looked more closely. Knights. They were knights in armor. Games. They were playing games, practicing swordsmanship and reenacting ancient warfare plots.

What were the odds that this would be happening on my twenty-second birthday at the queen's summer palace while we were both high as kites? Nevertheless, it was. In this fairytale land of beauty and madness, there were both topless Danish maidens and knights in shining armor. The only things lacking were court jesters and dwarves, and I would have settled for the latter.

Alas, all good trips come to an end. Kevin and I paced back to his house, getting lost in the quiet blue to our right, in the dense forest to our left, and in the beauty of an interconnected, hope-filled future ahead of us. Then I stepped on a giant bee. My foot swelled like a balloon and I limped the whole way back.

That sobered me up real quick.

Chapter 7

THE SNOOKER HOOKERS OF CHIANG MAI

After my adventures in the jungle of Koh Phangan, where Weightlessness first manifested, reality reared its ugly head with the realization that freedom is best adorned by cash, of which I was quickly running out. I transitioned to Chiang Mai and formed a plan that would kill two birds with one stone, one that would both further my training and put some cash back in my pocket. Despite preparing to move on, it was those remaining days in Chiang Mai that would teach me just how little I understood about sex, love, and openness.

"I'm going to be celibate again," I said. "So I'm not sure where that leaves us." As I said this to my future ex, I realized that I had discovered the single best break-up method in the history of the universe. The worst thing a man can do is leave a woman for another woman. The second worst is to leave her for no reason. It seemed I had just discovered a loophole. A truly neutral parting.

"Full-blown celibate?" she asked with incredulity. "What do you mean?"

"No ejac', no prejac', no getting it in," I explained.

"What in god's name for?"

"Qigong. Master Su is a bit of a stickler. So it doesn't make sense for you to go with me. It would be torture for both of us."

"Can I go with you and study qigong as well?"

"Well, the thing is, he's a hardcore monk. I don't think he can touch women."

"He's going to be touching you?" she asked.

"No, you're twisting things," I said. "You know what I mean. He's got rules."

"This is so extreme."

"Yeah, but where has the middle path ever gotten anyone? You go blue ball or porn star and you may learn something about yourself. You maintain the status quo and what do you have?"

"You can't have sex at all? Not even once in a while?"

"Nah. Believe me, I'd like to, but it has to do with my qi, you see."

The plan was immaculate. Move to Jiangxi, teach English at the University of Science and Technology in Ganzhou, and sculpt young Chinese minds, endowing them with the knowledge of keeping it real. Then I would relocate the infamous Master Su, my mentor, qigong master, and soft weapons instructor of the Shaolin torture center.

Regrettably, the plan was half-baked. Or perhaps I was half-baked when I scribbled the details on a notepad full of diagrams, sketches of warrior monks, puerile calculations, and arrows pointing nowhere and decided pursuing enlightenment was a good idea. After a few months of teaching, I'd realized I had made a tragic miscalculation about my disposable funds. A salary of $500 a month wasn't enough to live on and pay a monk to relocate and teach me full-time.

I also realized celibacy wasn't for me.

Instead of taking the path of the straight and narrow, I informed Master Su that money was too tight and our reunion needed to be postponed. As an alternative, I worked my magic and got Kevin (yes, tin man Kevin) and his girlfriend Anne jobs teaching along with me at the university. This turned out to be a bit like releasing a toddler on a buffet of candies and sweets, and lining up a bunch of smaller toddlers around the room with cool toys for him to commandeer and annihilate. The destruction that Kevin caused in the first few months as a 'foreign expert' was truly awesome.

Kevin is a natural educator, full of insight and inspiration. You merely need to look past the madness, which can require very good vision at times, such as when he tried to start a fight between the dean of the university (a respected qigong man himself) and me after drinking himself blind on baijiu, the hardest alcohol in China. It didn't make sense to Kevin that there were two martial artists in the same room and we didn't conclusively know who was better.

Kevin then mistook the servers for prostitutes and smashed several glasses with overzealous cheersing. His Welcome to the University dinner wrapped up with me pinning the dean in a wrist lock on the ground after all attempts to avoid puerile what-would-you-do-if-someone-did-this chops and punches within a circle of curious faculty members, causing gasps and cries from his disillusioned fans. It created an indelible divide between the rest of the faculty and me for approximately… forever. Kevin tackled whoever came near him, screaming "Ireland fighting!"

As only Kevin could manage, this open show of spirit won him many new fans and friends, among them the pinned dean.

There was also the time he vomited out of a third-story window twice in one day, during two different lectures, while horrified students stared in disbelief. Following a tragic night of violent sickness, Kevin refused to cancel classes that day because he was scheduled (self-scheduled, that is) to teach the film *Groundhog Day*. The lecture would go on, come hell or high water!

There was also the time he set a Christmas tree on fire and threw it out his window into the quiet confines of the women's dormitories.

But I digress. My aim is to tell a different tale, a tale of friendly snooker hookers and the merciless beating I gave them in the seedy bars of Chiang Mai. It all took place during that remaining week post-breakup, before moving back to China for the hurricane of glory and madness that would ensue.

Several streets in Chiang Mai are lined with a certain kind of bar. In these bars reside an ubiquitous species of Thai, infamous bar girls with curvy bodies and high-pitched sensual voices that remind you of the high school crush you were too timid to talk to. I've never been one to pay for sex and to this day have managed to avoid an overt transaction (though I admit the lines are a tad blurry in Asia in general, as relationships between foreign men and local women are often financially driven).

I don't mean to condemn the institution of prostitution, which I have no real qualms with, in so far as it's undertaken willingly. However, I have seen brothers selling their young teen sisters to dirty old men for a weekend of hell that is undeniably scarring. This practice should be eradicated with fire and brimstone. For me, the prostitutes of Chiang Mai were just good old-fashioned fun. They were friendly, lively, and always up for a game of pool. They were up for more. *A lot* more than pool in fact. This led to problems one night after I schooled the entire harem and they interpreted it as foreplay. It wasn't.

There was one bargirl, plump and heavily made-up, who gave me a real run for my money. She was called from the back like a fighter being called in to defend a title after I'd knocked down a couple of her cohorts. She lumbered up the wooden stairs and chalked the cue, eyeing me with a sultry and confident smile, well-honed by picking up grizzly old white men who didn't need picking up.

We sank ball for ball. Girl had game. But I pride myself on my pool skills against bargirls and to this day not a one has gotten the better of me. Beating her ended my fun on that particular strip, as I quickly established a reputation for beating hookers, without happy endings.

Gods be praised, there were other strips, and I had a few days left to kill. Adjacent to the night market was a small street with more bars. Some bars in Chiang Mai were obvious, with bar girls wearing uniforms that screamed, "Buy one get me free." But some bars were more subtle. I thought they were proper bars that focused on getting people wasted. I was naive.

Ten minutes into my beer, a tall, gorgeous Thai woman sat down next to me. She was wearing tight black spandex, black high heels, and a tight t-shirt that left little to the imagination. But she wasn't trashy. She carried herself well; she had perfect posture, clean, subtle makeup, soft shoulders, and a feminine neckline. Her outfit, while tight, could work in any nightclub without screaming *pro*.

Not sure at first whether she was a working girl, I welcomed the opportunity to practice my Thai. Our conversation lasted a good forty-five minutes and comprised titillating topics like favorite colors, hobbies, food, and other banalities that are the focus of a beginner Thai language class. Every few minutes, I found her inching closer, gently running her fingers over my thigh or holding my arm. The British bar owner eyed me suspiciously, with a strong 'buy her or get out' vibe. It was a message I didn't receive quickly enough.

With every drink, I found it harder to cut it off. She was intoxicating, sweet, sensual. She told me about her son, a good boy, three years old, who she was working to provide for. Her mother and father too had little money. She lacked the education that would provide her with another form of decent income. Her eyes were black, deep, and innocent. She was not a lost soul grabbing for easy money. She was making the hard call. She asked if I wanted to take her home. I couldn't lie, I did.

She asked how much I wanted to pay. The conversation so naturally moved to financial transaction. I said I had no money, which she knew was a lie. She wasn't cheap, and I certainly didn't have enough on me to take her home that night. Funds would continue to be tight until I landed in the madness of Ganzhou. My mind stalled with confusion, a stand off between two stubborn heads. I'd reached the limits of my ability to dissect, filter, and interpret my present experience. This was a moral quandary the likes of which I hadn't faced since my ethics classes at the university.

Do I sleep with her and rescue her family, indubitably validating and perpetuating her decision to sacrifice her body for the greater good? Or do I leave her, both of us, wanting, and deny her family a week's worth of food? It was a quandary that I could not answer with my rational mind amid the petting, the slight intoxication, and the party in my pants that was sending invitations.

It is in such moments of mental constipation that intuition sometimes finds a work-around stemming from a clear and unconditioned view of the immediate present.

When the Zen disciple is asked to identify the sound of one hand clapping, or what happens when a tree falls in the forest and no one is there to hear it, the master is assaulting the rational mind with the intention of destroying the disciple's ego. What is left is an empty self, free of judgment, habitual responses, and rationalizations. What is left is an empty vessel capable of being filled with the truth and beauty that resides before him.

This state of mental stuckness, this disconnect with one's immediate experience, isn't unique to navigating the tempting propositions of prostitutes. It surfaces constantly, daily, for all of us in countless ways. Shall we go for pizza or burgers? Should I quit my job or stick it out for a while in high hopes of greater compensation? Should I work things out with my partner or look for an upgrade? Should I go for higher education or travel the world? Our unconscious proclivity to make sense of the world, and our experiences therein, all too often confine our creativity in decision-making to obvious binary options.

This proclivity makes sense when it comes to rapid, high-stakes decision-making like that of early man fleeing a tiger or contemplating the probability of getting poisoned by a mushroom. Our neurology is built for streamlined decision-making. The more we think or do a thing, the more likely we are to do it again, and with greater ease. But the stuff of insight and personal growth lies outside of well-paved, concrete neural pathways, outside of habitual acts and repetitive thoughts. When we allow ourselves to step back for a moment, rather than act on autopilot, and observe the options before us without emotional attachment or desired outcome, clarity of a qualitatively different order arises.

My own moral *koan* severed the line between my rational, moral self and the monster in my loins jonesing for a wild ride. So I stopped thinking. I stopped weighing the situation on my scale of egocentric judgments.

I corrected my posture. I breathed into my abdomen. I relaxed. I sensed.

I saw her, her soft shoulders, her lovely black eyes staring back at me. I saw her as she was at that moment – a mother, a daughter, a lover – not as the object I wanted her to be. A wellspring of empathy arose, and in that meditative moment there was only love.

She worked hard to further the discussion, inching closer, gently caressing, dropping her rates. Twenty-five percent lower. Fifty percent. Seventy-five percent. I no longer had an excuse on financial grounds. Back in the US I might spend more than that discounted sum on a first date, quite likely with the hope of closing the deal. This was a relatively clean exchange. No pretense, no games, clear mutual benefit. My mind, after running a million miles a minute mere moments before when weighing my options, had crashed into the brick wall of emptiness. There was no dilemma.

When the bartender told me to take it or leave it, with a look that would rival Medusa, I took her hand and left her the money I had on me. And I left alone. A third option. A night of ecstasy with her might have been a memory of a lifetime, or it might have left me empty and lost the following morning. Both were possible. Neither was guaranteed. But most importantly, I was not bound by either one.

I was free in that present moment – free of my compulsion for lust and free of the fear of regret. On another day, things may have gone another way. And if accompanied by an equally encompassing awareness, they could have been just as insightful. But in that moment I wanted for nothing. My mind was full.

What I took away was the memory of that vivid moment, the beauty of a woman with an open heart set against the neon lights, classic rock, muggy warm Thai air, and the vacuum of eternal beauty, which exists in all moments of clarity.

Chapter 8

THE DICE CLUB

A Sledgehammer Approach to Mindfulness

One night, Michael, hero of the section *From Businessman to Beast*, threw a curve ball at our typical post-martial arts training beer and burger session, during which we normally discussed everything from philosophy to business development. He wanted us to introduce dicing for a more aggressive approach to living and for the expression of minority selves.

After delving into the principles and efficacy of mindfulness, as we are sometimes guilty of after a beer or two, he told me that a decade earlier he'd spent two years living his life at the roll of a die after reading the disturbingly profound *Diceman* by Luke Rhinehart. The book details the autobiographical exploits of a man who makes every decision possible based on the roll of a die.

After his conversion to the religion of the die, Michael was your run-of-the-mill businessman by day, and hipster chaos pilot by night. He found himself dicing on grandiose as well as menial life choices. The rolls made him fast for days, direct work projects, scheme his way through the underbelly of Amsterdam, have conversations with jazz pianists on the meaning of life, and slam drinks with Russian models. A Tuesday evening might involve spring-cleaning or it might involve cigars and whiskey. Nothing was predetermined. His fate was dictated by the whim of the die.

> *Weightless Tangent*

Perhaps the biggest inhibitor of effective meditation is the inability of many to view the present independently of the biased perspectives of the ego. More often than not, even the decision to sit and meditate, to practice a state of egoless, selfless perception, is ego-driven. It is a paradox that requires depth of insight or diligent practice to bypass. In the beginning, almost everyone falls into this trap.

One of the most effective ways to bypass this self-sabotage is to embrace randomness and roll the die. At any moment, there are a multitude of possible actions, but our minds consciously or unconsciously reduce our options to a few rational choices, as most possibilities seem to have little benefit or relevance. At our beer and burger dice evenings, I could at any point attempt a headstand on the table, smash my beer glass, ask the attractive girl at the bar for her phone number; there's an infinite number of possibilities. But a lifetime of conditioning removes these real options from my plausible action list.

So why should you care?

Because we don't know what's really good for us!

Because we perceive many options as irrelevant, our minds ignore real options in favor of engaging in common conversation, listening to music, compulsively checking our phones. Every option ignored, every impulse denied, is the suppression of another side of you, a minority self. These alternative possibilities often harbor the greatest chance for a profound experience of the present, not to mention upward mobility in life (through real option creation).

These alternative possibilities are poignant vehicles for uniting with the present with a full and open mind, much in the same way that getting lost in a foreign country results in fresh experiences and vivid, unforgettable memories. These possibilities are also infinite. Your habitual self is limited to those thoughts and actions most consistent with your identity, with who you think you are. If you shatter that reflexive mirror of self you realize the freedom and power of not being you, if even for a short time. This allows you for brief stints to be the well-connected millionaire, the prolific writer, the disciplined athlete, the dedicated parent, the selfless partner.

By embracing randomness, you stop living by an ego-driven formula.

The similarities between mindfulness meditation and dice rolling as practices of nonjudgmental awareness and unconditioned experiences of the present are undeniable. Yet they are extremely different activities. I've never seen a monk roll a die. I've never seen a gambler breathe deeply and watch indifferently as snake eyes materialize. But mindfulness practice and committing to randomness both give rise to curiosity, passion, and innocence.

The connection was so strong that dice rolling became a mind-liberating tool on par with our weekly meditation sessions. We did beer and dice on Friday at a local microbrew pub and serene and conscientious introspection on Sunday morning at Enso Temple. They became inextricably linked as our mild curiosities grew into a lifestyle practice. We became dicemen.

We began showing up to beer and burger nights with lists of wants, dreams, and curiosities. All of them were things we'd like to do or think would make us better people, but for reasons of self-conscious inhibition, busyness, or laziness simply hadn't made a priority. Occasionally we included spontaneous musings or gave expression to our minority selves. Those selves might not be concerned with the greater good, but were tickled by the possibility of picking a fight, skipping out on a bill, eating ten eggs a day, or punishing tiresome habits with absurdly irrelevant penalties. All options were usually given weight on the die, although some options were given unequal weight if the compulsion to try them was exceedingly strong.

And then the die was rolled. The number that appeared would dictate our assignment for the week to come. Because we made a game of the things of life, we could approach large tasks without the fear of failure or success. After all, it was just a game. We each broke down barriers and mental blocks, and accomplished tasks we'd thought would take months or years to complete in just one week.

This process was aided by our strict penalty system of five hundred push-ups or a kamikaze tequila on all failed missions. For those of you fortunate enough not to know, a kamikaze tequila requires you to snort the salt, drink the shot, and then squirt the lemon in your eye. It's fucking insane and has spurred me to success on several difficult challenges, for fear of going blind or getting brain damage. Michael, on the other hand, likes that shit from time to time and treats it as a cure-all vaccine that makes the rest of life seem pretty pleasant.

"Remember," started Michael one Friday evening. His eyes were ablaze and his abdomen was slushing with microbrew. "Remember when you were young, how time seemed to stand still? You'd wake up in the morning and the day was a gift of opportunities. Limitless. So much fun to be had. The idea of a week – what couldn't be done in a week, which was made up of seven of these long days of limitless potential? To think of what you could do in a month, or a season, that much time, it was unfathomable."

"Absolutely," I said.

"We've forgotten the value of time. We ignore the freedom of opportunity and instead fill time with heavy breathing and frustration. But remember when you were young. Time and the choice of options it gave you was awesome. So here, tonight, I humbly submit a new category of dice rolling: the category *Awesome*. We must give *awesome* a chance so that we can complete a challenge that for all intents and purposes seems totally impossible within a week's time. We embrace that bright-eyed hopefulness of our youth, and make a game of life again. If we fail, we fail at a game undertaken with passion and lighthearted optimism. In all likelihood, however, we'll make tremendous headway in a short time toward goals we perceived as vastly out of reach. If we succeed, well, *awesome!*"

Thus began the category *Awesome*, and a series of chance-given accomplishments that both of us, once we discarded the fear of failure, knocked down and mastered in just a week's time. Mind you, these were assignments that we believed were well out of reach and impossible to accomplish in a week. One assignment was the completion of my soft weapons curriculum, a comprehensive curriculum of whipping, shooting, grappling, throwing, choking, and pinning with the use of innocuous soft things like belts, ties, sashes, and chains. It was a project I believed would take me another five to ten years to formalize. I finished it in one grueling week of research, analyzing techniques accrued over a decade of soft weapons training and personal reflection.

Michael's own attempt to reduce his body fat percentage from 17 percent to 10 percent in three months, as well as his first seven-figure contract, were given a chance on the die, rolled for in successive one-week challenges, and accomplished with passionate focus and curiosity. We completed subsequent goals with an unwavering commitment to follow that number on top, no matter what it represented.

The book you are reading right now was also born of the die. It was one of several options on my weekly list a mere four months ago, one I was deathly afraid of rolling. The book was also the recipient of consecutive dice rolls for the following several weeks purely by chance, causing a catharsis of pent-up passion and creativity.

In Pursuit of Weightlessness was born of the die.

As much as the creative spirit shirks the confines of pressure and limitation, more often than not the crystalline sparkle of passion is refined under pressure and stress. A diamond is the hardest natural substance known to man. It is pure, clear, concentrated carbon, refined by extremely high pressure in the Earth's mantle. Pressure, when embraced with that lighthearted curiosity of non-competition, leads to profound creative expression. You become youthful again, challenging your older brother to a game of basketball, knowing very well that you stand no chance of winning, but challenging him nonetheless. Why? Because maybe, just maybe, this time is different. Should you fail, well, you bug him until you have another chance.

But if you win, well... awesome!

Now, it isn't the fact that these tasks were *accomplished* that makes this method so brilliant, although I imagine it could be used as a powerful tool for corporate productivity. What makes it so spectacular is that the game brings excitement back to mundane tasks and challenges. It assumes imperfect knowledge. It assumes that there may be experiences worth having and lives worth living that are not self-directed or well understood. Consequently, embracing uncertainty and treating the stuff of life as a mere game naturally awakens a very mindful state of processual awareness. Not all tasks resulted in noteworthy results, but every task resulted in an educational process marked by the vitality and energy of youth. We began to paint the canvases of our selves.

Chapter 9

MINORITY SELF-EXPRESSION

You. Yes, you.

At the end of this brief chapter you're going to make a list with a minimum of three entries and a maximum of six. The list will be actionable and empty of ambiguity. If there are fewer than six options, you may weight them according to personal interest or perceived benefit (i.e. one option gets more than one number, if it's very important).

At least one option will involve doing something you are currently committed to doing, only with greater mindful awareness and aggressive organization. You will make this project or commitment sing.

At least one option will give *awesome* a chance. You'll select something you want to do, something you don't believe you can accomplish in one week. It must be theoretically possible, though practically incomprehensible, given only one week for completion. Should you roll this item, you are morally obligated to stop at nothing to accomplish it. Perhaps you want to learn the tango. Perhaps you want to read *War and Peace*. Perhaps you want to write a novel and writing the first chapter intimidates the hell out of you. Whatever it is, you will give *awesome* a chance.

At least one option can contain a personal goal, interest, or curiosity that you've been too lazy to initiate. Should you roll this item, you'll take the first steps toward demystifying and mastering that thing over the course of the following week.

Other options may involve absurd curiosities, personal challenges, or doing absolutely nothing for extended periods of time. They can involve brash, impulsive, or spontaneous actions that deviate from your known persona. You can tell someone you care deeply about and who may not feel it of late that you love them.

Armed with this powerful list of actions that can express your minority selves, your challenge is to commandeer a die (there are even phone dice apps these days) and let chance be your guide.

Illustration for the Unoriginal (Try at your own peril)

Die roll 1: Ask your boss for a promotion

Die roll 2: Write to a friend and lay out how you will realize a life's goal in one hundred days

Die roll 3: Call your mother or father and convey your love for them in depth

Die roll 4: Visit the closest orphanage

Die roll 5: Eat only veggies and protein (no grains or sugars) for a week.

Die roll 6: Break a routine (different paths to work, different meal selection)

Chapter 10

IF YOU FIND A BUDDHA, KILL HIM!

The Magician and the Rabbit

So there I was, ten years old, rockin' a neighborhood garage sale with piles of worthless crap. I did have one gem, however, that I'd been fixing to unload since my second hour of owning it.

I've always been interested in magic. Even today, for my money, it doesn't get better than a Chris Angel or David Blaine street performance. Whereas they were endowed with gifts of insight and mystery, I had a crummy magic set of cheap tricks. I mastered them in two hours and realized I'd been scammed. It wasn't real magic.

Nonetheless, it made for a good garage sale prize. It was practically new and I'd practiced the connecting rings and disappearing balls well enough to impress a few people. By a few, I mean one. Enter dopy neighborhood girl Jenny. Jenny was a simple, innocent thing, with big square glasses if I recall correctly. She was quickly drawn to my magic set, as I would have been. So I put my top hat on and started to dazzle. It was amazing. She couldn't believe it. Balls disappearing, solid rings linking together. *Guy's a savant...and I can have that power.*

"But," she said, "I don't have enough money right now. How long will it be here?"

"I'm not sure, Jenny," I replied. "It could go at any time really. It's pretty cool."

"I get my allowance tomorrow, can you hold it for me?"

"That's a big ask. If you don't come back, but I have other interested buyers, what am I to do?"

"All I have right now are the silver dollars I've been saving up for years. Birthday gifts from my grandma."

"Is it real money?"

"Yup."

"Well, you better go get them, Jenny!"

She got the coins and that day became the proud new owner of a deluxe magic kit, guaranteed to win friends and woo fellas. Guaranteed. I became the proud new owner of a silver dollar collection, which I used to practice coin rolling techniques on the back of my knuckles, like a gangster. I stockpiled the silver dollars for guilt of scamming a naïve little girl. I didn't have enough guilt to give them back, mind you, just enough to not spend them for eight more years.

In the weeks that followed our exciting barter, legend has it that Jenny took magic to heights I couldn't have imagined. She quickly graduated beyond the rings and balls and such, and integrated live animals, a little bunny to be precise. I imagined it had something to do with a hat trick, one that would no doubt dwarf my humble demonstration in grander and pomp. But it seemed that rabbit had other more nefarious plans, and took her nose for a carrot one fateful practice session. And that was the end of Jenny's magical dreams.

I didn't know enough about investigation at that time to look into things more deeply, nor have I learned anything about investigation since, so I still cannot confirm or deny the ironic aftermath of being blindly intoxicated by magic. Nor can I confirm that these events were inextricably, or even causally connected.

Let's sum up the moral of the story as seen through the eyes of a ten year old. It's a story of a little girl's ambition and the retribution it elicited. You desire the power of magic? Don't be surprised if a rabbit bites your face off.

Suffice it to say that the Buddha was right, desire leads to suffering.

Actually, just disregard everything in this story except that last sentence and let's get back to business.

Meditation is not...

... sitting cross-legged, quietly forcing your mind to empty and avoid capricious thoughts. It is not the rigid application of philosophical dogma, ethical rules, or external physical postures. It is not striving for a state of mind that is beyond your immediate grasp. The meditative mind is alive with passion and free of desire that leads to suffering.

I often hear from people with some modicum of experience that they meditated for an hour this or that day. I've been meditating for over twenty years, and I'm exceedingly happy if I can sustain a meditative mind for ten minutes. Meditation has nothing to do with fitting the mold, with sitting quietly while your mind jumps from work to sex to work to shopping to breathing back to work. It's a concentrated state of awareness where the mind is sensitive to the sensate world and its own internal operations. To maintain a state of concentration for five minutes is highly advanced. For ten minutes or more, elite. People may try to stay put, sit quietly, and 'meditate' for extended periods of time, but to believe that meditation means a wash of randomness and whimsy interlaced with brief moments of heightened awareness is very misleading.

Furthermore, the domain of meditation is often relegated to natural or monastic environments that remove external distractions and reduce the stuff of living to a bare minimum.

My little nephew runs around like a maniac on crack. Sometimes he bonks his head or takes a hard spill. Everyone in the room gasps. He looks around, unsure how to process what just happened. Clearly, it hurt like hell. He starts to tear up. But when my sister rushes over, picks him up and brushes him off, and gives him a soft loving smile – boom, he's all good. That bonk will never live to be retold. It was never felt longer than a moment.

As adults, we turn a bonk into a weeklong event, telling friends and family, fanning the flame of self-pity, and looking for sympathy from everyone and their dog. We replay the event looking for all causes. We try to find out who was really responsible. We fill our suitcases with the dead remains of countless experiences and we drag those bastards to every meeting, conversation, and new experience. Kids don't do this, and therefore are free to experience the continuum of beauty, excitement, and unique life experiences that flow ad infinitum.

Where a child has a meaningful experience of an event, and the events that follow it, most of us 'mature' adults spend minutes, hours, days, processing momentary events that carry little weight. It could be a workplace conflict or a fight with the spouse that causes us to pass over countless fresh, unfiltered experiences of sensitivity, awareness, curiosity, and beauty. We don't see the man, we see the color of the man's skin, which we know to be bad because it is different than ours. We don't see the country, we see the political or socioeconomic system, which we know is different from ours, and therefore bad. We don't see our lover, we see the stupid off-hand comment that was unintentionally offensive, and we drag them through the gutter for days until we feel vindicated.

Imagine the energy you'll have after emptying your suitcase of attachment and starting over. You'll become a wealth of knowledge and experience unburdened by negativity, pain, and fear. Your mind will be so free and clear that a single day will seem infinitely long, awarding you countless opportunities to play, study, watch, ask, and learn.

Imagine the pillow of intellect and judgment that has slowly been asphyxiating you being suddenly lifted from your face. Imagine the breath that comes in the next moment. Imagine the gratitude, depth, and fullness of that breath.

This is the life ignored.

Your compulsion to rethink and process an experience, your commitment to carrying the past into the present, is the practice of living death before the big game of Death. Life is now. It isn't in the memory of your first painful injury, your first kiss, your first dance, or the first death of a close relative or friend. It is right now.

In addition to the words passing before your eyes, it is also the sound in your environment, the pressure of the seat beneath you, supporting you. It is any subtle scent, any spontaneous thought arising in the moment. Life is in your relationship to the words before your eyes and the breath that sustains you every moment. Life is that beautiful innocence of the baby in the carriage.

If You Find a Buddha, Kill Him!

Zen master Linji was quoted as saying, "If you meet the Buddha on the road, kill him." Before you get too excited and grab your bashing stick, Linji was not advocating homicide. Or maybe he was, you never know with Zen monks. But for our purposes here, what matters is that regardless of your religious affiliation, or lack thereof, the Buddha resides as an indelible image of peace, serenity, and enlightenment. For Buddhists in particular, this image is sacred. But holding on to the idea of the Buddha, who was merely a hand pointing the way to enlightenment, will prevent you from ever becoming a Buddha yourself. To realize your own potential, to become your own light, the Buddha must be killed.

Dreams, values, and ideologies give us hope and drive us in life. They also bind us to static concepts that don't necessarily promote happiness and fulfillment. Whenever we view a person, idea, or fact as gospel, we place an indelible gap between them and us. We make excuses. In some cases we view others as smarter, luckier, and more talented. In other cases we view them as ignorant, base, or inferior.

It should be glaringly clear that egotism creates conflict, that politics create division, and that ideologies create war. Labeling something as *different* is the easiest way to justify erasing it, or worse, prostrating yourself before it. It's easier to quit your job if your boss is an asshole. It's easy to laugh at someone's pain if they aren't close to you. It's easy to follow a guru if they're considered enlightened. It's easier to wage a war on Muslims if you're a Christian.

Naming is blaming.

This is a fundamental problem with epistemology in the West. Divide and conquer is the path to understanding. Knowledge is a dialectical battle of opposing forces, argumentation, and scrutiny. It destroys the present in front of us, breaking it into its composite parts in order to construct meaning. The paradoxical outcome of this learning process is that the more we learn, the more we become disconnected from that which we aim to understand.

Western medicine, for example, treats the disease (or more often, the symptoms). If a man has cancer, you kill the cancer. What caused the cancer is less meaningful than the fact that it exists and the danger it implies. Above all, it must be eradicated. In some cases, the individual is cut open and part of him or her is removed. In other cases, cancer is treated by poisoning the patient. Kill enough cells, and you'll kill cancer cells. Hopefully the patient survives.

In Eastern medicine the individual (and cancer within) is treated as a whole. Qigong energy healing and acupuncture have been curing chronic conditions longer than Western medicine has been around. They do so by treating the person, not the disease. Disease is not considered an independent, malicious force, but the consequence of stagnant energy or an unbalanced whole. Eastern medicine practitioners aim to reconstitute vital energy flow and to allow the body to heal itself. In so doing, the body becomes stronger through this supported, self-regulating process.

Treat the person, not the disease. See the present in its entirety, not as the sum of numerous disjunctive parts. See the man, not the skin color, political view, or religious affiliation. Don't feel compelled to break up your world into intelligible pieces. These pieces give you the fuel for powerful arguments. They also lead to the compulsion of analysis, hypertension, and depression. The biggest battle for a warrior is internal.

Breaking down the web of constructed ideas, beliefs, and lies that bias our experience so that we can live fully in the undivided present is a freedom that few outside of monasteries and insane asylums find. But it doesn't need to be this way. We are all entitled to this freedom.

Beauty. Love. The Good. God.

The very concepts kill the things. When we define beauty it disappears. When we rigidly adhere to the good, we cease to be. When we possess love, it dies. When we pursue enlightenment, we wind up with a handful of dust. Attachment to fixed ideals separates us from the ephemeral nature of reality, even if that ideal is enlightenment (or the Buddha). Attachments prevent us from living with power and focus, which arise naturally from nonjudgmental awareness. Our greatest freedom, our greatest passion, our fullest life, exists within our immediate relationship with the present.

The unfettered mind accepts the transience of life and relinquishes conditioned habits, comforts, and beliefs. It boldly embraces the present, undivided moment in all its wonder and beauty. If I had been unable to release my desire for comfort and security, the primal innocence and freedom of the Steppenwolf would not have surfaced. Had I just said no to fungi, I would not have reunited with the interconnected whole that resides beneath the veil of normal experience. Had I predetermined that consorting with hookers is unwholesome, and refused to look beyond my desire to bed a sultry Thai prostitute, I would not have seen self-sacrifice personified or experienced unconditional love.

And had I been unwilling to surrender self-doubt, to face my inhibitions head-on, and to roll the die (accepting chance-dictated assignments), the creative energy and all-consuming passion that coalesced in this book would not have been released.

Experiencing the present through a veil of conditioned habits and beliefs is like viewing a sunset through cracked, dirty eyeglasses. Freedom exists in replacing your cloudy lenses, in a willingness to challenge long-held biases, and in openness to fresh, unfiltered experiences. The weightless person resides on the precipice of uncertainty, and diligently works to see that which is before her. She lets nothing stand between herself and the freedom, peace, and beauty at her fingertips (even if that freedom and beauty are sheltered in pain).

To fully recognize the beauty of the present, we must release fears and insecurities, relinquish comfort and control, and destroy all ideals that prevent us from actualizing our greatest freedoms and fullest potentials.

To become a weightless, guiding light unto yourself, you must remove all others.

I implore you, if you find a Buddha on the road... *kill him*!

BOOK 4

Weightlessness

Theory, practice, and allegory integrate the disparate elements of Weightlessness.

In *Weightlessness* your trainer submits his manifesto on human flourishing. Your own pursuit is sparked with a call to action. A day in the life of a weightless man.

Two traveling monks reached a river and met a young woman. Wary of the current, she asked if they could carry her across. One of the monks hesitated, but the other quickly picked her up onto his shoulders, transported her across the water, and put her down on the other bank. She thanked him and departed.

As the monks continued on their way, the first monk was brooding and preoccupied. Unable to hold his silence, he spoke out.

"Brother," he said, "Our spiritual training teaches us to avoid any contact with women, but you picked that one up on your shoulders and carried her!"

"Brother," the second monk replied, "I set her down on the other side, while you are still carrying her."

A Zen Parable

Chapter 1

TOM FAZIO'S WEIGHTLESSNESS MANIFESTO

The Future of Mind-Body Fitness

Illustrations By

诸海波
Zhu Haibo

Weightless Nutrition

The aims of Weightlessness nutrition are to support health, strength, and lean body mass. It allows for a clean, detoxified body, a clear head, and efficient metabolism.

Your genetic code hasn't changed markedly in forty thousand years. The foods that nourished our hunter-gatherer ancestors are unparalleled in nourishing your body today. Modern processed foods, including grains, while containing energy, lack the essential nutrients for optimal health and metabolism, and should be avoided.

Method: The Big 3

- Eat real things, things that had a head or grow from sunlight and earth, with a primary emphasis on dark green vegetables and those with bright colors.

- Oscillate caloric intake for a dynamic and resilient metabolism. Eat satisfying and nutritious dinners. Embrace hunger. Embrace full satisfaction.

- Avoid grains and sugars.

Animals that eat meat assimilate nutrients while at rest. The order of energy turnover is energy expenditure, then consumption, then rest. Carnivores don't eat before they play or hunt. On the other hand, fruits and vegetables may be grazed on throughout the day for energy maintenance. As omnivores, humans should find a happy medium, grazing on veggies as cows do, on fruit as primates do, and occasionally indulging in high-protein meals as lions do. Dinner is the most important meal of the day, as your body is most capable of absorbing and utilizing nutrients consumed while at rest. Weightless warriors should be concerned with getting sufficient protein and micronutrients in the evening for recuperation and growth.

Super Strength

Strength should be understood as an adaptation to environmental stresses. In the beginning, one may implement extreme sessions that lead to local or systemic failure, but they should only be seen as the initial phase of building base strength. In this phase you are akin to a child standing for the first time, or taking their first steps. Every step is an act of maximum strength and coordination. There is no alternative to failure. But after these basic skills are acquired, children grow as they play. Their all-out efforts become a series of squats, lunges, and sprints impulsively repeated throughout the day, strengthening the body and honing the nervous system.

You are no different.

Our bodies are built to push, pull, squat, and press. The first exercise of a baby is a push-up of sorts. It is the foundation of total upper body strength and fitness. The second is a squat. It is the foundation of total lower body strength and fitness. If you aren't pushing and squatting, you are not training. In an ideal world, you would have adequate weights dispersed through your house. Even better, you would have a job or hobby that requires the use of physical strength, performing repetitions as the logic of your environment implied.

For those who work demanding jobs and sit at desks:

- Focus on the big five vectors: push, pull, squat, press (overhead), and twist. One heavy exercise in each vector is sufficient for total body health and strength.

- Intensity and tension are of greatest importance, achieved through very high resistance and very short duration (if it cannot be sustained, it is by definition intense).

- Strength is best stimulated through environmental needs (a child at play, constantly standing and lifting).

- Do three to five sets with three to eight repetitions per exercise. Doing this two to three times per week is sufficient to increase strength. You must want to increase strength and strive for heavier lifts. There are no other rules. Three days per week with a day to rest in between is fine. It's also okay to lift five times a day, several days per week, or as little as once every two weeks (given sufficient intensity). Simply try to best your one-to-five-rep maxes. Play. Eat well. Recover and grow.

An Indestructible Body

From Static to Dynamic Flexibility

Static stretching should be engaged in as a form of meditation and relaxation. It keeps one connected to the body and constantly aware of tension.

Dynamic stretching is crucial for activating your fullest physical freedom. It deconditions the stretch reflex and allows you to move through a full range of motion at top speed without injury. Without it, all strength, speed, and insight acquired through Weightlessness training may only be a recipe for self-destruction.

Perform static stretching until range of flexibility is satisfactory for health and performance. Proper alignment, with an emphasis on a straight spine and an untucked tailbone, is paramount for safe and productive gains. One should not 'stretch' the body, but instead focus on relaxing and releasing the tension that prevents your natural length from manifesting.

For improved dynamic flexibility, perform three sets of three to ten repetitions of dynamic stretching. Swing the leg straight up in front of you, spine erect, both legs straight. Do not snap the legs. Practice this three to six times per week. Once speed and height plateau with strict form, begin to add weight to each ankle. Progress slowly, and continue for one to three years until you can perform several sets of full-speed rising kicks with ten pounds on each leg.

Modern living creates tremendous tightness in the hamstrings. Sitting for extended periods of time leaves the hamstrings at their shortest length. They are the key to a feeling of relaxation, to maintaining general back health, and to safe ballistic mobility. Static stretching, such as dangling forward from the waist by drawing in the navel and breathing up to the crown of the head, will add years to your life. Consult a yogi for principles of spine elongation, the nuances of downward dog, and the forward bend. Find a martial arts instructor for the full range of rising kick options and dynamic flexibility.

Peace, Passion, and Freedom

Mindfulness Meditation

There are no rules.

Meditation begins wherever you are, whenever you are. It can begin as you read these very words.

Be still.

Listen.

Feel.

Observe your breath. Be aware of its length and depth. Don't force it to be other than it is, just be with it. Allow your awareness to extend to sounds, temperatures, and pressures, without reducing or narrowing your scope. Let your experience expand to encompass a plethora of sensations at once and be fully present. Should your mind wander, don't judge it.

There are no rules.

A free mind does not force itself to adhere to rules, postures, and structures. To forcefully pull your thoughts back to your breath is an act of egotism. To be with your thoughts, no matter how anxious, ridiculous, depraved, or unholy, will result in genuine insight and innocence. Your thoughts, like your sensations, are immediate experiences. Observe them and be aware of them, as you are of your own breath. Be aware of the *you* that is thinking. When your thoughts run their course and dissolve, you will find peace, awareness, and strength.

There are no rules, but…

Sitting or standing with an erect spine and good posture is conducive to proper deep breathing, as well as maintaining a state of nonjudgmental awareness. Closing the eyes initially helps reduce sensations and distractions, allowing less-dominant senses to surface and come to life. If there is any value in the seated lotus position, it is that it can lead to sustained stability and allows the lower abdomen to have free play. There is no sacred pose, position, or stance. No one can teach you how to feel. You must step boldly into the present and surrender all security and comfort.

Forever Young

The Secret Science of Cheating Strength

Millennia ago, men did not pump weights up and down. They lifted things, hung from things, stabbed things, thumped things on the head and dragged them home. When lifting, their muscles were contracted and relaxed. Otherwise, they were held statically in the strongest range of motion until the burn could not be sustained. Biceps bend the arm by way of a third-class lever. Lifting in the strongest range of motion allows for more weight, recruits more fast-twitch fibers, and leads to greater strength. Quadriceps extend the leg by way of a first-class lever and are at their strongest as the leg nears full extension.

To find the strongest range of motion, find the prime mover (the muscle(s) doing the bulk of the work) and place it at full contraction, where it nears its shortest (the big squeeze). That's your strongest range. Due to the limited range, reps can be higher in number than standard strength training numbers. You can go as high as twenty to thirty reps. For rehab, three to four sets of eight to fifteen reps are generally sufficient. The aim is to stimulate, not exhaust. For rapid strength gain and bodybuilding, six to eight sets of ten to thirty repetitions are recommended. Alternatively, a static hold in the strongest range of motion is just as effective when chasing progressively heavy weights and longer durations (fifteen to thirty seconds is sufficient, given enough weight).

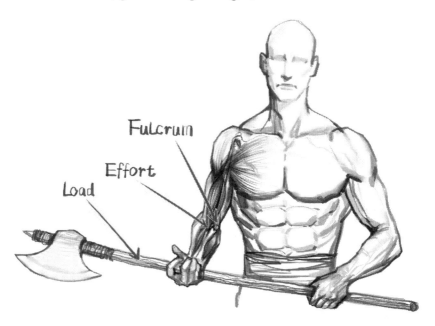

Fulcrum

Effort

Load

Rules for Cheating

- Concentrate on the big five vectors.
- Target fast-twitch fibers and strengthen connective tissue by lifting heavy weight in the strongest range of motion with short-range partial repetitions (or static contraction).

- Do not train to failure (for rehab).
- Increase caloric intake substantially, with a focus on a variety of vegetables and complete proteins.
- Supplement with balanced micronutrients (lots of vegetables and fruits or regular multivitamin supplementation) and omega-3 fatty acids, to ensure you have sufficient resources to reconstruct tissue and reduce inflammation.
- In cases of inflammation or acute post-workout pain, ice the region in fifteen-minute intervals.

Energy Development

Qigong

Observe a child breathing; the abdomen still pumps as if drawing life through the umbilical cord. This is your energy breath. The seat of energy, the *dan tian*, is located within this region. It's the human battery. Fill it with energy from the universe, breathing in through the nose and visualizing energy flowing to the lower abdomen (despite the fact that our lungs don't extend that far down). Sit or stand with an erect spine, head lifted as if drawn by a string from the crown point (top-center of the head). This should relax and drop the shoulders, releasing tension throughout. Lightly press your tongue to the roof of your mouth, just behind the palate. This connects your conception and governing vessels on the front and back of the body, allowing for smooth energy circulation within the small universe. Keep your mind focused on your *dan tian*, about an inch and a half below the belly button and an inch and a half within the body. This is a general guide and starting point. Your exact energy center may vary.

Your breath should travel slowly down the body, expand the lower abdomen, and create a pressure that is not muscular. When you exhale, that pressure within the lower abdomen should not diminish, and the qi stored does not exit. It's trapped. Every breath fans the flame of energy. When you exhale, the diaphragm and thoracic region should contract, expunging air and leaving a ball of pressure and fire in your abdomen. One should practice daily for three to six months to acquire genuine sensations of energy.

After this time, you may add more advanced elements, such as holding the breath for an equal breath count or tensing a part of the body to draw energy to that region.

Men should conserve their qi. Sex can be enjoyed liberally, but ejaculation should be reserved. Women, however, are strengthened by orgasm.

Lightness Training

Speed Running Skills

For legendary lightness skills, begin with unweighted running or leaping. Each of these skills alone is sufficient for total body strength and health. Together, they create a monster of speed, power, agility, and stamina. You must train these skills frequently for two to three months and reach a point of diminishing returns before adding weight. Furthermore, there must be no pain in the joints of the lower body or lower back before resistance is added.

For speed running skills, begin by adding three pounds to each ankle. Begin every run with five minutes of running lightly in place, sinking your breath into the lower abdomen, and concentrating on the *dan tian*. Take a mental survey of all tension in the body, and release it. With every inhalation, draw energy from the universe into the vacuum of your *dan tian*. After five to ten minutes, begin to sprint at 100 percent of your ability until fatigue sets in. Do this one time only. Repeat daily, each time sprinting a little farther than the time before.

Alternatively, jog for distance to warm up, rather than jogging in place, but total length should not exceed fifteen minutes. Ideally, the jog lasts less than ten minutes and finishes with an all-out sprint to fatigue. Gradually add more weight to the ankles as your current weight becomes imperceptible. Your Weightlessness initiation is one hundred days. For legendary warrior-monk skills and permanent Weightlessness, continue for two to three years.

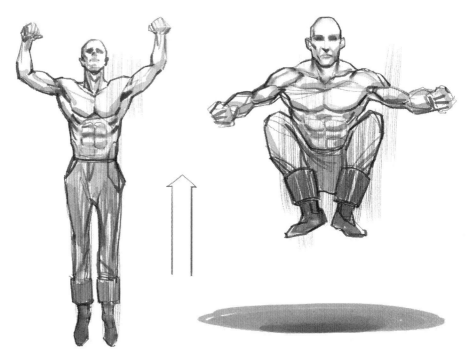

Leaping Skills

For extreme leaping skills, begin by digging a hole three feet deep. Stand in the hole and breathe deeply into the lower abdomen for three to five minutes. Focus on the *dan tian,* allowing energy to enter every pore in your body and accumulate there. Take a mental survey of all tension in the body and release it. Begin by adding three pounds to each ankle. Relax fully and leap out of the hole with one all-out effort. Repeat this until fatigue sets in. Perform only one set to fatigue. Every morning remove a bit of earth from the hole with a rice bowl (don't take this literally. Box jumps, and any other shelf or level will also suffice, so long as small incremental changes can be made to the height). Gradually increase the weight on each ankle and, if so inclined, add weight to the torso. Your Weightlessness initiation is one hundred days. For legendary warrior-monk skills and permanent Weightlessness, continue for two to three years.

Alternatively, for those living in our modern world, buy a box or find a park bench. Not everyone can afford a hole these days.

Lightness training can be applied to all manners of physical performance, but is most suitable for gross motor movements like pushing, pulling, pressing, squatting, leaping, twisting, and running. These skills are transferrable to all possible movements under all possible scenarios, despite the fact that they may not be sport-specific. These gross movements are the quintessence of human biomechanics and teach the application of fluid power in all possible vectors.

To apply these theories to enhance your particular craft, gradually add weight to the movement in question, never train to failure, and repeat daily. Avoid movements that snap or force a sharp contraction as a joint nears its maximum range. For example, a front snap kick should be avoided (unless performed slowly and with control), while crescent or wheel kicks are acceptable at full speed. Throwing (a baseball, say) should be avoided, while swinging a weighted baseball bat is acceptable. Always start with a foundation of leaping or running to ensure sufficient total body strength and stability. For a disciple of Weightlessness, one or both of these skills must be incorporated as a foundation in the art of physical lightness.

Into the Mystic

Third eye activation

For third eye activation, begin concentrating and accumulating sufficient energy in the *dan tian*. It will eventually be accompanied by jitters, temperature changes, swirling sensations, and a host of other abnormal sensations in the lower abdomen. You will also feel an increase in overall body temperature. After concentrating qi in the lower abdomen as you would throughout a standard meditation session, you may bring your concentration to the point above your eyebrows, in the center of your forehead. There is no active manipulation of energy at this point, merely concentration. This should be accompanied by sensations of pressure behind the forehead. Continue this practice until your seeing, healing, and channeling powers are fully developed. Follow your intuition.

Channeling

To channel energy to the extremities for martial or healing purposes, begin with an extended practice of qigong until sufficient energy is accumulated in the *dan tian*. If you are not sure if you have reached this state, then you have not reached this state. Continue to focus on the fundamentals. This state will be accompanied by jitters, temperature changes, swirling sensations, and a host of other abnormal sensations in the lower abdomen, along with an increase in your overall body temperature.

When you feel ready, extend one or both hands in front of you, shoulders relaxed, palms pushed forward. Your inhalations should concentrate on drawing energy from the universe through all pores of the body to the *dan tian*. When you exhale, draw your focus to the center of your palms and, using your intuition as a guide, will your qi to the center of your palms. Continue this cycle until your palms tremble with energy.

To project this energy beyond the palm for martial or healing purposes, imagine resisting against an external force. Visualize the walls in the room closing in on you. With outstretched, relaxed arms, supported only by your skeleton (as if empty of all muscle and connective tissue), resist the wall with only your qi. No muscular force. After sufficient practice, the hands should feel alive with energy, but the heat previously felt should be extended beyond them. One may also practice by extinguishing a candle at a distance through qi projection alone, using the same method just described. One should be willing to commit decades to this study.

Qi follows two paths:

1. Physical Tension: Tensing a muscle (clenching a fist, for example) will draw energy (bioelectric current) there. Actually, tension is a bit like damming a river. Once tension is released, or the dam destroyed, a flood (of water or energy) occurs. You might inhale to the *dan tian*, clench your fist lightly, and focus your mind on it. Then relax and exhale, allowing energy to flow freely to and through that region (this is similar to how acupuncture works).

2. Intuition and Will: Concentrate on a region of the body (your palm, for example) and will your energy there while remaining physically relaxed. This requires significant sensitivity and awareness of natural energy flow prior to effective training.

The Weightless Man

The businessman removes his burden of weight, takes the podium, and speaks with unwavering conviction and confidence.

The poet unshackles her wrists, releases all inhibition, and expresses her naked passions in permanent ink.

The politician, unswayed by public approval, leads with heartfelt compassion, wisdom, and insight.

The athlete removes her ankle weights and, with liberated limbs and a lightness of being, competes only with herself. She has surrendered all concern for success and failure. Her only remaining ambition is to leave her heart on the field; her only itching thought is "win or lose, they will remember my name."

The prisoner removes his chains, and like the mighty phoenix is reborn from the ashes of his prior self. Today is a new beginning, but it will be lived as if his last.

The lover forgets all transgressions, and gives unconditionally, unreservedly, completely.

The Weightless Man,
Indelible beacon of human flourishing,
Brimming with concentrated energy,
Raw, unbridled power and effortless speed,
A calm, compassionate, and uninhibited mind,
And an indomitable will,
The Weightless Man is.

Chapter 2

YOUR PURSUIT:
A CALL TO ACTION

Here we are at the moment of truth. Will you take the stories and information that preceded as mere entertainment and insight, or as a call to action for your coming transformation? There's no middle ground, unfortunately. You now know, due to the antifragile nature of your mind-body complex, that stress and discomfort are required for growth. You also know that the skill of non-attachment is essential for combatting stress, for liberating the conditioned mind, and for living a passion-filled life.

And you know that skin in the game is required for growth.

These aren't practices and capabilities that can be fully understood or remotely developed by reading a book. They can only affect personal change through first-hand implementation.

So here we are. The case for Weightlessness has been made. It's your turn.

In theory, there's no difference between theory and practice. In practice there is. - Yogi Berra

Integration doesn't occur in theory. Theoretical understanding, as we discussed in *If You Find a Buddha, Kill Him*, is a process of rational abstraction, not integration. Theoretical understanding separates and divides, thereby killing the essence of the whole. This is useful in many cases in life and is one of humanity's greatest gifts. But in matters of wisdom and true insight, it only gets us part of the way. These fractured and disparate parts can only reunite in the conscientious practitioner. It's in the consistent application of Weightlessness tools and principles that practice becomes far more than theory.

Weightlessness is nothing if not a call to action. The programs and workouts provide the tools and structure of integration and peak performance. This is something that cannot be internalized or embodied intellectually. It requires first-hand experience and skin in the game. The reason this chapter is nestled between the Manifesto and a portrait of a weightless person is to highlight the fact that one cannot merely leap from insight to personal growth without skin in the game. The necessary segue is implementation and consistent practice.

Placing the workouts centrally in Book 4 and giving them a chapter unto themselves should suggest to the reader that training is not a footnote or appendix to theoretical understanding. This game cannot be played from the benches. Everything you've read thus far shouldn't remain a passive experience. It's time to join the tribe.

Books 1 through 3 are perhaps better framed as appendices in disguise; the science and support for your journey ahead. The true depth of Weightlessness doesn't lie in open source information or the innovative compilation and application of physiological facts; it's in the integrated framework of Weightlessness workouts and protocols.

On Integration

It's rather easy to assume that Weightlessness training is the sum of several parts, by reading about the various categories, principles, and tools that make up the training regimen. It's easy for someone with fitness experience to assume they just need to meditate and stretch more, or for a meditator to lift more. But this risks missing the profound mind-body integration that can occur through the cultivation of all elements in tandem and in appropriate degrees.

The diametrically polar impacts of strength and flexibility, and of strength and meditation, are such that if trained in isolation you'll likely experience fallout. Strength training creates tension in the body that can cause inflammation, tightness, and wear and tear. Flexibility and meditation counteract this by relaxing tight tissue, remolding and integrating your myofascial structure, downregulating your sympathetic nervous system, and improving blood flow and oxygen utilization.

Meditation trained in isolation can indeed lead to stillness and peace... in isolation. The grand insight of Weightlessness is that to apply meditation under more volatile, high-stress circumstances – where it truly matters most – requires a resilience to stress and a mental fortitude that can only be developed through hardship. Physical training is the safest laboratory of stress exposure, for it allows us to measure and quantify the degrees of applied stress, and thereafter to make incremental changes that guarantee internal growth. It's also an indispensable building block of health and strength in its own right.

A monk with decades of meditation experience in solitude will crumble if dropped in New York City and told to survive. He might be alright for a day, maybe a week. But the pressures of survival, the stress of social tensions and conflict, and the inability to control the conditions of his environment will test every ounce of his being. The monastic tradition has propagated a verifiably weak model of mindful awareness and non-attachment that don't assume real conditions. As such it commits basic model errors, and leaves the practitioner exposed to long-tail risks.

On Assets and Liabilities

We all gravitate toward our interests and proclivities, and we avoid those things that challenge us in a personal way. One glaringly obvious pattern has manifested over the last few years: those who excel in the physical domain will gravitate toward it and emphasize it in their training, often underemphasizing the flexibility and meditation protocols.

And vice versa. Those who have learned to rely on their minds, who have gained a sense of confidence in their intuition or their ability to manage their emotions and manipulate their environments, will commonly avoid pushing themselves in physical training. The pressures of an escalating resistance within training cannot be controlled with the rational mind. You cannot deceive yourself into thinking it's easy when your entire being is being tested. All those who deadlift know this. Training destroys the rational mind with deep prejudice, and only honors conscientious effort, adaptability, and will.

Meditation, which is egoless practice, without the cultivated will and discipline of strength training, is unlikely to become a regular part of life, due to a lack of focus and drive. It will also cease to be applicable as soon as stress and pressure rise beyond your capacity to manage them. Strength and conditioning increase your stress threshold, buying you the opportunity to implement meditation (and non-attachment) in real time for stress management and creative problem-solving.

These pillars are inextricably linked in the whole person. And the results go far beyond the sum of individual parts. As such, each Weightlessness protocol contains three core pillars – strength, flexibility, and meditation. Lightness adds the fourth – ballistic weight training.

Weightlessness does have a series of progressive metrics that allow us to assess our strengths and weaknesses and to program their balancing and integration. This is largely the focus of *The Essence of Lightness.* This doesn't undermine the programs below; it merely alludes to the depth of what's currently available for those who want to master the art of Weightlessness. But I mention it here as a word of caution and support. To truly develop yourself, to truly test yourself in this domain, you must be conscious of where you feel most comfortable, and you must consciously develop the 'other.' Rapid growth and integration lies not only in advancing points of interest, but in addressing those mind-body liabilities that hold you back.

The Progressive Nature of Weightlessness Training

For those looking to capitalize on the blood, sweat, and tears (and consequent method refinement) of the early pioneers of Weightlessness, below are sample workouts that take into account everything that has happened since the first publication of this book – since the organization and implementation of the Weightlessness methodology as a coherent, fully integrated framework. The updated programs below are not meant to be universal, fixed workouts. They're snapshots into different developmental stages. You can use them as a reference to help you visually organize the myriad tools and techniques discussed in Books 2 and 3, or you can give them a try in their entirety.

Keep in mind that Weightlessness isn't a static workout (nor is the experience of weightlessness a static state), but an evolving prescriptive framework of personal development. These workouts can still serve you well for quite some time, but the serious trainee will outgrow them as a snake sheds its skin or a butterfly its cocoon. Your sense of weightlessness will lie in the constant uphill battle against increasing resistance, not in standing still.

Weightlessness protocols aren't just workouts. They're medicine prescribed to meet the trainee exactly where she is. They organize the complex worlds of strength and conditioning, flexibility, and mental development into a single progressive framework that takes into account individual difference and personal imbalances over time. It has taken me over 30 years of training, 20 years of teaching, and five years of exclusive Weightlessness coaching to fully organize it.

Most people specialize. Programming for strength isn't so complicated. Programming for meditation isn't so complicated. Fitting these different domains into an organized, progressive framework that acknowledges individual differences... well, that *is* complicated. And I know of no other system that does it effectively.

Reframing Your Mind-Body Training

You stand on the shoulders of like-minded truth-seekers who have put skin in the game to elevate their minds and bodies, as well as inform the ever-growing system of Weightlessness. You can allay your concerns and skepticism as to the efficacy of the training regimens in eliciting promised freedoms. But you must get off the bench and play the game. This is about you, not about me, abstract theories, or lofty ideas. It's about you and your story of change. Weightlessness protocols are not an isolated domain in the world of personal development. They directly speak to your preparedness and capacity to face uncertainties in life with a sense of power and grace. And this requires practice.

It's your turn.

Beginner Weightlessness Workout: Foundations

Perform three days per week. Should not exceed forty minutes per session.

Warm-up

- Five minutes of jumping jacks or jogging.

Strength

- Chest press or push-ups: Four sets of ten to twelve reps.
- Rows: Four sets of ten to twelve reps.
- Weighted squats or Lunges: Four sets of ten to twelve reps.
- Shoulder press: Four sets of eight to ten reps.
- Plank: Three sets of one minute each.

Stamina:

- Burpees: 3 sets of 15 reps

Flexibility

Work through this sequence three full times. Hold each stretch for 20 to 30 seconds until the initial tension subsides and the stretch reflex surrenders. Make sure at all times that your spine is straight (tailbone is untucked), and your feet-knee-hip-shoulder alignment is square. With each set, try to sink deeper into each stretch.

- Forward bend – Focus on hamstring relaxation, do not bend the lower back.
- Deep squat – With feet straight, work the knees as wide as possible with the elbows.
- Hip flexor stretch – Essentially a front split with the front knee bent at 90 degrees.
- Front splits – Use blocks to elevate your hands and support your weight. Gradually lower yourself down and extend further over time.

Mindfulness

- Ten minutes.

Intermediate / Advanced Weightlessness Workout 1

Intermediate / Advanced Weightlessness workouts should alternate between workout 1 and 2. Due to your increased strength, it's important to periodize body parts to ensure enough intensity per workout and time for recovery. Ideally, each is done twice a week, four total sessions. Three sessions is a minimum, and if intensity is high enough may be enough to elicit ongoing growth. Workouts should not exceed fifty minutes per session. Additional stretching and breathing can always be added.

Warm-up

- Five-minute jog followed by 100 squats.

Strength

- Vector: Push 1 | Suggested exercise – Bench press
  » Reps per set: 15, 10, 5, 5, 5
- Vector: Push 2 | Suggested exercise – Dips
  » Reps per set: 15, 10, 8, 5
- Vector: Pull | Suggested exercise – Pull-ups
  » Reps per set: 10, 8, 5, 5, 5
- Vector: Twist | Suggested exercise – V-sits
  » Reps: 50

Stamina:

- Burpees: 4 sets of 20 reps (1 minute rest between sets)

Flexibility

Work through this sequence four to five full times. Hold each stretch for 30 to 40 seconds until the initial tension subsides and the stretch reflex surrenders. Make sure at all times that your spine is straight (tailbone is untucked), and your feet-knee-hip-shoulder alignment is square. Each set, try to sink deeper into each stretch.

- Forward bend – Focus on hamstring relaxation, do not bend the lower back.

- Hip flexor stretch – Essentially a front split with the front knee bent at 90 degrees.
- Front splits – Use blocks to elevate your hands and support your weight. Gradually lower yourself down.

Dynamic:

- Add three sets of dynamic front rising kicks, five to eight reps each. Start low and slow.

Mindfulness

- Fifteen to twenty minutes.

Intermediate / Advanced Weightlessness Workout 2

Intermediate / Advanced Weightlessness workouts should alternate between workout 1 and 2. Due to your increased strength, it's important to periodize body parts to ensure enough intensity per workout, and time for recovery. Ideally, each is done twice a week, four total sessions. Three sessions is a minimum, and if intensity is high enough may be enough to elicit ongoing growth. Workouts should not exceed fifty minutes per session.

Warm-up

- Five-minute jog followed by 100 squats.

Strength

- Vector: Squat/Pull | Suggested exercise – Deadlift
  » Reps per set: 10, 8, 5, 5, 5
- Vector: Press | Suggested exercise – Shoulder press
  » Reps per set: 10, 8, 5, 5, 5
- Vector: Weighted Squat | Suggested exercise – Squats
  » Reps per set: 20, 15, 15, 12
- Vector: Twist | Suggested exercise – Crunches
  » Reps: 100
- Vector: Twist | Suggested exercise – Bicycles

» Reps: 100

Stamina:

- High Knees or Mountain Climers: 8 sets of 40 seconds (20 second rest between)

Flexibility

Work through this sequence four to five full times. Hold each stretch for 30 to 40 seconds until the initial tension subsides and the stretch reflex surrenders. Make sure at all times that your spine is straight (tailbone is untucked), and your feet-knee-hip-shoulder alignment is square. Each set, try to sink deeper into each stretch.

- Forward bend – Focus on hamstring relaxation, do not bend the lower back.
- Deep squat – With feet straight, work the knees as wide as possible with the elbows.
- Center/Straddle splits – Hold as wide as possible, making sure the toes and knees are pointed straight up, and the tailbone is untucked.

Meditation

- Ten to fifteen minutes of qigong followed by five minutes of mindfulness.

Lightness Protocols (Advanced Weightlessness)

Perform four to six days per week. Movement elements should not exceed forty minutes per session. Cycle for sixty to one hundred days of training, then rest for a full week. Each cycle should result in higher leaping and heavier weights for all exercises.

Lightness

Jog for eight to ten minutes. For the last 100 meters (up to one minute), sprint at 90 to 100 percent. Begin with three pounds on each ankle, and work up to eight to ten pounds (this is very advanced). If you struggle against the weight, it's too heavy for you. It should be imperceptible. Your stride should be light and free of tension. Your breathing should be abdominal, not upper chest. If you cannot sprint under these conditions, you are not yet ready for fruitful lightness training. The emphasis here is not in getting it done, but in how you do it. This is a long journey.

After a short rest, proceed to weighted box jumps. Add three pounds to each ankle and work up to eight to ten pounds. Perform only one set to fatigue, allowing for deep meditative breaths in between each repetition. Follow the guidelines in the Weightlessness Manifesto.

Dynamic Flexibility

Dynamic stretching. Five to eight sets of three to five front vertical leg swings with erect spine. Begin slow and low, and increase height and speed with each rep and set. Begin with three pounds on each ankle, and follow the same progression as above (only after you are proficient without weight and can swing head-height with a straight back). This training bares risk; please seek a qualified teacher of alignment and dynamic stretching to ensure correct (safe) mechanics in the beginning. Essentially, you'll move from the Lightness component into dynamic stretching after a short rest, wearing the same weights.

Alternate the strength and meditation components from session to session. Do **A** *one day,* **B** *the next, and* **C** *the next.* Follow the guidelines for strength and meditation in the Weightlessness Manifesto.

Strength A

- Vector: Pull | Suggested exercise – Weighted pull-ups
  - » Reps per set: 5, 5, 5, 5, 5
- Vector: Push | Suggested exercise – One-arm push-ups (assisted)
  - » Reps per set: 3, 5, 5, 3
- Vector: Push | Suggested exercise – Push-ups (controlled)
  - » Reps: 100 (made up of sets to failure)

Strength B

- Vector: Squat/Pull | Suggested exercise – Deadlift
  - » Reps per set: 5, 5, 3, 5, 5 (set 3 uses your heaviest weight)
- Vector: Press | Suggested exercise – Shoulder press or handstand push-ups
  - » Reps per set: 5, 5, 3, 5, 5 (set 3 uses your heaviest weight)
- Vector: Pull | Suggested exercise – Bicep curls (for men. Women may not want the extra volume / bicep growth)
  - » Reps per set: 10, 8, 5, 5, 20

Strength C

- Vector: Squat | Suggested exercise – Barbell Squat or pistol squat
  - » Reps per set: 8, 6, 5, 5, 5 (set 3 uses your heaviest weight)
- Vector: Twist | Suggested exercise – Cable wood chops
  - » Reps per set: 10, 10, 10 (each side)
- Vector: Twist | Suggested exercise – Cable crunch
  - » Reps per set: 20, 15, 10, 8, 8

Meditation

- Qigong: Fifteen minutes.
- Mindfulness: Five to ten minutes.

Lightness Notes

At this stage you should be very in tune with tension in your body. Maintain static stretching as needed, based on what you've learned through the earlier stages of training. You may not need much if you've activated both front and center splits already. But it's okay to add static stretching after your meditation, or at other times of the day as you have a short break. Regularly putting your body in extended positions is the best way to remold your form. I also highly recommend hanging from a bar as much as possible, and practicing back bends or back extensions if you have appropriate experience and knowledge of safe form.

Don't consider static stretching a protocol; just integrate it whenever and wherever you can. This goes the same for meditation. At this stage you should be very connected to your breath, and practice will wind up spilling over into daily life, as it did for me on the streets of Florence or in the bars of Chiang Mai. When you're walking down the street or sitting in a business meeting and realize that your mind is aware of the *dan tian*, that you're relaxed and you feel energy within while simultaneously being receptive to your environment, then meditation becomes a living practice outside of training. That's when you go from training to being.

Metrics for Levels of Training

You might be wondering which program is appropriate for you if you've got experience. Here is a very brief assessment for the uncertain among you.

Metrics for Level 2:

Can you jog continuously for 10+ minutes?

Can you hold a static squat (90-degree bend in knees, 1.5 shoulder width feet apart) for 1+ minutes?

Can you deadlift 80% of your bodyweight at least once?

Can you do 20+ full-range push-ups in a single set?

Can you hold a plank for two minutes?

Can you touch your toes in a forward bend?

Can you enter a full deep squat (ass to heels)?

If you answer yes to all these questions, you can undertake intermediate/advanced Weightlessness training with promising results. If you answer no to any, spend some (weeks to months) time working through the beginner workout.

Lightness Metrics:

Do you have any joint pain in the lower body? If yes, not ready.

Can you deadlift your bodyweight or heavier for five reps or more?

Can you run a mile in under 6.5 minutes (or a kilometer in under four minutes)?

Can you do five full pull-ups in a single set (for men)?

Can you do 30+ full-range push-ups in a single set?

Can you hold a static deep squat (ass to heels) for 5+ minutes?

Can you do the full splits?

Can you take 10 full, continuous, slow abdominal breaths or fewer in eight minutes or more?

If you answer yes to all these questions, you can safely start Lightness training. If you answer no to any, spend more time at the intermediate level and emphasize your lagging metrics.

Chapter 3

A HUNDRED DAYS LATER

Noah turned to face the alarm with twenty minutes until lift-off. He looked around, alert and very well rested. He saw a slight glow on his ceiling from distant streetlights, felt a subtle draft, and awoke with a genuine appetite. He no longer dreaded the shrill beep that dictated his waking hours. He hadn't needed it in weeks. He hadn't known this kind of energy since childhood, ready to spring from bed first thing in the morning. He remembered birthdays, Christmases when there were things to do, toys to play with, a beautiful day of opportunities ahead. Lying in bed was an insult to the spirit of youth.

Cool water drained the last bit of sleep from his eyes as his hands cupped his face. Noah took note of the ongoing changes in the figure who stared back at him in the mirror. He noticed the clear, passionate, and focused eyes, the chiseled body of a competitive fighter. He felt clean, lean, and strong.

Three months prior, these moments were not without an element of mental turmoil. There was the back and forth, the internal struggle between well-ingrained habits and a vision of becoming something different. He remembered these moments, the time between sitting up and slapping the alarm, throwing on his running gear, and traversing the apartment to the door, beset with a pair of blue ankle weights.

The weights could not be avoided. They demanded respect. In that groggy, anxious, uncomfortable state, it required tremendous effort to fasten the weights and dive into the cool early morning dark for a jog. Today, however, would not feel like *today* without them. Without them, something would be missing and it would gnaw away at him.

Noah plunged into the dark, spontaneously choosing one of several possible directions that would have him back home in less than fifteen minutes. He began with a slow, relaxed stride, warming up to the added weight. He sank his breath deep within his abdomen, conscious of points of tension that needed releasing. With every minute, his pace quickened slightly but his breath did not. His eyes were fixed ten feet ahead, assessing terrain and helping him make adjustments to move from sidewalk to crosswalk to alleyway. The distant swooshing of traffic reminded him he was never alone. Shadows danced before him, a faint ray illuminated the peaks of the city's tallest brick buildings. These quiet, addicting moments became a life unto themselves.

Eighty meters from his building entrance, Noah narrowed his sight, lengthened his stride, and raced with all of his being, the weight around his ankles shredding his core. His recovery time had increased profoundly over the months prior. Twenty seconds was more than enough to feel at ease after his sprint. Before ascending, he did a few rounds of vertical leg swinging, beginning with modest height and speed, and increasing the vigor and height of each successive round. He'd circulated his blood, woken his muscles, and earned his breakfast.

Noah had surrendered a number of useless habits recently. He had become more attuned to his body's nutritional needs, the extent to which he needed rest, and the drain of energy that television and music sometimes were for him. Despite the fact that he no longer required caffeine to start the day, he did love the taste of coffee and found the process of brewing it an ideal time for quiet, focused breathing on his balcony. Breathing deeply with a focus on his lower abdomen, fanning the flame of energy he'd become intimately aware of, Noah released any lingering tension and grounded himself before the long day ahead.

To counteract the acidity of his addiction, Noah began breakfast with a tall glass of cool, freshly squeezed lemon water to alkalize his stomach and allow him to absorb and utilize the proteins in his eggs and bacon more efficiently. He'd given up bread and other grains entirely, realizing that nothing beat fresh fruit and a splash of caffeine for sustained energy throughout the day. He'd also ceased reading the morning paper and checking the markets while eating. He'd found that this simple beginning provided a contentment that couldn't be equaled by the chaos and hustle of daily noise. His only object of attention that morning, a diamond ring seated in a small, antique wooden box, lid ajar, was sparkling.

Noah had spent years in the jungle of finance, in violent struggle to survive and conquer, to claim his place as the king in a major investment bank. There had been treacherous encounters, shady politics, and indeed numerous casualties. But it was war, and no one wins a war without dropping a few bombs. Despite the fact that the jungle had not changed and its inhabitants continued to remember him, fear him, and aspire to be just like him, his own sense of power and pleasure had become increasingly internal. The dialectical struggle for power and the pressures of a chief strategy officer had been relegated to a day job. Pressures were ever-present, but Noah seemed impervious to the stress, unmoved by the gravity of catastrophe after catastrophe.

He approached his work like a ten-year-old at play. Challenges felt like opportunities. Problems were titillation, and he was filled with joy in confronting them. Wins and losses were out of his hands, after all; he could only affect the process. But affect it he did, and more than ever before. His acumen was undeniable, marked by increasingly efficient processes and effective decisions. The lion that built his empire had been contained.

However, to all those around, those who knew how tough and ruthless he could be, he only seemed more powerful, untouchable, passionate. But this wasn't by means of imposing his will. It was with an air of calm that couldn't be pinned. His interactions had become far more acknowledging. He would listen generously and talk less. His gaze would remain fixed without agenda on the eyes of those he was with, giving them a sense of importance. And he spoke with little excess on matters of importance.

Days like that day were common, with common catastrophes, pressures, and anxieties promulgated by everyone and by each project. There was an urgency to maintain. But the lion had moved beyond his compulsion to be constantly on the move, to kill and conquer. In light moments between meetings, urgencies, and problems, he could be seen sitting quietly in his office doing next to nothing, the eye of the hurricane. His boss would have called him on what seemed to be laziness, had his new habits not been accompanied by greater effectiveness. Nothing could be said. That day, a little extra groundedness was needed to keep him from fixating on the little wooden box in his jacket pocket.

His relationship with Sarah was never the smoothest. She was fiery, passionate, intelligent, and ambitious, a spicy blend of Colombian and American descent. She could make an argument feel like the world was coming to an end, and she could make a quiet night of light-hearted conversation over a glass of red feel like nothing else mattered. On those nights, time stopped, life was good. They'd had their struggles, their ons and offs. But if there was a *one*, Sarah was *the* one. Over the last couple of months, their time together had become more cool and calm, fun and easy. This was no doubt in part due to his newfound awareness of his egotistical impulses, sensitivities, and his insistence on being right all the time. He began to let the small things slip. He began to see the woman he first fell in love with all over again, forgetting silly spats and living contradictions.

Noah was no longer an *overtimer*. He put his work in and unless there was a legitimate emergency, he clocked out before seven. Tonight, however, Sarah was caught up and he stayed on a while to keep his mind from fixating on commitments to come. His favorite sushi restaurant, where he'd taken Sarah on their first date five years earlier, was fifteen minutes from the office. He wanted to be early.

He remembered their first date. He was still himself then: confident, conquering another challenge. But her quiet reserve, her thoughtful questions and answers, and her mood and pace declawed him. The nerves drained from him, and he was able to relax with her. She wasn't going to be like the others. He had to work for this one. And for once, he was okay with that.

On the subway, he felt himself being eyed by younger, rougher, possibly tougher city kids. They were rowdy and aggressive, without concern for the space they took up and the nudges and bumps they imposed on the passengers around them. Hoodlums. Occasionally, income disparity caused trouble for Noah. He dressed to the nines and played all the games to project his success. But there were people who were in many ways similar to him, but stood on the outside looking in. Other lions. Younger, untamed, hungry for the kill. He felt their eyes and observed discussions that seemed pointed. Predators always stalk their prey.

Noah exited the subway two blocks from his restaurant, but he didn't exit alone. A subtle over-the-shoulder glance picked up four bodies following in suit. It was uncertain, probably nothing, but Noah was from the streets and knew that readiness trumps wishful thinking any day of the week. He knew this area well. He knew there was an alley fifty meters from his exit. He kept a regular pace and an open ear. As he neared the alley, he quickened slightly, tucked inside, removed his leather belt, and wrapped his left hand and forearm. He could hear footsteps quickening, infantry on the gallop. If there were knives, this shield would give him a fighting chance.

Adrenaline filling his veins, the hair on the back of his neck stood high. His eyes were focused, his gut full of butterflies, his abdomen burning with fire. It was the first time he'd noticed that heat outside of training, that burning within his abdomen. It wasn't just nerves. He'd been fanning that flame in silence every morning and night for months now. He tightened the grip on his briefcase. He could use it as a ballistic to distract the first guy and free up a second to attack the number two, before numbers three and four could find an angle. Still uncertain, probably nothing. But ready.

Noah corrected his posture. He sank his breath into his abdomen. He released the tension from his shoulders and bent his knees slightly, connecting with the ground. He sensed.

One man entered sight. And the second. But they all continued past in testosterone-laden joviality. They were late for a game. They were pumped. They were young. They were brash. They were not his enemies. As quickly as his body had prepared for action, it fell back into a state of calm awareness. Muscles filled to the brim with blood and adrenaline deflated on his empty skeleton. Blood slowly returned to his midsection, stabilizing his organs and digestion, removing his butterflies. He'd need only another few minutes for full release and he'd be ready to enjoy a dinner with Sarah, a dinner that, with all hope, would be their most memorable.

To Noah's surprise, Sarah had arrived early and was already seated with a glass of white wine at the same table of their first date. She seemed a little tense, but managed a smile of sorts. Must have been a tough day, Noah thought. He gave her a kiss and sat facing her, his heart pounding almost as much as it had several minutes prior.

Anticipation.

"I need to tell you something," she said. "I've been thinking."

"Are you okay?" he asked. Her expression was austere, her shoulders folding forward.

"I can't... we need to end it." A glass of white arrived in front of him. She had preordered for him. He was going to need it.

"End... us?" he asked in disbelief. "But I thought... I mean, recently, we've been..."

"We've been good," she said. "That's why this is so hard for me. I can't point to any one thing."

"Yes, so..."

"There's distance, Noah. I feel it. It's growing. I don't understand it. I love you. I do. But you've been changing. And we have been changing. I don't know what to make of any of it, because I see that the ways in which you're changing are not bad, not in any way. If anything, you're a better person. But I feel deeply that you just don't need me anymore."

"You're right, Sarah. Need is the wrong word. There was a time when I needed you. And now I don't. Now I want you. I choose you. I choose to be with you. The difference between these two is incomparable."

She took another sip of wine.

"I know what you mean," she said. "I know what the words you're using mean, at least. But in my head and my heart I don't know what this means for us, for a relationship. I *want* to be needed. I *need* to be needed. I need to complete somebody. What you are now, you don't need me. You are completing the circle, with your weird new habits, your simplicity, and your diet. I'm around you, and our time is great. But I know that if I was not around you, your time might still be great."

Sarah's eyes were tearing up. She recalled his gradual changes, all stemming from his obsession with that goddamn book several months prior. At first, it was just a dramatic shift in his exercise regime. Who can complain about that, though? He was hot. He was fit. These were good things. But it had evolved into a ritual of solitude, where her presence felt more like an obstruction than a partnership. She began to hate the mornings.

He had got rid of many common conveniences, *inessentials* he called them. The first bit made sense. Drawers filled with old electronic devices, wires, and attachments were dumped. Later, his clothes started disappearing. Anything he didn't wear on a regular basis was tossed out. Then, one at a time, the microwave (cancer beams), guest bedroom bed (replaced with a rustic barbell set), the fucking DVD player (which wasn't needed after the television was unplugged) – they had all vanished.

'There's nothing wrong with a minimalist life,' she thought. He was a big hitter at work, so she could see the logic in needing to simplify his externals and clear his mind for such a demanding lifestyle. But the biggest change had come at social events and gatherings. He was clearly avoiding old friends and casual conversations. He opted to talk more to the stand-outs and eccentrics, delving into new domains and expanding his horizons. It was unintentional, but resulted in alienating their inner circle and damaging long-held friendships. After these events, when it came time to analyze conversations, to judge people for their selection of attire, partner, or political stance, Noah was ghostly.

'Who,' she wondered, 'after meeting friends, drinking, and chatting, leaves a party without a wellspring of gossip and slander? Who isn't anxious to knock on everything *other*, to feel better about oneself for being smarter, better dressed, or more cultured and tasteful? More sexy and powerful?' She had a sense of comfort in the order of things, in the relationships she held, in knowing who fit where. She was intimidated by what might lie beyond those neatly defined structures. He was changing at a rate she couldn't keep up with.

Noah was a powerful man, it couldn't be debated. At these times, however, he felt like a man without an identity. His presence felt vacuous. There was no ill will. No slander. No feeling of frustration, anger, or contempt. 'Who was he?' she pondered. 'Even more, who was *she* now in relation to that man, a man who seemed to think nothing and feel nothing about the world we live in?'

She knew this wasn't entirely true. Of course he felt. He seemed more sensitive to subtle tastes, to music, to literature, to her moods and needs. But he was abandoning the things that defined them. He was upsetting the natural order of how things work. So what if he looked at Sarah with greater openness? So what if he spoke with greater sincerity?

'Who can really love someone without needing to possess them?' she considered. 'Why didn't he want to control her, to own her, to inquire after her with jealousy and anger? Can you love someone and not feel jealousy?'

"Noah," she started, "I wanted to do this in person. I owe you that much. We've been through so much."

"Sarah," he interrupted. "It sounds like you're about to break up with me. Let's order something before this goes any further. We can sort everything out. I'm sure of it."

"It's really over, Noah. I'm sorry." Sarah stood up, lowered her eyes, and warmly placed her hand over his on the table.

And then she left him.

Noah was speechless. He couldn't insist further, not in her current state. And he too needed time to process things. He had seen this potentiality, but hadn't believed things had gotten to a point of no return for her. He knew she was uncomfortable with his changes, or more accurately, his rate of change, but he had no expectation of her to be anything other than who she was. The proposal did carry a sense of urgency for him. He had thought the symbol of commitment in his breast pocket could reassure her of his love, could buy them time to settle into the changes. Despite all his shifts, his feelings for her were the one constant.

It didn't feel real. They were characters in a play, acting out their roles. He hadn't received his next lines or the subtext of emotion with which to speak them. He felt her phantom warmth on his hand, and was left with nothing but emptiness. His other hand, unfrozen, cupped his jacket pocket. It was still there. She was gone. No action to follow, no place to go. Noah finished his drink and sank into the moment. Aware of his breath, he sensed.

Returning home, Noah removed his shoes and dropped his briefcase by the door. He'd normally take a few minutes to unwind, get changed, and organize himself before starting his evening routine. But what did routine matter, considering the events of the day? He lifted his pant legs and fastened his blue weights. He removed the ring from his jacket, placed it gently beside the coat rack, and replaced his suit jacket with a forty-pound weight vest. He ventured into the guest bedroom and stood before his leaping box, now a good four feet high. He took a mental survey of tension through his body, relaxed his shoulders, and breathed deeply into his lower abdomen, fanning the flame of energy within.

After a few cycles of breathing, Noah leapt up onto the box and back down, resting briefly between each effort until he began to fatigue. He swung his legs aggressively in front of him, stretching his hamstrings after a day with a respectable amount of sitting. He crushed his deadlift sets, which were at 70% of max as scheduled. He dropped to the hard wood panels to perform a hundred push-ups, spaced out over a few sets, with forty extra pounds on his torso. A few minutes of quiet breathing on his balcony marked the end of his effort for the day.

Noticing slight pangs of hunger, but with no real appetite to speak of, Noah poured himself a glass of red, put on Van Morrison's 'Into the Mystic,' and sat, gazing out at the city skyline. The song was on repeat. On repeat. On repeat. The sparkling panorama danced generously before him. Every note, every cry a new moment, a new beat, lights blinking at him. Ever repeating, ever anew. Pains and beauties defining us, fixing us. But never repeating, every moment new. Van cried, "Let your soul and spirit fly... into the mystic." Lights dazzled in orchestral levity. The deep red dried, sweetened, and soothed.

An eternal moment. How sweet it tasted.

Epilogue

The Missing Threads

THE BUSINESSMAN AND THE MARTIAL ARTIST

In a last-ditch effort to integrate the disparate strands of Weightlessness into a single unified whole, a businessman and a martial artist convene in a local bar tucked neatly away on Chengdu's ancient Wide and Narrow Alley. The martial artist, for fear of leaving his faithful readers with what may seem a mere (captivating) autobiography or (enlightening) travel narrative, has thrown structure to the wind and resolved to expose in brash discourse the invisible strings that bind his vision, to turn this weightless odyssey into a working model of personal development and, dare he say, a coherent framework for the future of mind-body fitness.

After a first glance at the rough draft of this book, in all its unchecked gore and profanity, and in which he plays a key role, the businessman has a few lingering questions. No stone is left unturned as the martial artist and the businessman delve – deeply, mind you – into the four pillars of Weightlessness. They discuss the antifragile underpinnings of personal growth, the finality of death, the brilliance of life, and the necessary struggles required to become weightless in mind and body.

The ambience is as absurd as the mission at hand: Chinese pop blaring from the speakers, beach sand on the ground both indoors and out, but no beach to speak of within a thousand miles. A cold, consistent drizzle keeps them under an outdoor canopy where they enjoy pints of imported microbrews. Funny little waitresses do funny dances every thirty minutes, like toddlers doing their first choreographed Teletubbies follow-along. But they are all nice enough and service isn't terrible.

August 8th 2013: 9:42 pm

MICHAEL: Let's talk about weightless Tom. When did the notion of Weightlessness first occur to you?

236

ME: I think from a young age I've always been extremely open-minded, if not naïvely optimistic, about human potential. I've always been quite open-minded to Eastern mysticism and the abilities of wise martial arts sages. From a young age, I've believed that the abilities of the human mind and body are far from being actualized. That ridiculous cartoon tale of what in the Shaolin tradition is termed *qing gong*, lightness training, was what gave me a coherent vision for the concept of Weightlessness training. It contained one small sentence within a training anecdote that tied together all of the fractured parts of my ten to fifteen years of training at the time. It was the pivotal shift in my understanding. It is what showed me that we can activate our potentials methodically, not merely with the hope that something great will happen.

MICHAEL: That was a cartoon, a comic book?

ME: I'm sure the author was trying to relay something more content-based, but I'm certain that for the majority of readers it would seem like complete bullshit, to be frank. The majority of the book contained cartoon sketches, one large sketch per page, with short descriptions of how to actualize and perform that particular feat. It included scaling walls, running on water, lifting extreme weight, or, as I highlight in the manifesto, leaping and speed running.

Some of these traits were laughably mystical. However, I could see and feel that a few of them might not be so much of a stretch based on my understanding of martial arts and fitness. I felt this passage contained the missing pieces.

MICHAEL: It was about monks doing crazy shit. By jumping...

ME: Jumping ten feet in the air. Sprinting ten miles without fatigue. Yeah.

MICHAEL: How old were you when you read that book?

ME: I wish I could say I was eight, but I was actually twenty-two when it blew my mind. [Both laugh.]

MICHAEL: Of those extraordinary skills, it seems you've selected only two physical practices, leaping and speed running skills, to include within your manifesto and training regime. Why is that?

ME: Because they are exceedingly practical movement skills. Either one of them can lay the foundation for total lower body strength, health, and power, as well as being vehicles for methodically actualizing one's higher potentials. Dogs run and bite. Cats leap and climb. Simply put, humans squat, run, and leap. These are innate skills dictated by our unique biomechanics.

When trained methodically, with progressive resistance on the ankles and possibly torso, each of them can teach you how to release physical tension, acquire extreme coordination and physical awareness, and develop the explosive, fast-twitch muscle fiber required for extreme speed and sensations of weightlessness. This doesn't mean there are not many other theoretical applications, like weighting a dancer's legs or a boxer's fists and applying the same principles. It just means these are universal human movements that should be a launch point for integration.

Likewise, both of these skills are gross and compound, meaning the entire body is working together to produce power. They result in strength and speed that is transferable to other, unrelated movements. It's similar to why football players squat to help them sprint from the line, and boxers bench press to improve the muscular strength, power, and integrity of connective tissues required for all types of punches. We're talking about the source of all power, not the specific manifestations or implementations of it. Therefore, at least one of these two skills must be selected in order to learn the essence of lightness, as well as to become a conduit for long-term weightlessness.

MICHAEL: Let's look closer at some of your pillars. Do people need flexibility?

ME: Do people need flexibility? Well, certainly the majority of people out there survive with very little flexibility. Let me think of a good analogy.

MICHAEL: Let me help you along. On one end of the spectrum, my grandmother before she died, as some people do as they age, had an accident and wound up in a wheelchair. It compromised her walking. Once she was in the wheelchair, she eventually had the problem that she couldn't stand up, because...

ME: Her hamstrings were too tight.

MICHAEL: Exactly, her hamstrings were too short. Beyond the ability to stand up and walk, do people need flexibility?

ME: Do they need it on a survival basis? I mean, Weightlessness is not a platform for becoming fit only. It's designed for people who care about *flourishing*. You know, you might have a plant or a flower in your home, you might forget to water it for a few days, and it will start to wither. It doesn't die, it just sits there on the windowsill and turns a bit brown and gray. It starts to curl up a bit, but it's not dead. It just survives and maintains and... that's most of us.

The difference between that and a flower that's flourishing, alive, and vibrant, colored and blooming, is huge. I mean, people buy flowers for that reason. Nobody buys a dead wilted piece of shit on a windowsill.

MICHAEL: Fuck you, Granny. [Laughing.]

ME: Sorry Grandma, get your shit together. No, that's horrible. [Both laugh.]

ME: Let the record show Michael is laughing. He started laughing before I started laughing.

[Also, let the record also show that Michael was generous enough to allow the transcription of our dark humor on the condition that I make very clear that he deeply loves his grandmother, and I mine.]

The point is, I'm not talking about your grandma, I'm talking about us, you know, people. The royal grandma. We need to choose in life. Is the point of life just getting through? Is it checking off the boxes and saying, okay, I went to college, I got married, I got my two-car garage and my two-point-five kids, a decent job, and what do they call it... money in the bank.

MICHAEL: Savings?

ME: Right. Is that it? Or is there something more? I have in my mind that the human race has a higher calling.

MICHAEL: Hitler.

ME: Oops. We all waste time, and I think to live a life where we simply maintain the status quo and choose to get by in comfort without challenging, testing, and growing, that for me is the life of a wilting flower. There's something beautiful about a person who is willing to accept a little bit of discomfort and pain to become a fully flourishing human being. One who tries to actualize their potential, to become creative, to be loving, passionate, and compassionate. There's no comparing these two types of people.

The one you could spend an incredible evening with, telling you great life stories and providing beautiful insights. The other one you're going to be bored to death with and need a bottle of whiskey just to make it through an hour. But I think I'm on a tangent.

MICHAEL: I can sympathize with that. It's a great answer to a different question, perhaps: "What is Weightlessness?" A mediocre versus an awesome life? You're not just getting by and surviving.

ME: Got very side-tracked. Where were we?

MICHAEL: Do people need flexibility?

ME: To bring it all together, if you're going to look at the two types of people, you've got your wilting flower and you've got your bright, vibrant, blooming flower. Flexibility is important if you want to be a blooming flower or a flourishing human being. On a very basic level, I deal with a lot of people who have a great deal of tension throughout the back and the hamstrings due to sitting all the time. They haven't been active enough over the years, and are very inflexible. I haven't read much about this, but I see very clear patterns between those who have tight hamstrings and those who have lower back and upper trapezius problems.

I believe that relatively flexible hamstrings will add years to your life. If not actual, tangible years, they will at least increase one's quality of life for many years. The differences I see between people who have hamstring flexibility in terms of their gait, strength, posture, and neck and back health, there's no comparing them. I've worked with a wide variety of clients that I get to see operate in these realms. I've helped rehab many clients with back problems by extending their hamstrings. There's a direct correlation. I think one's quality of life improves tremendously by improving hamstring flexibility, for example.

If we're talking about maximizing potential, I think that having dynamic flexibility, and what we might call ballistic flexibility in a full range of movement, opens the door to an infinite potential of physical expression. It allows you to move spontaneously and creatively with extreme power and precision, without injury. Even though it needs to be trained and conditioned somewhat, your body intuitively knows where it's going to break down. That's why most people don't spontaneously start sprinting or jump too much after they're teenagers. They just sit around and don't do anything.

But if you watch kids, they are naturally flexible. They haven't generated enough muscle mass and created enough tension in their legs to where they're in danger of pulling and tearing things. They still have tendons, ligaments, and cartilage that could be jeopardized, but because they're so fluid and relaxed in their muscles, you rarely see kids get injured from all the crazy falls and jumps that they do. And they do some crazy things. If they will it, their bodies generally perform it.

It's this accumulation of psychological and physical tension over the years that eliminates the body's ability to move in a wide, full range of movement with freedom and power. And do we need it? No, you'll survive without it. But I would argue there's a great intrinsic value in being able to have the physical freedom of a two-year-old, to be able to jump and play and run and have fun. Even if you're a grandparent, it's great to play with the grandkids in the same way, to kick the ball around, to sprint with them through a field. These are the good parts of life, not sitting in a chair unable to move because you're too heavy or too tired. It's why dynamic flexibility is a pillar of Weightlessness. Even if it is practiced independently of the other pillars, I think it adds quality years to your life.

MICHAEL: So where are you at today with your view of fitness and personal development?

ME: Where am I at today? I realized a major transformation in my own understanding of the world of fitness honed my methodology of training others (and myself) to a single concept, *stress*. When I'm asked about why people should train with me, or what my particular method of rapid body transformation is based on, I tell them that the only factor determining transformation is stress. I tell them that I have a method for quantifying stress and that it allows me to assess and prescribe the exact workouts that will lead people to a specific end.

Fitness is something that damages the body. I view the real process of fitness as an adaptive response to pain and to stress. I think that when fitness is viewed in this light it takes a very different tone. A lot of people go to the gym to work out and burn calories. They go to get big and buff. As soon as you view fitness training as something that temporarily damages the body, then you are armed with powerful information that can lead to extreme transformation. Our bodies are extremely resilient and adaptable, and the true story of fitness is not what happens in the gym. It's what happens in the twenty-four to forty-eight hours after beating the hell out of yourself in the gym.

I've known a lot of trainers and coaches, and studied a lot of methods. I believe there are few people that believe as deeply as I do in this process of deconstruction and consequent adaptation, or what we might call the stress-adaptation cycle.

MICHAEL: Cool. Did you ever purposefully have sex without ejaculation?

ME: Speaking of stress. I have, yes.

MICHAEL: Purposefully?

ME: What? You think I'm misfiring all the time? Yeah, I did.

MICHAEL: Did you ever have an orgasm without ejaculation?

ME: Uh... no.

MICHAEL: But this is one of the old methods of qi development?

ME: Some people talk about the possibility of climax without ejaculation. Someone even coined the term reverse ejaculation, which is, well, it just makes my stomach churn. Not really sure what that's about. More historically, the approach is to get within seconds of climax and then to hold that energetic state so that you can harness the energy for greater qi storages or spontaneous enlightenment.

MICHAEL: Will that make you weightless or frustrated?

ME: I'm of the frustration camp, I'd have to say. I think that if you're going to bust a nut, don't play games. Do the job. Make everybody happy.

MICHAEL: Okay, that one was my tangent. Let's come back. Why fast-twitch muscle fiber?

ME: Fast-twitch muscle fiber. On a basic level, it's the muscle fiber of strength, and is improved through high-tension, high-intensity resistance training. Slow-twitch muscle fiber is the fiber of fine motor skills and endurance activities: picking up a glass of beer, walking, or even jogging sometimes. Fast-twitch muscle fiber is called into play any time you are required to move quickly, or if you're fighting against considerable resistance that slow-twitch fiber is not capable of accommodating.

Where this becomes meaningful is that our bodies wear out. When the body does things consistently all the time, connective tissues wear out because they're overused or unsupported. If you're active and don't have sufficient fast-twitch muscle fibers – or, we could simply say, enough strength – there's a great chance that you'll wear your joints out, stressing ligaments and cartilage to a great degree. This is why you commonly find copious joint problems among duration runners, and considerably less so among sprinters. Once an activity is sustained past the point of muscular fatigue, joints cannot be stabilized or protected.

Fast-twitch muscle is crucial for powerful movement, general strength, and body composition. For me, the biggest factor is that it prevents injury, as it is preeminently responsible for securing and stabilizing joints and protecting connective tissues. This is what holds your body together. Another pillar of Weightlessness, high-tension resistance training, justified. Fast-twitch fiber is the foodstuff of explosive movement and lightness training. The more of it you have relative to your bodyweight, the lighter you perceive yourself to be and the faster you move. On both sides, building and maintaining fast-twitch muscle fiber is the key to remaining injury-free, staying young and healthy forever, and it is also your path toward weightlessness.

MICHAEL: I'm on my fourth liter of beer. Last few questions for tonight. First, some people are advocates of bodyweight training, and others favor gym training, or heavy load resistance training. What's your view?

ME: I think the pinnacle of resistance training is bodyweight training, but I also think that bodyweight training is uniquely challenging and requires a great deal of focus that you can bypass if you're using equipment. I've seen Shaolin monks do two-finger push-ups on one hand alone with strict military form, and it was unfathomable. I never believed it was possible before I saw it. Everybody has seen the videos of Bruce Lee doing his three-finger push-ups. His push-ups were crap. His arm was way out in front of his shoulder, body twisted, feet spread apart. When I say that this monk had strict military form, his feet were less than a foot apart, his arm was to the side of his chest, and his other arm was tucked behind his back. It was pristine.

MICHAEL: You saw this in person?

ME: I saw this in person and he was busting these out as if both hands were pushing and he was on his knees. They were unbelievably effortless. To get to a level like this, there is no comparison. This is the type of man, when you talk about the old-school martial arts skills like pressure point fighting, this is a man who can drive his fingers through your sternum. We're not just talking about strength or lifting weights, this is a man of extreme physical power. He's able to support his bodyweight on his index and middle fingers stuck together.

The challenge though, to put things in perspective, is that if you can do twenty to thirty push-ups, the resistance isn't significant enough for you to use it exclusively as a strength-building tool. If you're not strong or coordinated enough to do a good one-armed push-up with strict form, you should be using equipment to bridge the gap. If you get to a point where you can graduate up to a one-arm push-up, by all means you should be training this skill. It's a valuable skill that not only requires considerable upper body strength, but it forces all muscles in the body to contract in order to stabilize the activity and counterbalance the torque. You want great abs? Do one-armed push-ups.

It's even better because you're not only becoming very strong, you're also using your body as it is built. You're recruiting stabilizing muscles to support the primary effort. You're simply practicing moving your body through space with power.

This is one of the fundamental aspects of performance. When you sit in a machine or lie on a bench pushing a bar, these activities are not related directly to physical performance. The strength transfers, the specific movements do not. Moving your own bodyweight in a variety of ways transfers to the application of strength and physical performance in the real world. This is fitness.

MICHAEL: You talk about value and worth in the second chapter of Book 1, *The Phoenix*. How does the inherent worth or value of people relate to Weightlessness?

ME: I think that to practice any mind-body art, including Weightlessness, you need to have some perception of human dignity. You need to respect humanity as incredibly complex and capable. Weightlessness is an acknowledgment of our innate value and worth.

MICHAEL: Can you think of anybody you know that would have a greater sense of self-worth if they embraced Weightlessness?

ME: I wouldn't propose Weightlessness as a viable option for mind-body training if I didn't believe it can improve the life of anybody who practices it. The thing is, I don't see it as an external thing. I see the pillars of Weightlessness as fundamental to our biology and the make-up of our minds. I believe that they are the most fundamental and essential tools for personal development. If someone doesn't feel strength training or meditation is for him or her, it's as confusing to me as if they felt that food isn't for them. We don't exactly get to ignore that and still have a fair probability of health and longevity. I've reduced these principles to the bare minimum of what I think is necessary to actualize mind-body freedoms.

MICHAEL: I hate it when people talk about spirit, and half the time the term *mind* is bullshit. Physical is very real. I enjoy the division between metaphysical and physical. These are two clear domains for me, and I am a very cynical asshole. In these two realms, and I think you do this extremely well in your book, you cover both. Maybe not explicitly in terms of what goes where. But this is one of the tremendous things in your book – you embrace both. Many attributes are exclusive to the physical domain, with many hilarious stories about how Weightlessness relates to the physical domain. Especially for those people who don't think they need to embrace spiritual concepts, what is the most important metaphysical concept to consider in your discussion of Weightlessness?

ME: Good question. I'll reduce it to two values: *peace* and *power*. The first metaphysical benefit – that is, the first tangible psychological benefit of the meditative practices – is having a mind that is calm, still, confident, independent, creative, and non-attached. All of these things allow an individual to experience reality as an immediate relationship with the present. This is difficult to justify conceptually, or to speak about with language, which is the reason I use narrative in Book 4.

However, those who have practiced meditation and have been able to bypass the ego (the judgmental persona that we spend most of our time operating in) would probably argue that it's intrinsically valuable, that it doesn't requires much justification. I think they would ask: Why don't we spend all our time in this state?

There's an experience of peace and contentment that occurs in this state, during which, in spite of all things, everything feels right in the world. You don't wish for more, you don't wish for less. You simply *are*, and can see the beauty before you. I think that this state of being is enriching and useful for all people. It allows in everybody in all walks of life; in a lot of ways it democratizes spirituality. It gives an even playing field to even the poorest people on Earth. Everybody can appreciate the world before him or her in some way.

On the other hand, there is the spiritual benefit of power. I believe there are meditative components of power. But power is something that also stems from your physical transformation, or as I put it, the rebirth of the phoenix. Elements of energy work (qigong) and some of the transcendental elements of actual physical training lead to a psychology and confidence of a warrior. They create a person who is indomitable, someone who has the strength and confidence to carry out their will.

I can't think of any reason why we all shouldn't carry that kind of confidence and strength with us. I think people should live boldly and stand behind their ideas. They should think freely and creatively and come to their own conclusions. Having a body that can carry out our will and having a mind that cannot be manipulated are powerful attributes relevant to every walk of life. The combination of these two – peace and power – lays the foundation for a complete human being. I'm leaving aside for now the discussion of internal energy development and what some consider more esoteric metaphysical experiences.

MICHAEL: Let's speak briefly about this concept, as Nasim Taleb defines the term, *antifragility*. Antifragility is the idea that there are some things that actually benefit and become stronger when stressed. Or more accurately, they gain from disorder. Fragile things break, like a porcelain cup. Those things in nature that are robust simply ignore stress, like a sponge or a book when dropped on the ground. However, there are some things which neither break nor ignore stress, but which become stronger, up to a point. Are there any parallels with antifragility and your philosophy of Weightlessness?

ME: Weightlessness presupposes this concept and uses it as a working theory of personal development. You might accurately say that Weightlessness is antifragility applied to the mind-body domain. The way in which Weightlessness implements it is to make sure you're constantly exposing your body to small stresses (and the occasional larger one), so that over the long term you become more powerful than you can imagine.

More explicitly, our bodies don't simply compensate for stress. They *overcompensate* for stress. When we stress our musculoskeletal and nervous systems, our bodies don't simply build enough muscle and coordination to handle the stress that broke us down. We respond and then some. We build stronger connective tissue so that we can handle more weight than we previously could have handled.

In that sense, we're not just adapting to that stress, we're becoming much stronger in spite of it. That's antifragility. In the same way, by breaking bones through methodical hand conditioning, you don't simply repair bone so you can do the same thing. Your bones become thicker, denser, and stronger, so you become increasingly resilient. I say *resilient*, but the truth is your body is overcompensating for those stresses and preparing for even greater ones.

MICHAEL: Right, and you also talk about life quality. I think it's a terrible term but I don't know what to use otherwise. So let's take options trading, for example. You dabbled in coffee futures trading. As a coffee bean trader, it is not enough to have some variance around the medium, or around the expected value. You need to have tremendous potential upside to be able to make any sense of the investment or speculation you're dabbling in.

ME: Right.

MICHAEL: I think for investors and business people, this is what they obsess about. To me this is a central theme in Weightlessness. If Weightlessness were just about having a slightly better outlook on things by doing these practices, it wouldn't be worth it. It would lack the leverage that sophisticated individuals, businessmen, and investors strive for in every endeavor in life. But I can see a clear path in terms of how it brings with it not just a bit of overcompensation, but allows tremendous upside. How do you look at that?

ME: I believe what you're referring to is nonlinear payback, where the whole is greater than the sum of the parts. I do believe that this occurs when one embodies the four pillars of Weightlessness. We're not talking about one plus one plus one equals three. The potential payback for time and energy input is considerably higher. The gains are disproportionately high compared to the sum of specific efforts. We wind up with a magic combination of parts that empower the whole person to make decisions and face problems with a loaded gun, so to speak.

I remember my father telling me when I was young that not every member of the Beatles was a great musician, but when they came together they became a superband, something much more than the composite parts. He may have been jealous and not wanted to give each one enough credit. I think he had a thing against Ringo. But it's fair to say that the Beatles were a magical band, and I think it's fair to say that the pillars of Weightlessness have a similarly profound union. Where they're practiced independently, each provides considerable health and strength benefits, but when they're developed together there's a nonlinear payback in that your quality of life, performance, and mental capabilities extend well beyond the sum of the composite parts.

MICHAEL: Can you give any concrete examples?

ME: More concrete than the Beatles? All right, if we take high-speed resistance training, or ankle weight training in conjunction with the meditative practices of mindfulness and qigong (leaving aside for now the strength training and flexibility components), we wind up not just with enhanced speed, but what feels like, in some cases, super speed marked by effortless ease. One's ability to release physical tension, an outcome of meditation practice, in conjunction with refined neuromuscular coordination that stems from ankle weight training, results in enduring states of effortless super speed and stamina. Ankle weight training without relaxation, focus, and breath control may result in a short-term phenomenon of improved speed. But in conjunction with meditation or qigong, it leads to an altogether different state of physical awareness and sensitivity and produces a lasting, extreme speed.

That's in the physical performance domain. In other domains, these pillars coalesce in a different type of clarity and presence. I refer to integration throughout the book. It's an impossible term to define clearly because it's a state that precedes abstraction or conceptual reduction. You can't merely discuss it as the sum of parts, even though we can cultivate it through practice. But structure and strength in the body, a lack of physical tension, a deep and regulated breath, a clear and focused mind – these reflect the presence of the Steppenwolf, a powerful and free creature that chooses to play the social game. It's a powerful presence that is not merely internally felt, but is felt by those nearby. You are able to think and act from a stable center, and not react from a place of insecurity or fear.

MICHAEL: Are there any psychological upsides to this?

ME: In the physical performance domain, there's an odd thing that occurs when you become faster. One of the reasons that I emphasize speed in Weightlessness is because when you become faster, things begins to appear in slower motion. It's like the theory of relativity. The feeling of slowed time is just a byproduct of moving faster. Intuiting and perceiving things faster, your mind operates at a faster pace, with the odd consequence that it buys you more time. And as resistances are streamlined in the body through coordination, attachments are reduced in the mind.

When I used to fight, I had been practicing meditation, qigong, and ankle weight training over the course of about one year when I noticed my martial arts skills had transcended previous levels by a considerable margin. On many occasions, I had the sensation that I could read the minds of my opponents. I don't know if my intuitive mind was much more acute or whether I perceived very subtle movements early, the minutiae that are the origins of physical movement. Moving faster requires (and generates) a faster processor.

Imagine being in a fight and being able to slow down the movements of your opponent by 50 percent while you're still operating at full speed. That's essentially what Weightlessness does. Only you operate at 150 to 200 percent while everyone else is average. They appear slow. Imagine the psychology of a man who lives in that state but who can also turn it off and on at will.

In the domain of life, this may resemble the eye of a hurricane. Life is, or at least can be, chaos. Everyone is caught up in the news of the day, in personal fears and ambitions. The man or woman who isn't attached to outcome (this doesn't mean you don't strive for certain results; it means your self worth isn't defined by success or failure) can be patient and discerning. Just as the stronger, faster fighter can wait for the right opportunity to strike, so too can the weightless person play in highly volatile, high-pressure work environments with a clear, unburdened mind. With confidence in a body and mind that adapt, and the knowledge that pain and struggle are growth triggers, the integrated person thrives in environments that others fear.

MICHAEL: If I were the CEO of Google, why should I buy your book?

ME: Um... it's a good book, man. [Both laugh.] I don't know.

MICHAEL: Well, this is a pretty serious one.

ME: Do you know the answer already? Because I kind of feel like... is it because you're overweight?

MICHAEL: Well he's the one who needs it the most.

ME: Ah, of course. Yes. I concur. Good save.

MICHAEL: This brings us to something else. I'm from the business world. Elite career people, very strong-minded vocational people, why should they embrace Weightlessness? I mean, on a very egoistical level, if I was a CEO of a big corporation or a director climbing to the top, why would I want to do this?

ME: Great question. I think there are a few strong reasons. One is grit. Weightlessness is a safe way to cultivate resilience and adaptability without the devastating exposure that comes with business risks. It's a microcosm for the world at large, a laboratory for growth that transfers to all other domains. I'm speaking here from personal experience, because I work with people on that level on a regular basis.

On a superficial level, Weightlessness is an extremely efficient mind-body training methodology. I think it exceeds all of the other options out there in terms of efficiency and in terms of results for time spent, if you can look at it in that way. On a deeper level, it's a way of preparing for and managing uncertainty in life.

I think that executives and businessman are in a unique position to be able to understand and appreciate the efficiency of the training, while at the same time being in a unique position to benefit tremendously from precise inputs in terms of physical conditioning, mental training, and stress management. Of all the people I train, those most curious about and interested in meditation are those who have extremely demanding lifestyles and jobs. They're the ones who have a hard time balancing the stresses of work with something that could be called a good quality of life. They wind up living for their work and sacrificing a great deal of themselves for their jobs. They have a hard time tasting the strawberry while being threatened by tigers.

Likewise, it's hard for them to maintain a state of physical health and fitness, because they believe it takes a lot more time than it actually does. I believe, given the components of Weightlessness training, that only three or four short sessions per week can provide unparalleled results for the time spent. To repeat, I would argue that it's the most efficient and effective program for physical health and fitness, as well as mental balance, peace, and confidence. This isn't merely a fitness discussion; it's a life discussion. I also think, on a principle level, that the spirit of Weightlessness speaks loudly to people in high-stress, volatile occupations because it provides unique, robust solutions for navigating uncertainties in life.

Do you feel like the principles of Weightlessness have helped you? I mean, you're in that world. You're a CEO yourself.

MICHAEL: Well, let me talk about some specifics. Business is full of randomness, noise, and clutter. A nonjudgmental view on many things is tremendously useful for negotiating, for cutting a better deal, and for having greater clarity in your head. It's also great for avoiding ulcers and being able to sleep at night. Just the basic fact of having a body that can perform (let's forget about health for a minute), that you can feel comfortable in, is an asset for anyone trying to make a million. Stimulants and poison can only get you so far. You can only get so far with coffee. You can only get so far with alcohol or whatever it might be.

In the long haul, there's nothing to pull you through but your own sense of well-being and weightlessness, if you will. The long haul is what matters, at least for entrepreneurs. For executives who want to go to the top, I think it's very similar. For executives who just float around and mooch off their companies, perhaps not. But if you want to survive as an entrepreneur, every aspect of Weightlessness matters. In particular, you need a body that's very healthy and a mind that is unfettered, as you say. Shit hits you every day when you're trying to do business. If you panic, you're fucked. There's not much to do about it; volatility is going to hit you every day. You're an entrepreneur as well, you know. This shit can kill you. You can get depressed, anything can happen.

I think we are understating how this is something high-powered, high-charged CEOs and career people could use. Do you have some people you work with who fit the bill?

ME: Sure. You would be a concrete example. You know, a lot of people practice the strength training components of Weightlessness in other arenas like CrossFit, calisthenics, or general resistance training, with a focus on lean body mass and improving their strength-to-weight ratio. Dynamic flexibility and speed training are implemented less frequently in more specialized domains like martial arts and dance, and I therefore tend to reserve them for my martial arts students or advanced Weightlessness trainees (studying Lightness training).

I've certainly worked with many businessmen in terms of meditative techniques. It's not uncommon among people who have high-stress lives. I've worked with people on the fringe or people recovering from extreme burnout who needed extensive rehabilitation. The problem is they just can't re-acclimate to a work environment and maintain. They've been overrun; they've lived for years on caffeine and not enough sleep. They've fucked up their adrenals and their hormones are out of balance.

Without maintaining a steady mental focus and state of calm, without techniques for breathing and tools for emotional control, they regress very quickly. I find those are the two most commonly valued components, strength training as it relates to lean body mass and energy maintenance, and meditation for stress and burnout. But again, custom prescriptions pale in comparison to integrated training. It's very hard to self-correct by learning or developing the skills needed after an event or systemic breakdown. It's like trying to rebuild a ship at sea. Black swans and mental or physical fallout can only be pre-empted by well-rounded training. Correction after the fact is extremely difficult.

MICHAEL: So, let's tear a new one for meditation. Horrible, right? I mean, *meditation* as a term.

ME: Yes. One-word answer. I think on a lot of levels it's applied to so many different things that it retains very little practical meaning. However, even I use the term to envelop the two types of mental practices within Weightlessness training: mindfulness and qigong (or more accurately: awareness and concentration respectively). But these are diametrically opposed approaches to meditation, at least in the early stages of training.

One may argue, and I may tend to agree, that after extensive practice, these two forms of meditation lead to a similar end. They are two paths leading to the same mountain peak. But the initial practice of each is radically different. Where it becomes difficult is when people have a very rigid definition of meditation that encompasses the physical postures, practices, and states of mind that are quite exaggerated, and have nothing to do with the actual experience of a meditative mind.

A lot of people have an image of a monk sitting in solitude in temple, sitting in the lotus posture and maintaining that for extended periods of time. Still, I have people tell me they meditated for an hour. I've been meditating for over two decades, and an hour sounds insanely long to me. I'm quite happy if I can maintain focus for over ten minutes, which I consider an elite level of concentration.

I think people need to come back down to earth and treat meditation like it is something internal to us. It's something we do naturally as very young children. Infants are constantly meditating. They're constantly seeing, feeling, touching, and asking questions. They're curious and alert. All of the things that meditation tries to reactivate, we do naturally as children.

We are connected as children because we don't have names for things or fixed habits and beliefs. We don't have egocentric judgments and well-formulated interpretations of our environment. As we age, we view this pre-intellectual state as something external to us, if not a mindless state of experience, and that's a big problem.

Meditation is innate and intimately a part of us. Even without five minutes of formal practice, it is intimately a part of us. It refers to a qualitatively rich state of experience. We might do it naturally when overwhelmed by an emotional movie, while making love, or when tasting a new food in a foreign country. There are many situations that make it easier for us to experience the present with an acute sense of awareness, curiosity, and passion. But all of them, in that moment, exceed our model of the things itself, thereby liberating us from egocentric experience.

The practice of meditation itself should not be more than this. It shouldn't be inflated to a point where you're practicing a 'thing' external to yourself or trying to access something altogether 'other'. But that's commonly how it's perceived.

MICHAEL: Do you ever use meditative techniques when you're not sitting in a room quietly?

ME: For sure. And I know that you do as well. The scope of meditation, anything you do in life falls into the domain of meditation. It isn't distinct from you. A meditative mind is one that is aware, sensitive, passionate, nonjudgmental, and yet highly focused. The narratives in Book 3 are meant to demonstrate the spontaneity and originality of meditative moments. They're meant to demonstrate its relevance. You tend to find this kind of mind in the meditative arts that are monastic and in holistic lifestyles, albeit after long periods of training and cultivation. Sometimes you find it in elite athletes, fighters, or soldiers, because they need to be very aware within the moment.

Certainly I've used meditative techniques when I've been walking down the street, watching a movie, fighting, or eating dinner. It's the degree to which you are connected to reality in front of you. The degree to which you experience the moment, relinquish your doubts, fears, judgments, and biases, and view the present innocently and with full awareness, is the degree to which you are meditating. It's perhaps better approached as a qualitative spectrum rather than a distinct concrete state of being. It's not as simple as a light switch that you turn on and off, more like those that have gradations of brightness.

MICHAEL: The concept of a nonjudgmental consciousness, well... I think it's a beautiful thought. But how do you practice it? Even when we talk about other people, family and friends, are you nonjudgmental toward them when you see them hurting themselves?

ME: Not at all. I'm by no means a saint. That's why I'm as much in need of Weightlessness as anybody else. They say necessity is the mother of all invention. There's no doubt I've needed and still need Weightlessness to unburden myself of things that weigh me down. This is ongoing. But I've experienced the power of nonjudgmental awareness, and I've experienced friends, relatives, and loved ones with that sense of non-attachment and nonjudgment. It can turn almost any experience into something extremely profound. Nonjudgment doesn't need to be another moralistic, dominating framework. Consider it a powerful tool with which to reframe your current experience.

If a car is careening toward you and you're standing in the middle of the street, I think that the meditative mind is the one that can think and operate at the speed of light. It's not an all-accepting moronic state of being or that of a deer caught in headlights. I would argue that if you recognized a car careening toward you, it's quite likely that your reaction would call on faculties you were probably not aware of. People in near-death experiences talk about time slowing down and noticing every detail. It's the samurai warrior who can see the blade of grass in the distance, where all things come into focus. Without attachment there's a reduction of noise, and more time and energy to act and react with immediate insight.

Again, nonjudgment doesn't mean there is not action, that you are immobilized, or that you are not intelligent. It simply means that you act from a state that is not preconditioned. We all have a wealth of life and experience that weigh into any decision. They even weigh into the decision to sit down and not make decisions. Internal conflicts arise when we hold tightly, usually with a modicum of emotion, to outdated interpretations and ideas at the expense of new experiences and insights.

In many cases, like that in the Snooker Hookers story, I entered a new experience with an old lens, and it kept me from seeing what was directly in front of me until I shifted. When the rain freed me from the fear of discomfort, I was able to embrace the streets of Florence from a fresh and unfiltered vantage point.

I would also argue there is an important place for judgment in life. So my advocacy of direct experience is in no way a rebuttal of rational thought. We need both. Many people in meditative traditions talk about one overarching value, whether it is love or compassion or nonviolence. But you and I have talked about the importance of survival in life and in business, and I think there are certain times where you need to take care of survival before you can focus on quality. These rely not only on different cognitive states, but on different regions of the brain as well.

There is no progress in the tangible matters of the world without the ability to form hierarchies of thought, moral or social, and filter or judge the relevancy and benefit of information and events. Our prefrontal cortexes evolved out of necessity to solve the forecasting problem – how we go from personal experience or information to predictive modeling, strategizing, and planning – even in very rudimentary things. We cannot deny ourselves the advantages of rational thought.

This is a dichotomy that you initially raised in one of our evening conversations when we were dicing. I couldn't agree more with it. If there are ways of living in a mindful state all of the time, I personally don't have enough life experience or wisdom to speak intelligently about them. I think there is a place for ego-driven judgment in terms of survival. When you go to a convenience store and buy toothpaste, you try not to buy the stuff that makes your hair fall out. When looking for a partner in life, it's good to filter out the self-destructive masochists. But regardless of the extent to which someone can live in a state of mindfulness, the benefits of mindfulness practice, even when adopted as a regular practice in non-attachment, are extremely enriching.

MICHAEL: You talk about breathing in the book. Breathing is very fundamental, but what does it mean to you? If you strip away mindfulness and qigong and so on, what's it to you?

ME: Good question. If we strip it away from all these things, I would immediately gravitate toward two responses. The first is that, traditionally speaking, the breath is always the first focal point of meditation. The reason being that if you don't breathe, you die. So the breath is a conduit for experiencing one's present reality. It occurs in the present moment by necessity, it doesn't stop. It's incessant. There are very few things like the breath that are in constant flux, yet ever present. Not to mention that it's the source of all life, or immediate life. To be aware of that is intrinsically valuable because it connects you to present reality.

On a side tangent, from a martial arts and health perspective I think a great deal of stress, tension, and anxiety come from upper chest breathing. If you watch a baby breathe, most of them breathe from their lower abdomens. This changes around five or six years old, but most toddlers breathe from the lower abdomen, where there is little movement in the thoracic region and their bellies oscillate tremendously. It's almost as if they're still breathing through the umbilical cord. I believe this is the source of enduring energy for most children.

It has a few undeniable benefits. One is it expands the diaphragm fully and extends air well into the lower lungs, developing the musculature required for full lung capacity. It improves digestion and maintains healthy organ function, balancing hormone release and improving healing abilities. There's not a lot of literature on this, but regular abdominal breathing (as well as advanced breathing techniques) also improves oxygen uptake and utilization, which can lead to greater performance and help people maintain lean body mass. Oxygen is a key factor in mobilizing and utilizing body fat for energy.

The other point worth mentioning is that of emotional control. If you notice any time that you're angry, frustrated, afraid, anxious, or nervous, if you're having trouble with the boss, if you're about to ask a girl out on a date or give a public speech, you'll find your breath is invariably drawn into the upper chest. The lower abdomen becomes tense and perhaps even drawn inward while inhaling. This is a form of high-stress breathing that is natural among competitive athletes. It's the huffing and puffing that occurs when you're fighting or any time you're under great physical stress. It's a form of power breathing but it indicates a state of high stress.

Within the context of sports performance, it's useful and powerful. However, when it is applied (often unconsciously and habitually) while doing work or thinking about deadlines, it creates tension and increases anxiety and stress. It can even lead to hormonal imbalance and depression. Learning to breathe from the lower abdomen can reverse this cycle and regulate the autonomic nervous system. It can reduce stress, remove tension, and allow for much greater emotional control.

People can almost immediately reverse their mood and psychological outlook by simply increasing the length and depth of their inhalation, increasing its duration relative to the exhalation. In short, independently of the perspective shifts that occur through meditation practice, we should consider breathing as a foundational practice on these merits alone.

MICHAEL: Let's turn to Book 3, *The Unfettered Mind.* I expect that some may complain that it is not specific enough on what you're trying to express. You've compiled stories, good stories, humorous stories, provocative stories, but they leave you wanting for instructions of how to go about meditation.

ME: Okay, let's do this. I think that meditation is one of the most misunderstood and misapplied terms in the English language, as we discussed. One of the biggest problems is that people have an impression that it is formulaic, dogmatic, and that there are certain rules and techniques to follow. People think that there is a *way* to meditate, that there's a context for meditation, and that it belongs in a temple, forest, or yoga studio. And many others wrongly assume it isn't for them.

The stories I've selected, which I hope are challenging for some readers, are examples of meditative experiences in unconventional settings. There is no domain for meditation, and no technique that truly matters at the end of the day. Meditation addresses the quality of connection one has to the present, regardless of company or setting. If someone is unwilling to face his or her own assumptions and see beyond egocentric values, then all the meditation practice in the world will provide no benefit. But this is rarely put to the test.

I purposefully focused on stories from my past that highlight taboo topics or 'undesirable' situations – lost and isolated in Florence, drug-induced transcendence, unconditional love with a prostitute, a felon with a missing insight, the ugly baby metaphor, and a gambler's tool (the die) to access novelty and improve awareness.

If someone doesn't complete the book or read our drunken discourse here, then I run the risk of readers missing my intention. It is not only to paint a clear picture of an unfettered mind (with it's momentary insights) in the real world in all its practicality. It is also to hold a mirror up in front of them, revealing the readers' own fixed assumptions and values. I gained many of my greatest insights in 'unsavory' circumstances with 'unsavory' people that challenged my values and worldview. I'm giving the reader that same opportunity in a way. Can they see past their sensitivities to the practical takeaways? Or are they busy judging the situations, characters, even my character? I took some risks here.

I took the risk, having framed the stories as I did, of seeming racist or narrow-minded for the story about Damon, despite him being portrayed as the unlikely teacher, and me somewhere between an ignorant, sheltered ten year old and a clueless adult who misses his insight. I run the risk of being accused of fat shaming for the thousand pound man story. And I run the risk of being seen as a misogynist for the Snooker Hooker's story, or stuck in the mental worldview of the young man who received those insights. But no one is truly safe in this book, including myself, and there are many unlikely heroes.

I hope readers will delight in some of the playful anecdotes and look past some of the taboo topics, accepting the sarcasm and attempted dark humor as a way of poking holes and making space for new insights. I'm not just trying to be provocative, and I certainly don't play the role of a provocateur in real life. I'm as sensitive to race and gender as the next guy, and have no tolerance for racism or sexism. But I felt that to do this job well, that is, to relay the message honestly that unburdening requires more weight, or freedom requires resistance, I'd need to frame these insights within tensions that strike deep, tensions that force the reader to let go. The rogue trainer would need to rear his ugly head a bit.

I wanted to express that the work we all need to do isn't soft, it isn't easy, it isn't flattering, and it doesn't accommodate our personal sensitivities. It requires challenging our complex worldviews. There's no way to avoid the deeply personal aspect of that challenge. We all have hang-ups, judgments, and beliefs that no matter how small, we don't really want challenged. They provide us a sense of comfort. 'You can touch my diet, but don't touch my lifestyle' type of thing.

'You can teach me to meditate, but drugs are wrong.' 'You can give me the insight, but don't touch my race, gender, or life choices.'

Weightlessness doesn't work that way. More often than not, the insight we seek is just beyond that comfortable attachment. We don't get to pick and choose when we're non-attached. Non-attachment doesn't exist in isolated pockets of life, it's a state of mind that is both cultivated and influential, or it isn't. It correlates with the plasticity of your neurology and the flexibility of your mind.

A meditative mind (a truly meditative mind) doesn't have the luxury of only connecting to reality when in a temple or in our greatest comfort zones. It transforms many of one's experiences, often at unpredictable times and in unpredictable ways. Sincere practice opens Pandora's box and challenges your well-formed identity, potentially penetrating the very core of who you think you are. It has to.

If your mind is clouded by the judgment that doing drugs is wrong, then you likely missed the insight that ego transcendence is the path to insight and understanding, with or without drugs. If you cannot imagine sharing a moment with a prostitute, or you felt I was unnecessarily naïve in my early understanding of women, then it's very likely you missed the insight that true love isn't about the object. It's a byproduct of non-attachment.

I hope the stories of Book 3 illustrate that meditation is something that has no domain. You can perform and practice meditation wherever you are. It's a part of you. It can enhance and improve the quality of any experience in life. The meditative mind can be activated or utilized at any time; it has nothing to do with physical structure (posture) or dogma. Your willingness and ability to connect with the present, to see, to feel, to listen without judgment, is paramount. This can be learned, but it cannot be taught.

After Book 2, *Enso Temple*, the reader is probably expecting a lot more meat, with clear descriptions, prescriptions, and recommendations on meditative practices. But this is not meditation at its core. I don't want to give readers something to hold on to (at least not yet) or a concrete how-to guide, because I don't want them to fixate on concepts or techniques. I want them to feel it, to learn it practically, not by rote. I don't want them to *understand* the strawberry. I want them to *taste* it.

MICHAEL: Cool, cause I thought you were a racist. [Both Laugh] So when I read this story about you being homeless for a night in Florence, what do I do with that?

ME: I think I can ask you the same question. What have you done with that? Not to be cheeky, but this is the point of the story. I want to leave people with an open-ended interpretation of an experience. I want to illustrate that an experience that most people, including myself, would consider full of pretty unfortunate circumstances, turned out to be one of the most vivid and deeply meaningful moments of my life. If I had put that evening in a box and simply labeled it as *bad* because I had no place to go, it would have been chalked up as a horrible, dreaded experience.

As far as the story goes, I don't want to tell somebody what he or she should do with it. But I do want them to consider their reactions to it. Are they able to embrace the possibilities I paint? Or do they dismiss it outright as an interesting story, but not their type of insight?

I hope there is enough meat within it to help someone reconsider his or her own beliefs as concrete absolutes, as I did with mine. Because maybe, just maybe, there's something brilliant on the other side. Can you empathize without analyzing? Can you feel without judgment? I gave you a meditative moment. Now it's your turn.

MICHAEL: So you studied philosophy. And you taught it a bit in China, to some extent. Philosophy and Weightlessness. Why didn't you pursue it as a career path? I mean institutional study.

ME: I'm glad you qualified that, because I would say that I did choose philosophy as a path. But as an institution... it was certainly one of many options. Henry David Thoreau was quoted as saying something like (and he said this over a hundred years ago), "Today there are no philosophers, only professors of philosophy." I can say that, based on the four years I studied philosophy at the university, his words are just as true today as they were then.

I wanted to be a genuine philosopher, somebody who lives his values. There may come a time or a day when I'm qualified to teach that unwaveringly and provide genuine value and insight regarding the world before us. But there is something substantially different between a man who teaches principles – that is, a man who teaches philosophical world views – and a man who stops at nothing to live his values. It's the difference between a man who has knowledge and one who embodies wisdom. I may never reach it, but I'd like to choose the path of wisdom, if I may be so bold.

MICHAEL: Good luck. There are many aspects of the book that deal with the notion of stress. You go out, you get broken down, and you grow from it. You rejuvenate and you become stronger and better. But one of the things that is striking to me about your life is skin in the game. I see you putting your skin in the game, beginning at an early age as a young competitive fighter. But it's persisted until today, whether it is coffee bean trading with the possibility of going bankrupt, or whether it's becoming an entrepreneur and starting a personal training studio in Shanghai, where you can also go bankrupt! Is this something that's relevant to Weightlessness?

ME: Yes, absolutely, on two important levels. The first has to do with Taleb's notion of antifragility – the idea that there are a great number of human attributes that become stronger when stressed. You don't activate those without a real risk of loss, pain, or failure. In terms of Weightlessness, the notion of skin in the game gives you the confidence to go through the process of deconstruction and growth that occurs in fitness and meditation. It's the breaking down of the body and the mind that makes you stronger and fitter. It's important that one acquires a confidence or faith in his or her antifragility. Otherwise the pains and discomforts of training (and growth) can be overwhelming. Perspective has a lot to do with how experiences hit you.

The other level at which it's important is that I believe there is something profoundly meaningful about committing 100 percent to your endeavors in mind and body, in living and committing fully to a certain path. I believe it's the only way to accumulate genuine knowledge or wisdom. In life, there's no logic in holding back. Everybody holds back. Everybody makes excuses. But you don't need to be that person. You can die for your beliefs. This is a beautiful freedom.

More often than not, when you step out and you take that risk, take that chance, you don't die. You become so much stronger than you ever imagined you could be. But you can't learn this from a book, from speculation or theory; you actually have to risk death. When you do that, there is a feeling of life that cannot be encapsulated in words. It's beautiful. It's the difference between unconditional love and fitting the mold. Weightlessness is about fighting for life, that unreserved commitment to life. It's about stopping at nothing to become stronger, fitter, and peaceful. It's dying and sacrificing for the love of your life without having any knowledge if you can actually win her in the end.

Everybody has to ask if that's a battle worth fighting. You don't know until you try. If you care, you have to put skin in the game to find out. You take the poor man who saves, scrapes, and sacrifices to make ends meet so that he can win over the girl of his dreams. He has skin in the game. Then there's the rich asshole born with a silver spoon in his mouth who buys his way through life, can get whatever he wants, and uses and abuses women.

It's a difference between a man who knows he can lose everything, puts all his eggs in one basket, and suffers for that one thing, versus the guy who doesn't suffer and who is playing games. I won't judge too harshly the man who plays the game. There is certainly some life and a good deal of pleasure in it, just like there is sometimes an illogic on the part of the guy who commits everything to the impossible.

But of these two, the man who sticks his neck out has integrity. And it's been tested. The man who has it easy, you just don't know. He may have integrity; he may be a good man, a passionate man with genuine love. But you just don't know, if he's never had to fight for it, never risked anything, never shown his commitment, if he's always had it too easy.

MICHAEL: This is central to people today. Certainly among my group of friends nobody is starving, but of course a few hundred years ago people were living on the edge, fighting for tomorrow's meal, and trying to prepare a future for their families. But today, at least in the developed world, there seems to be an abundance of 'stuff.'

That leads us to the story we've talked about a few times, which my father loves, which is the story about these people in a rescue boat, dying slowly of dehydration and lack of food. The captain ultimately decided to put a hole in the boat, which created a sense of urgency. It created real immediate skin in the game for everyone to get to a fucking island, to make it happen. And they made it happen.

ME: They began rowing furiously.

MICHAEL: They rowed like they never rowed before, probably destroying their arms, the skin on their hands. But they got there. How do you view this in terms of your hundred-day challenge to *Weightlessness* readers? Because most people are comfortable. Would you encourage most people to poke a hole in their boat and get skin in the game, to bring them on the path toward becoming weightless?

ME: Absolutely. I say this with the full realization that it is not easy for many. The natural motivation for most people is to seek comfort and security. It is a trait of humanity that we strive for an easier way of life. The irony is that after we find those comforts, once we're satiated, we cease growing. We stop being vital, adaptive, and passionate people. And since we cannot predict what may come tomorrow, comfort leaves us exposed and ill-equipped to manage uncertainty and risk.

I absolutely would encourage people to get some skin in the game. But I should give one word of caution. I can't promise you happiness with this path. I am not always happy. I suffer sometimes. There are easier paths. I think I'm a relatively intelligent guy. I think I could have several other potential career paths if I so choose that would provide a lot more comfort and security. But they would not provide me *life*. The path of Weightlessness cannot guarantee a constant state of happiness, but it can provide a rich, colorful life. It can develop men and women of undeniable character.

MICHAEL: How many days do you have left to bankruptcy?

ME: Two weeks. Well, at the time of this interview, rent is due in two weeks and I'm about halfway there. This does not include paying salaries or feeding myself. But this has been an enduring state since Enso's relocation nine months ago.

MICHAEL: That's skin in the game. But in the edited interview, in the transcript, it'd be cool if it just said *five days* or something like that. There have been moments when you've told me that.

ME: There have been moments in the last nine months where it's been one day.

MICHAEL: That has to go in the book. That's fucking skin in the game. So, my friend, we're getting to the very essence of stuff. Weightlessness is not a means of having just a mediocre life or simply getting by, but a way of transcending from the mediocre into the awesome, and to live a spectacular life.

ME: Right.

MICHAEL: In the book, you paint a portrait of a man who has taken up the torch of Weightlessness. So I'm curious where you would like to go with Weightlessness for yourself.

ME: Ah, Noah. I'm glad you brought him up. Speaking of holding up mirrors in front of the reader, this is perhaps the best example in the book. I've used this story as a reflection piece with clients in the past. Their interpretations, the details they choose to focus on, tell me which sticking points in their training still need to be addressed. It's a story charged with drama, a volatile day in the life of a Weightlessness practitioner that ends, well, in highly uncertain fashion. Some might say it lacks closure. It's been an excellent litmus test to determine how well someone can forego judgment and just empathize, versus read into the story from his or her own value center. Or rather, to determine which fixed judgments are preventing insight.

Some people find Noah's story inspiring. Some hate his character. Some don't understand why he let Sarah leave without a fight if he did in fact love her. And while there are breadcrumbs dispersed throughout that give the reader a chance to reflect on real-life implications of non-attachment and personal growth, the last line of the story is the real test. Despite the events of the day, where are you in this moment? Are you present? Are you obsessing about Sarah, or can you taste your wine, feel the music, and take in the dancing cityscape? On your worst day, despite everything, are you a crumpled mess on the floor, focusing on details of a very recent past, or can you taste the strawberry? I'll leave that there.

As for my own journey, I'd really like to take Weightlessness to its natural end and apply the principles relayed in the Weightlessness Manifesto in full for two to three years, which I must say is well outside the scope of my experience and understanding. It's uncharted territory. My transformation after a few months of Weightlessness training changed my life forever. I saw the world in a new light, and I could see clearly the untapped potential within me.

I'd like to pay homage to our warrior-monk predecessors by living the tenets of Weightlessness daily for two to three years. I realize this is a platform that is unrealistic for most people, and I don't think people need to make such an extreme commitment in order to find tremendous value in moderate doses of Weightlessness training. But I think that you stated it well: my intention is to present a clear roadmap for human flourishing.

I aim to share this message with every like-minded individual who wants a taste of the strawberry, but who may be lacking the tools to actualize their inherent peace, power, and freedom. It's not about getting by and being comfortable, about the two-car garage and two-point-five kids and all that jazz. It's about killing it. It's about becoming a man of real character, wisdom, and power. I gotta put more skin in the game.

THANKS FOR READING!

If the ideas and principles in this book appeal to you and you would like to go deeper in the study and practice of Weightlessness, you can find information on upcoming remote training programs, retreats, and workshops at: www.weightlessness.co

For further self-study or for those looking to go further down the Weightlessness rabbit hole, the following books will get you there:

The Essence of Lightness

...unveils the comprehensive philosophy and methodology of Weightlessness. It looks deeply at our mind-body hardware and proposes concrete, actionable life practices that empower us to navigate uncertainty with power and grace, while opening the door to incalculable upside in life.

Here Now Breathe

...is a story for children about the challenges we all face, big or small, and a reminder that the secret to being strong and weightless in life is already within us. It introduces mindful awareness as a tool for managing fear, pain, and change.

PLEASE CONSIDER:

As a self-published author I rely on word-of-mouth to market my books and creative content. If you feel this book has been of value to you, please recommend it to someone you think may benefit from it as well. Every review also directly impacts the book's ranking on Amazon.com, while giving prospective readers the information they need to make a decision. I would really appreciate your review on Amazon.com.

FOLLOW ME

Follow me on Youtube: www.youtube.com/user/ShaolinRopeDart

Connect with me on LinkedIn: www.linkedin.com/in/tomfazio/

Follow me on Instagram: weightlessness_by_tom_fazio